RESURRECTION
THE KIDNAPPING
OF ABBY DROVER

Also by John Griffiths

Fatal Prescription

RESURRECTION
THE KIDNAPPING
OF ABBY DROVER

JOHN GRIFFITHS

INSOMNIAC PRESS

Edited by Kate Harding
Copy Edited by Lloyd Davis & Liz Thorpe
Designed by Schrödinger's Cat

Canadian Cataloguing in Publication Data

Griffiths, John, 1944-
    Resurrection: The Kidnapping of Abby Drover

ISBN 1-895837-62-6

1. Drover, Abby - Kidnapping, 1976. 2. Hay, Donald.
3. Kidnapping - British Columbia - Port Moody. I. Title

HV6604.C3D76 1999   364.15'4'092
C99-930483-6

The publisher gratefully acknowledges the support of the
Canada Council and the Ontario Arts Council.

Printed and bound in Canada

Insomniac Press
393 Shaw Street,
Toronto, Ontario, Canada, M6J 2X4
www.insomniacpress.com

AUTHOR'S NOTE

QUITE APART FROM ALL ITS DRAMA, *Resurrection: The Kidnapping of Abby Drover* is very much a personal story for me, as well as for the heroic young woman in the title. My first involvement with the case came towards the end of a sixteen-year career as a newspaper reporter, just before I made a complete career change to spend the next sixteen years in the world of business.

I had wanted to be a writer ever since childhood, when I first smelled the inked ribbon of my late father's Remington typewriter. His dreams of a writing career sadly were derailed by the outbreak of World War II, but I know he was proud when eventually I fulfilled his ambitions and began to work for newspapers myself.

Subsequently, as a journalist in Europe and North America, I came to report on almost every imaginable sort of drama and circumstance affecting the human race — sometimes interviewing paupers, other times heads of state.

But never had I covered a story as memorable as that of Abby Drover. The circumstances of her case were so unforgettable that years later I still wondered about her — and whether it might be possible to tell her story in a book.

Originally, I doubted that I might be able to locate anyone in Abby's family after all these years. Even if they could be found, I thought, it seemed unlikely that I might obtain their cooperation these twenty some years later.

Thanks in part to the compliments of readers on my first book, *Fatal Prescription*, I began thinking about telling Abby's story as my next project. It was especially topical because it was nearing the twentieth anniversary of her disappearance and a bizarre discovery that made headlines around the world.

Although I had limited time to complete the book, I was especially motivated from a creative standpoint because I was, after all, one of those who had first reported the story those twenty years ago.

It is with thanks to the people mentioned here — and others too — that I was able to complete the project on time. Not only do I think you might find this as absorbing a story as I did, I hope it might also contribute to raising awareness about the dangers around us, and the ever present need for vigilance to protect our children. There is unfortunately much evil in this world, but in the end this is a book about survival and hope.

While this book is not intended as a clinical treatise, *Resurrection* does answer some of the questions that might be of interest to psychologists around the world. After her terrible ordeal, what had become of Abby? Had her experiences condemned her to life in a psychiatric ward? Had she resorted to drugs to repress the memories? Had she turned to prostitution? Would her story be a source of inspiration to others who might have suffered lesser adversity?

Insofar as I was able to obtain some of the answers, I express my gratitude to the Drover family, especially Abby's mother Ruth, a strong woman who almost always kept the faith and who generously spent many hours reaching back into her memory to make this a better book.

I also would like to thank Sergeant Wayne Smith and Constable Bill Reed of the Port Moody Police Department, as well as former Port Moody police officers Paul Adams and Rick Nelson, and Sergeant Peter Montague, media liaison officer with the Royal Canadian Mounted Police.

In addition, considerable thanks are due to Kathleen Selfridge and to former Port Moody Mayor Norm Patterson.

Other contributions came from the *Brandon Sun* newspaper in Brandon, Manitoba, as well as my former colleague Don MacLachlan at the *Vancouver Province*, who correctly predicted that I had ink in my blood and that inevitably, one day, I would return to writing. Thanks also for an excellent job of editing by Kate Harding of Insomniac Press. For their generous assistance, I extend special thanks to *CBC-TV* reporter Wayne Williams and former *Province* staffers Al Arnason and Peter Hulbert.

And most of all, I thank Abby Drover herself.

TABLE OF CONTENTS

1 LITTLE PRINCESS

RUTH DROVER GLANCED at the clock on the kitchen wall, the knot tightening in her stomach as the big hand approached quarter past four. Putting down the bag of groceries she had just bought on her way home from work, the tall, heavyset woman hurried to the living room window and craned her neck, anxiously looking for her youngest daughter.

Twelve-year-old Abby should have walked in from school by now. In fact, she should have been home a good half-hour ago. It wasn't like Abby to give her mother any cause for concern, especially when it was still late winter and already beginning to get dark.

The single mother and her three daughters had moved into the plain basement house at 1617 Barnet Highway less than four months earlier. On its own full-sized lot, it had seemed like a palace at first, compared with some of family's previous accommodations, but Ruth now felt a brief shiver as she surveyed the damp and dismal scene outside.

Surrounded by heavy underbrush, the house was actually located on the dead-end Gore Street, along with only four or five other properties clinging to a steep cliff well over a mile and a half from town. Suddenly, despite the comforting smell of smoking chimneys, it seemed to Ruth not only bleak but also very remote.

Frustrated, Ruth turned back from the window to express her concern to her eldest daughters, Kathleen and Robyn. "Abby should have been home half an hour ago," said their mother. "Everyone was coming out of school after I got the groceries. I waited to give her a ride but I didn't see her."

Unlike their younger sister, Kathleen, seventeen, and Robyn, fifteen, had remained in their previous school, travelling by bus each day to the neighbouring municipality of Burnaby. They knew Abby should have been home before them, but it seemed far too early to panic.

"She must be playing with friends up the street," suggested Robyn. "I'll go over and see."

Ruth was thankful for the suggestion. As a single mother, she hadn't had an easy time raising three children, but all of them had turned out healthy and fine, and the older girls always looked out for their little sister. Assuming she would find Abby safe and sound, Ruth watched Robyn put on her coat and returned to the kitchen to start dinner.

Lost in her thoughts, she glimpsed the sweep of Burrard Inlet through the tangle of leafless alder at the back of the house, observing the industrial townsite and its numerous oil refineries lying within the shadow of mountains on all sides. In the distance, railroad tracks and stacks of yellow sulphur, waiting for shipment to the far corners of the earth, seemed to blight its shorelines as far as the eye could see. Often shrouded in mist, it wasn't the location Ruth might have preferred but at least it was affordable.

MORE THAN ONE HUNDRED years earlier, Port Moody had been proposed as the western terminus of the first transcontinental railroad, touted by the local newspaper as likely to become "the grandest, most populous and thriving city upon the Pacific slope of the American continent."

Almost immediately, however, the tracks had been extended a dozen miles farther west to what would grow into the bustling seaport of Vancouver, leaving behind disgruntled investors in a backwater town that became just another suburb making up the Greater Vancouver Regional District.

Despite this, Port Moody retained certain advantages over the burgeoning metropolis further to the west, one of these being the fact that local real estate had remained comparatively cheap, which was the main reason Ruth Drover had bought her first ever detached house there in November of 1975.

With its yellow cedar siding and red asphalt roof, 1617 Barnet Highway was what most realtors would have described as a typical suburban box — practical, maybe, but possessing little if any semblance of architectural appeal. The only access to the house was via a steep and mossy dead-end street, lined with the winter scrub of bare alder, cottonwood and vine maple — presaging the chill and darkening nights of another oncoming winter.

The entire area, Ruth had noticed, was surrounded by dense, undeveloped bushland. While her older daughters could take the bus to school, Abby would have quite a long walk — almost a mile and a half to her new elementary school just off St. John's Street in downtown Port Moody. Surely though, she figured, all three of her children were plenty old enough not to get lost in the adjoining forest.

Abby's long walk to school was a bit daunting, but she was a cheerful, trusting child and there seemed nothing especially to worry about — other than perhaps the weather. When it rained on that section of Barnet Highway just below Gore Street, it rained with a vengeance. Low, grey clouds enveloped the edge of the mountain and discharged their contents with the volume and velocity of an automated carwash. Despite the dampness, however, the Drover girls were excited. The house, after all, was only one and a half years old.

"After some of the dumps we've lived in, I'd say it's pretty darn good," Abby had remarked upon moving in.

Abby, who had turned twelve the previous May, had grown to be a cute child — skinny, somewhat tall for her age, with auburn hair and green eyes. Ruth had raised all three of her daughters to be polite children, respectful of their elders, even though Abby had been prone to the odd bout of mischief. One time, her mother had caught her giggling hysterically as Abby played "knocky-knocky nine doors", ringing neighbour's doorbells, only to run away before the owners could answer.

Although she was a strict, no-nonsense mom, Ruth had found it hard to discipline her youngest child for such apparently harmless pranks. Life may have been a struggle for the single parent family but all of the sisters had developed a maturity about them, and Abby had recently been described by her classmates as a "little princess".

Finally, Ruth felt, things were starting to get a little better. Her daughters now had a big enough home where each of them could have her own bedroom. "But only," Ruth insisted, "if you keep your rooms neat and tidy."

Ruth had a good sense of humour and was happy at the family's sudden stroke of good fortune. Sometimes she seemed a bit rough around the edges, but being one of four sisters herself, she'd had to develop a bit of an attitude early on to attract attention. She had never been out of work and recently had started a new job as a bookkeeper with a local helicopter firm.

Co-workers found her a sensible, straightforward and sincere woman, who was deceptively talented. Having taken up oil painting, she could capture a subject on canvas with artistic flair, yet she herself was harder to read. A bespectacled woman with short, dark, curly hair, she didn't much care if nowadays she was somewhat overweight. She blamed her ex-husband for the dismal failure of her marriage and spared little if any time to thoughts of finding another man.

Ruth was born in 1938, some sixty miles east of Vancouver. Her own mother, Martha, had come from Russia aboard the *President Lincoln*, landing in New York harbour with her parents before moving to Saskatchewan. There, Martha had met Ruth's father, John Adolphe, son of Austrians homesteading in the flat, southeastern part of the province.

The Great Depression of the 1930s hit especially hard in rural Saskatchewan. Like many of their neighbours, the Adolphes were caught up in the dust bowl of the dirty '30s, battling successive crop failures while attempting to survive the vagaries of a harsh daily life.

It was not surprising, therefore, that soon after their marriage, Ruth's parents moved to Canada's westernmost province, settling in the mountain town of Trail, British Columbia, two miles north of the border with Washington state. On a hill overlooking the Columbia River, the Cominco company had built a huge smelter to refine lead, silver and gold, and there was plenty of work for most of the new arrivals.

The couple's first two children, Jean and Dorothy, were born in the shadow of the smelter, before the family moved to Chilliwack, where Ruth was born five weeks prematurely, after her mother was kicked in the stomach while milking the family cow. It was several weeks, however, before visiting friends realized there had been an addition to the Adolphe family. Baby Ruth was so small that no one except her parents seemed to notice her. Instead of sleeping in a crib, the infant was reposed under miniature blankets in an empty box of *Oxydol* laundry detergent in her parents' bedroom. Three years later, Martha gave birth to youngest daughter Delphine.

Eventually, the family made it all the way to the coast, where Ruth's father obtained a wartime job working on the railway. After a subsequent stint demonstrating in-home kitchenware, he became a realtor, listing and selling properties in Burnaby on the outskirts of Vancouver. The Adolphe girls grew up in a comfortable home, steeped in the values of sacrifice and frugality.

As members of the Seventh-Day Adventist Church — founded in Battle Creek, Michigan, in 1863 — Ruth's parents believed that Saturday, rather than Sunday, was the true Sabbath, and clung to their belief in the second coming of Christ, despite ridicule that their predicted day of the advent had passed without incident more than a century earlier. Ruth and her sisters regularly attended Saturday services.

In 1958, Ruth was married in the Seventh Day Adventist Church, to a man she had met just twelve months previously. At six-feet-one — tall, dark and handsome — Cecil Drover had attracted her almost from the moment she met him.

Four years older than Ruth, Cecil played the guitar and fancied himself a country singer. He had grown up in a family of five children in Newfoundland, on the opposite side of the country. With few opportunities other than fishing, he'd departed as soon as he could to work on ships on Canada's west coast.

At first, Cecil was a deckhand with Northland Navigation, delivering food and other supplies to remote settlements that could only be reached by ship, while later he worked as a quartermaster on the cruise ship *Prince George,* sailing the Inside Passage to Alaska. Frequently at sea, Cecil had little if any need for a car so, when he was ashore, most of his dates with Ruth Adolphe consisted of long walks in and around Burnaby.

Ruth remembered that it poured on the day of her wedding, and her enthusiasm was dampened as well by the fact, she recalled, that Cecil had lost his money in a shipboard card game — and a gift of $2 from Ruth's grandmother was the only cash available for the honeymoon that never took place.

By the time the newlyweds moved into a Vancouver basement suite on Seventh Avenue just off Main Street, employment had become scarce and Cecil found himself out of work. No sooner would she and her husband acquire a new piece of furniture than it would be repossessed for nonpayment. "There were always bill collectors at the door," she recalled. "Sometimes the kids and I would hide in the closet to pretend there was no one home."

Kathleen, the Drovers' first child, was born on January 16, 1959, and by the time Robyn entered the world fifteen months later, tension between Ruth and Cecil, exacerbated by concern over their lack of money, was tearing the family apart. One month before the birth of their third child, Cecil finally moved out.

Running low on food and unable to pay the rent, Ruth was given an eviction notice by her landlord. "This has gotten ridiculous," her mother finally told her. "You and the kids can come move in with me."

Ruth still listened to her mother, because Grandma Adolphe had always been an excellent parent. She may have been thrifty, but she always ensured that her daughters and grandchildren got all the extra attention they needed.

Although moving in with her mother eased Ruth's financial difficulties, Cecil found himself forced to spend his dwindling resources on the divorce, and Ruth still had no money of her own. If she and her kids were to survive, she decided, she needed to have the baby and find a new job as quickly as possible. Convinced her new baby would be a girl, she had already decided on the name Amy — or, as an afterthought, Abby.

Ruth had heard that castor oil might induce delivery and, hoping to speed things up, decided to put that theory to the test. Perhaps it wasn't just an old wives' tale after all; within a few hours, her own mother had to rush Ruth to Grace Hospital, panicking that her latest grandchild was about to be born in the front seat of her VW Beetle.

But they made it in time to the hospital where, compared to Ruth's first two excruciatingly long childbirths, it was an easy labour. Abby Rebecca Drover entered the world an hour later — early in the morning of May 3, 1963. Though she had only peach fuzz for hair, she was another healthy girl, weighing seven pounds, seven ounces. "After the castor oil," Ruth joked, "she came out like greased lightning!"

Abby's father visited the new baby at the hospital, but it would be one of the last times his family would see him for more than a decade. Later, Ruth tried to block out his memory. "I was pretty messed up," she recalled. "Robyn had gone to live with some friends and it was a real struggle."

When Abby was five months old, Ruth decided to upgrade her business skills and obtained a job as a bookkeeper with Van-Kam Freightways in Vancouver. In the meantime, she regained custody of Robyn and, for $40 a month, moved with all three girls into a dilapidated old house on Regent Street in Burnaby.

The street's opulent name couldn't have been further from the truth. The front porch of the house was falling off; rats ran through the building; and the pipes froze in the winter. One time, a visitor attempting to negotiate his way under the stairs to get to the toilet fell through the rotten plywood of the bathroom floor.

The landlord, a bricklayer, implied to Ruth that he might fix some of the deficiencies in the house in return for favours from her. Repulsed by the suggestion, Ruth dug in her heels and decided to make do. "We won't have to live here long," she consoled herself, although she was extremely disheartened. "Please, God," she prayed every night, "help us get out of this shack — maybe next month."

In fact, it would take seven long years.

Eventually, one of Ruth's would-be boyfriends moved in, but the girls began to feel he was showing more than a fatherly interest in them while their mother was at work. Abby had a schoolfriend named Sandy who'd confided to her about various sorts of abuse, so the young girl wasn't entirely naive about the boarder's suspicious behaviour, or the fact that he wasn't always dressed when perhaps he should have been. Finally, Ruth told him to leave.

The children, Ruth recalled, were embarrassed to let their friends see where they lived, and Abby, she remembered, even hesitated to invite friends over for a birthday party. "We never went hungry," Ruth said, "but I still didn't have a car and we had to walk everywhere. During the week, we had to get up especially early so I could walk the kids to babysitters or to school on my way to work. We walked miles and miles."

In 1967, Ruth finally got her driver's licence and, for $195, bought a well-used red 1959 Plymouth. It was more than a bit of a clunker, but it would surely make things a lot easier. Later, she applied for government housing, eventually qualifying with just over $500 down to buy a brand new, three-bedroom townhouse on Gannymede Drive, also in Burnaby, near Lougheed Mall. After renting the shack on Regent Street, the family finally had pride of ownership, and they kept the place immaculate. "You kids will have to help with the household chores," Ruth told them. "Abby can do the dishes, Robyn can vacuum, and Kathleen can dust. We all have to pitch in."

One Christmas in those early years, Kathleen and Robyn

were delighted when their father unexpectedly sent them bicycles. Abby was still quite small and her present was an unassembled tricycle that arrived in a box. Ruth didn't have the necessary tools to put it together, so the trike sat in its box for months and months and, by the time a neighbour offered to assemble it for her a year later, Abby's excitement turned to disappointment. "By then, Abby was too big for the trike," her mother recalled. "We gave it to the neighbour's son."

After those trying years, the modest house on Gore Street would seem like a dream come true.

RUTH LOOKED OUT the window again, still frustrated to see no sign of Abby. A bright, resourceful girl, Abby could certainly take care of herself — her older sisters had been known to playfully tie her up with scarves, and Abby could wriggle free as fast as the Great Houdini — but it was so unlike her to disappear without warning.

Most of the time, Ruth and her daughters got along reasonably well. On weekends, Ruth usually tried to arrange pleasant family outings with the girls. The big treat was going out on a Friday night once a month to McDonald's. At that time, recalled Ruth, $2 fed the whole family with hamburgers, fries and a drink.

The next day — in fact, almost every Saturday after church — meant ice-skating at the Trout Lake Arena. Dressed in bright red mitts and toques knitted by Grandma Adolphe, the Drover girls would skate round and round the rink, listening over and over to "Tiny Bubbles" being played over the public address system. Looking back, it might seem a bit boring, but at the time it was definitely what Abby was fond of describing as *bitchin'* — meaning that she and her sisters were having a great time. After skating, they'd each get a Wagon Wheel chocolate treat while Ruth warmed up with a cup of hot coffee.

Occasionally, for something different on weekends, the family would drop in at Brentwood Mall. Still short of money, they stuck together and spent most of their time window-shopping, but invariably, when they were ready to leave, Abby was nowhere to be seen and was presumed lost. Eventually, the family learned that Abby could always be found in the same place, sampling all the new fragrances at the perfume counter in Eaton's department store. No matter what the weather was like, Ruth later recalled, the family always used to have to drive home with the car windows all the way down.

These days, mother and daughters had even become business partners. For several years, Ruth had run a cottage industry out of her home, making wedding cakes. On top of her regular job, the home enterprise meant Ruth often worked eighteen hours a day, making hundreds and hundreds of cakes, some of them weighing thirty pounds or more. But the kids helped with the cakes — Kathleen or Robyn weighing out all the fruit while Abby counted out, lined and waxed all the pans. Although they helped, none of the sisters got an allowance — there was never enough money left over for that — but after the cakes went in the oven, there was always the bonus of being able to lick the bowls.

Fleetingly, Ruth wondered if her youngest daughter might be late home on account of rebellion. Recently, Abby had been unhappy about being made to wear "prickly curlers" and had expressed resentment that her mother would not allow her to wear jeans to school like the other kids.

The idea that her daughter might have run away, however, struck Ruth as being completely out of the question. Abby wasn't even a teenager. She was just a child, thought Ruth — a sweet little girl still very much in need of parental affection.

2 THE NEIGHBOURS

THE FRONT DOOR SLAMMED, signalling that Robyn had come back into the house. Normally, the athletic teenager would have bounded cheerfully up the stairs to the living area, but this time she came in with her head down. "I checked all the neighbours, Mom," she said dejectedly. "I asked all the kids and none of them has seen Abby since they got home from school."

Breathlessly, Robyn added that she had even spoken with the neighbourhood paper boy. If anyone had seen Abby, it surely would have been Brent Hay. The eleven-year-old boy lived at the top of the street and had crisscrossed the neighbourhood as always, delivering copies of the *Vancouver Sun*. He and his sisters were friendly with all the Drover girls — but he hadn't seen Abby either.

Sometimes, if Abby were late for school, Brent would lend her the money for the bus. His stepfather, Donald, sometimes picked both of them up after classes, and had done so as recently as the day before. "I didn't even see her at school today," Brent reported.

It might have seemed early to start worrying, but her mother's instinct told Ruth that something was wrong. This wasn't like Abby. She always stayed close to home. Ruth Drover and her eldest daughter Kathleen mirrored the expression on Robyn's face, each of them showing not just concern but the beginnings of alarm.

Suddenly, thought Ruth, the whole neighbourhood seemed eerie and foreboding. Her youngest daughter would never go anywhere after school without telling her. "This whole place," said Ruth, "is beginning to give me the creeps."

In fact, Ruth was thinking, things in the new neighbourhood had seemed strange even within days of her family moving in. Although she hadn't actively been looking for a new place, a realtor friend had found her the house she wanted with nothing down.

Over and above the moving costs, all Ruth would have to come up with were the legal fees to handle the conveyance. After being cramped in a three-bedroom townhouse, it had seemed like a good idea. And just as the realtor had promised, Ruth had been able to take over the relatively spacious, cathedral-entry home on November 30, 1975, simply by assuming the mortgage.

It had seemed like a great bargain until the problems began. First, Ruth awoke one morning to find that someone had been stealing oil from the tank that fuelled her furnace. After descending to the basement to investigate why the house was suddenly freezing, Ruth eyed the peacock mural that someone had painted on one entire wall of the recreation room during the tenure of the previous owner. Someone had told her it was bad luck to have peacocks in a house, and perhaps they had been right. Ruth had done a good job raising her family single-handedly, but she had to concede just now that it would have been good to have had a man in the house who could fix such things.

After returning upstairs, Ruth got on the phone and called the service people from Shell. The oil company serviceman arrived a short while later and checked the exterior tank beside the house. It didn't take him long to diagnose the problem.

"Tank's empty," he informed Ruth.

"That's strange," replied Mrs. Drover. "We just had it filled last week."

As the tank plainly was not leaking, the serviceman explained that someone must have been siphoning off the oil during the night. After refilling the tank from his truck parked on the street, he cranked on the cap tighter than ever, then attempted a smile as he adjusted his baseball cap. "If anyone tries to get that off again," he assured Ruth, "they'd make such a racket you'd wake up for sure."

It was somewhat reassuring, but the temperature was getting even cooler outside and Ruth shivered as she pondered the theft. Again, with no one but her in the house to protect the family, it wasn't a pleasant thought that somebody might have been sneaking onto their property at night while they slept.

Not long after that incident, the peace and tranquillity of the neighbourhood was abruptly disturbed by yet another incident. Ruth had continued to make the occasional wedding cake, and was in her kitchen decorating her latest creation when two loud bangs caused her to jump and wreck the colored icing she had so delicately applied.

Craning her neck, Ruth peeked through her dining room window to see if she could tell what was going on. Immediately, she could see that two teenagers, drunkenly staggering across the neighbouring property, were laughing as they shot at passing cars on Barnet Highway below. By the time she was able to call the emergency number at the Port Moody police station, the shooting had stopped. Although an officer came to the house immediately to question her about it, and she was able to point out the direction of the gunfire, she never did hear whether the police investigation resulted in any further action. "I realized the shots were coming from next door," she told the police. "It scared the living daylights out of me."

It seemed there were some strange people living in her new neighbourhood, Ruth reflected, but she soon forgot about it, getting up each morning before the kids left for school to drive the several miles along Barnet Highway to her job at Transwest Helicopters in Burnaby. She had worked for the helicopter company for the past year and was required to be there to activate the switchboard each morning at 8:30 a.m., before the owners arrived.

The work, Ruth found, was far from boring. One of the pilots who worked for the company had even treated her to a flight over Burrard Inlet. It was certainly a much more interesting job than working in the bank had been.

After Ruth set out in her old red jalopy each morning, Kathleen and Robyn would catch the bus to Cariboo Hill Secondary School in Burnaby. Abby was usually the last to leave the house. Being new to the area, she only had a few friends in the neighbourhood, and she didn't look forward to making the thirty-minute walk to her new school by herself.

Several of the other kids, wearing jeans, taunted her over the fact that she wore a dress, and one of them spat at her as she walked to school. Kids could be awfully cruel, she realized, but she tried to put it out of her mind as she set about befriending the rest of the children in her class. If any of her classmates were not feeling well, Principal Ed Parkachin noticed, the new girl would lovingly draw pictures for them or write them a poem.

But after school and on weekends there wasn't much for the Drover girls to do. Their house was isolated. With the exception of the few other homes overlooking the highway from Gore Street, the area on the outskirts of town was unpopulated and there wasn't even a corner store. Kathleen sought out parks in Port Moody to play tennis, while Robyn got to know a couple of teenage girls up the street. Perhaps in the spring and summer, they thought, the family could go on picnics or find a stretch of beach along the inlet to go swimming.

Meanwhile, Abby coped by befriending the neighbourhood boys. One Sunday, a football thrown to her by one of them almost knocked the wind out of her, but the five-foot-three, ninety-pound girl made a brave show of it. Being new on the block, she wanted to show Mike Hoce and the others that she could play as hard as the rest of them.

Abby hurled the football back at Mike as hard as she could. At times like these, she wished she were as athletic as her sister Robyn. She wanted to make new friends, and had liked Mike from the start. The same age as Abby, Mike was a husky, dark-haired boy who lived two doors up the street. He was in the same class as Abby at Moody Elementary School, and sometimes they had met in the playground during recess. Mike showed her interesting places to explore in the new neighbourhood and took her on her first ever "date", to a hockey game.

Four doors away, at the very top of Gore Street, Mike also

showed Abby a house with a big garage, owned by their neighbour Donald Hay. The garage was in fact a huge workshop, surrounded by trees and bushes. According to Mike, Mr. Hay worked there making camper units to fit into pickup trucks. He was a good carpenter, Mike told Abby, and he would often fix things for kids in the neighbourhood.

But Mike went on to tell Abby about a scary incident at the Hay household two years earlier. "I've heard he drinks a lot," the boy confided. "He got mad with everyone in the house one night and held them all at gunpoint. He cut the telephone wires, but his wife and kids escaped to the neighbour's and called the police."

According to Mike, the errant father had spent the night in jail but, as far as he knew, nothing more had ever come of the incident. Apparently, things had calmed down and life had carried on as usual. Wide-eyed, Abby said nothing but looked down at the Hay house and its detached garage as Mike concluded his story. Nestled in the trees, the buildings seemed a depressing shade of brown, forbiddingly situated far below street level.

Nonetheless, Donald Hay went up greatly in the Drover sisters' estimation shortly afterwards when he intervened to save Robyn from a potentially serious situation. It started out happily when Grandma Adolphe came over to do some more Christmas baking. Robyn set out eating one of her grandmother's freshly baked cinammon buns later that afternoon on her way to visit the Hay children at the top of Gore Street. As Robyn walked up the hill, a large brown dog belonging to another of the neighbours ran up to sniff the food. Robyn was sharing her bun with the animal when the dog suddenly attacked her, knocking her to the ground.

Screaming for help, the child felt the animal sinking its teeth into her flesh. As the dog ripped her rubber boots and bit her arm, she feared for her life when Hay — bringing home his stepson from school — suddenly arrived in his pickup truck and scared the animal away. Although her arm subsequently swelled up, Robyn reckoned that the helpful neighbour had probably saved her life.

Christmas came and went, and the Drover girls expanded their circle of friends as they entered the New Year of 1976. While they never let on that they knew about the hostage incident, eventually Kathleen, Robyn and Abby all got even closer to the children at the Hay residence up the street. The youngest, Brent, had met Robyn first, while he delivered newspapers after school, and had invited her over to the Hay residence to meet his older sisters Wendy and Jackie.

Afterwards, all three Drover girls frequently went to the Hay residence to visit their new acquaintances. They learned that their new friends lived with their mother, Hilda, a petite, slightly timid woman with long mouse-brown hair, and that Mr. Hay was in fact only their common-law stepfather. Jackie, at seventeen, was a quiet, studious sort of girl, while fourteen-year-old Wendy, a scrawny yet attractive blonde girl with green eyes, was more outgoing. But the whole family seemed friendly.

Contrary to the scary stories they'd heard about him, Don Hay was especially friendly and pleasant. In his early forties, he was a dark-haired, balding man with sideburns, fairly slim and just under six feet tall. Sometimes, he was attired in a clean white shirt and slacks, but mostly he wore old work clothes and forgot to shave before he fired up his power saw to build yet another camper in the garage.

Abby had never really known her own father and obviously appreciated the fact that Mr. Hay was almost exactly the same age as her dad. She also appreciated how he took a fatherly interest in her, doing little things for her, such as the time when he fixed her broken rock tumbler. Often, she would help him in return by passing him the tools he needed as he worked in his garage. Even if she could smell liquor on his breath, it never seemed to make any difference, and she would giggle as he occasionally picked her up to play-fight. Despite having the grey pallor of a hard drinker, he was surprisingly fit and agile.

It was nice to have a friendly male neighbour, especially when Mr. Hay told all three Drover girls that the workshop door was never locked and they could come and go as freely as they wished. It was almost like having their own clubhouse to hang out in. The girls liked and trusted Mr. Hay, who became annoyed with Mrs. Drover one day because she wouldn't let Abby accompany his family and the other two Drover girls up the mountain. The bad feelings quickly passed, however, and Mr. Hay continued to show a special interest in Abby's well-being. "You can come and hang out here any time you want," he repeated, as she watched him build his campers.

WITH ROBYN UNSUCCESSFUL in finding Abby, Ruth felt a rising sense of panic. Immediately, she phoned the Moody Elementary School, only to be gripped by outright fear as first one of the teachers and then principal Ed Parkachin confirmed that Abby had definitely failed to answer roll call that morning. "No, Mrs. Drover," they confirmed. "No one can remember seeing Abby here all day."

Kathleen and Robyn felt the same sinking feeling in their hearts. Normally, by now, the girls would have been busy helping their mother peeling potatoes and getting ready for dinner, but suddenly they weren't the least bit hungry. As three rambunctious sisters, the Drover girls may have had their fights, but when it came to looking out for each other, they were extremely close.

At 6:30 p.m., Ruth called the police.

3 MISSING

CONSTABLE PAUL ADAMS turned his police car from St. John's Street onto Barnet Highway, acutely aware of the vastness all around him. Off to his right, the lights of the oil refineries across Burrard Inlet were a faint blur in the distance, the intervening deep salt water invisible in the broad expanse of darkness. Only a ridge of trees far above the highway signified the steep mountainside to his left.

If there was a moon that night, it was hidden behind a blanket of low clouds and, as his car headlights picked off the roadside reflectors, Adams pondered how difficult it might be to find a missing child in such a vast expanse of undeveloped land and sea. He had just begun the evening shift on March 10 when his car radio crackled to life. "This is Car 2," Adams responded. "Go ahead."

The dispatcher's voice was flat, apparently emotionless as usual: "Can you attend at 1617 Barnet Highway? We have a report of a missing child. Speak to the complainant, Mrs. Ruth Drover." Adams responded affirmatively. Concerned for the welfare of a missing child, he was also intrigued by the prospect of investigating something more important than usual.

Sporting fashionable sideburns, the dark-haired policeman was still trim and athletic in his early thirties. In four years with the police department, Adams had been required to break up the occasional bar fight, but he'd never been called upon to attend even as much as an armed robbery.

This call was different. At last he'd have the chance to deploy some of the skills for which he'd been trained, but his mind was racing as he contemplated the questions he'd have to ask. As the father of three young children himself, he could imagine stepping into every parent's worst nightmare, but consoled himself with the knowledge that the majority of missing persons turned up safe and sound.

The policeman pondered the variables as he continued along the rain-slicked highway. Missing adults, he knew, had the right to disappear if they wished, and usually no police action would be taken for at least forty-eight hours. The same might be true of teenagers with a history of running away from foster homes. Sometimes, a child of divorced parents who didn't like the mother's new boyfriend might have run away to be with a father or grandparents.

In cases involving very young children, the policeman knew, it could simply be that the child had gotten lost. The first place to search might well be in the house itself; children who thought they were in trouble with their parents sometimes hid under a bed or in a closet.

The most common explanation was that the child had simply overstayed a visit at a friend's house, forgetting to call the parents. Adams realized he would have to be sensitive and tactful as he posed such questions to what would obviously be a distraught family.

As he headed towards the Drover residence, Adams was alone. With only twenty members, including Chief Len McCabe, the Port Moody Police Department was relatively small. One of the members might be on vacation, another possibly off sick, so usually there were only one or two patrol cars on the road at any given time. Unlike in big city police departments, the officers seldom had the luxury of a companion to back them up. A twelve-gauge shotgun slung horizontally across the partition behind the front seats afforded some compensation. "It was a pretty intimidating weapon," Adams recalled to me later.

Only the last of the homeward-bound rush hour stragglers passed him as he approached Gore Street. It would have been easy to miss the steeply inclined street in the dark, but for the fact Adams knew that it was the first turnoff he would reach on his left-hand side. It was a dead-end road and only the few residents who lived there would usually have reason to make the turn. After signalling to drive up the steep road, Adams noticed that there were only four or five houses, all of them to his right, atop the cliff overlooking the highway. On the other side of the road, there appeared to be nothing but trees and bushes.

Adams used his flashlight to pick out the house numbers as he ascended the dark, remote street, quickly finding the Drover residence approximately halfway up the incline. Although the address was 1617 Barnet Highway, the only vehicular access was from Gore Street. There were no sidewalks, and the policeman immediately ascertained there was nowhere to park on the Drover property. He pulled his cruiser as far to the side of the street as he could. Although it had stopped raining earlier in the day, the policeman had to avoid mud and damp undergrowth as he approached the front door.

Through glass panels beside the door, he could see someone hurtle down the steps to the entrance hall as soon as he rang the doorbell. "Come in," said a pretty teenage girl, sighing with relief at the sight of the uniformed officer. "Mom's in the kitchen."

Adams introduced himself, but doubted that Ruth Drover or her daughters even caught his name. The family was in a state of panic and confusion. Ruth felt numb; her head was spinning, and she was overcome by feelings of guilt. "If I wasn't a working mom, this might never have happened," she told Adams. "I could have driven her to school. Maybe I expected too much of her."

Attempting to reassure her, Adams leaned casually against the kitchen counter as he began to make notes. Keeping his questions as gentle as possible, he was interested to learn that Ruth was divorced and that Abby's father lived in another province. The family, however, seemed absolutely sure that Cecil Drover had nothing to do with Abby's disappearance.

"He hasn't seen Abby since she was a baby," said Ruth. "She never asks about him. All I know is he's remarried but I have no idea where he's living. Let me know if you find him."

Surveying the room, Adams ascertained that Ruth was clearly fulfilling her responsibilities as the working head of the household, while Kathleen Drover, who had opened the door, seemed almost like a second parent assisting her mother in the running of the home. Robyn was quiet, but her expression showed appropriate fear and concern. The home was neat and tidy. As far as Adams could tell, the family seemed normal and stable, with no obvious problems other than the terrifying fact that Abby was missing.

The phone rang and Ruth started, but her hopes were dashed. Instead of a call from Abby, it was one of the neighbours asking if the girl had shown up yet.

The Drovers had moved to Port Moody only recently, Adams noted, and he wondered if that might have been a factor in her disappearance. "Was she having any trouble adapting to her new school?" he asked.

Ruth confirmed that Abby hadn't been seen at school all day, but doubted any suggestion that she might deliberately have played truant. "She didn't like walking to school," Ruth conceded, "but she had an excellent attendance record. She never skipped classes."

There was still the possibility, Adams suggested, that Abby might be staying overnight with a friend, in which case she would surely catch it when she got home.

Ruth shook her head in exasperation. "Abby never stays out late at night," she insisted. "She's never been missing before. She doesn't accept rides from strangers. She's not the type of kid to run away. She's never given me any trouble at all."

It seemed a strong possibility to Ruth that her daughter may have been in an accident. There was no money or extra clothing missing from the house. "She's a happy, loving little girl," said her mother. "She always stays close to home. Abby is an affectionate child. She loves people."

Adams assured the Drover family that the police department would do everything it could to find the missing girl. The dispatcher, he promised, would contact the neighbouring police departments in Burnaby and Coquitlam, as well as check with neighbourhood hospitals to ask if any of them had admitted a twelve-year-old girl who might have been in accident.

The policeman still wondered if the Drovers had checked with all of Abby's friends and whether he himself had covered all the bases. Could Ruth Drover be holding back something vital? It was still too early for pessimism, the policeman felt, because so many children reported missing turn up safe and sound. "They usually show up soon after nightfall," he told Ruth. "As soon as it gets cold, they miss the warmth and security of their beds."

Having exhausted his questions about Abby's family background, Adams turned his attention to obtaining a physical description of the missing child. Abby, said her mother, was about five foot three, with collar-length light brown hair. She had blue-green eyes and a slim build. "She weighs about ninety pounds," added Ruth.

Ruth returned from the dining room buffet with two or three photo albums. Although recent family pictures showed that Abby was an angelic-looking child, Adams was disappointed to see that most of the snapshots of her were somewhat blurred. The pictures would have to suffice, he decided, and might make a good missing poster montage if the girl were not found within a day or two.

The policeman's final questions pertained to what clothing Abby had been wearing when last seen at home that morning. Helped by Kathleen and Robyn, Ruth Drover was able to reconstruct a detailed description, which Adams recorded in his notebook. Abby had been wearing a beige turtle-neck sweater and blue buttoned vest — both made by her grandmother — a gold-coloured ski jacket, navy blue Fortrel slacks and brown boots.

After returning to police headquarters, Adams found himself unable to dig up any good news. Neighbouring police departments and hospitals had no information that would be of any help, so he sat down to prepare a full report for his supervisor, Corporal Archie Connell. Adams liked the thin, balding corporal. He considered him a fine policeman. Never having learned to type, Adams wrote out his report in longhand. He took care to keep it legible, wanting to be sure that Archie Connell would have a clear report, with all the pertinent information, on his desk first thing in the morning. Meanwhile, Adams arranged with an on-duty corporal to have at least one Port Moody police officer out all night checking known hiding places.

As Adams finished his shift, he knew it was still too early to reach any definite conclusions. There was no reason to think of the case as being particularly out of the ordinary. Still, as he arrived home and looked at his own young children fast asleep, he regretted he hadn't been there to read them a bedtime story. Quietly, he leaned forward and gave each of them a goodnight kiss.

4 FRIENDS IN NEED

"IS THERE ANYTHING at all we can do?" asked Don Hay.

Surrounded in the living room by his wife and stepchildren, the home handyman had phoned the Drover residence to offer his help and support to Abby's mother.

Although balding in his early forties, the friendly neighbour was a lean, good-looking man — still quite youthful in appearance with his dark sideburns not yet showing any signs of grey.

As he spoke to Ruth, stroking the stubble on his chin, his family gathered that Abby's mother had already called the police and didn't think anyone could do anything else to help.

Don's own wife nodded approvingly, however, as her husband persisted: "I can take the kids out looking for her in my truck," he said. "We'll come right over."

Hilda liked that about him. Not only was he considerate, he could be a good husband and father when he wasn't drinking — and he'd been sober now for almost a month, ever since Valentine's Day. It was nice, Hilda reflected, that he still cared about special days like that, and could be such a stalwart supporter of his family, friends and neighbours.

Hilda had felt fortunate when Donald Hay had come into her life six years earlier in Lethbridge, Alberta. Recently divorced, she was not unattractive but hadn't really expected to find anyone who would be willing to take her on with three young children of her own. Although her daughters Jacqueline and Wendy were then eleven and nine respectively, her son Brent had only just turned six.

Originally from a churchgoing family in Manitoba, Don had impressed Hilda as a hardworking and talented craftsman. He was fond of kids, and obviously regretted that his drinking problems had led to the breakup of two previous marriages and caused him to lose contact with his three natural children. Hearing that his second wife had been unfaithful, Hilda gave him the benefit of the doubt and began living with him on November 1, 1970.

The following year, with Hilda's consent, Don took Wendy and Jacqueline to British Columbia, where he rented a house in Port Coquitlam before sending for Hilda and her youngest child. Hilda then purchased the house at 1601 Gore Street, and Don did well until he succumbed once more to alcohol.

Losing two jobs in succession, he tried to make a living selling Amway products door-to-door but frequently took off for days at a time to consume as many as three bottles of vodka a day at various downtown hotels. Although he seldom *appeared* drunk, Hilda had threatened to leave him, which had caused the October 2, 1974 incident in which he held the family at gunpoint.

Hilda had never been afraid of him until then, but a psychiatrist at the Port Moody police station ascertained that her husband wasn't suffering from any serious mental disturbances. Placed on probation with an order to abstain from alcohol, Don showed remorse and agreed to enter a detoxification program at Riverview Hospital.

"I'll never drink again," he promised Hilda when finally he returned home. "It was awful drying out and going through withdrawal. I never want to go through that again."

What he needed to stay sober, he said, was a new challenge. If he kept his overhead low by working from home, he could create his own business and cash in on the booming recreational vehicle market by building camper units for pickup trucks. All it would take, he convinced Hilda, would be a detached workshop that they could build themselves in the backyard. "I've even got the perfect name for the company," he added. "*Hayvan* Campers Ltd."

Then forty years old, Hay had been anxious to get started, renting a cement mixer on North Road in New Westminster and applying to Port Moody City Hall for a building permit. He intended to do things properly and submit the proper applications.

Don had immersed himself in the project as soon as Hilda

had given her approval, renting the cement mixer again six months later as the wooden structure neared completion. The large building with its high overhead door had gone up sooner than expected. The kids had pitched in for the final touches, painting the new workshop a rich, dark brown with turquoise trim to match the house. With Donald Hay's craftsmanship, there'd never been any doubt that it would turn out to be well-built and designed.

When it was finished in 1974, all of them stood back to admire their handiwork. Bristling with pride, Hay erected a pole beside the workshop so that he could fly the Canadian flag. Stepdaughter Jackie helped him to sweep out the workshop and keep it clean. "Don's very nice when he isn't drunk," Jackie told her Mom.

Hay remained sober as he equipped the workshop with an ever increasing inventory of materials, tools and paints. He extended electric and water lines from the house, and installed a separate oil furnace in the shop so that he could work there year-round. Then he lined the walls with shelves, with lots of upper and lower cabinets for extra storage space.

The business started to show a profit, and Hay quickly developed a good reputation. It was clear to Hilda that he had finally begun to turn over a new leaf. In addition to filing all his sales and income tax reports, he continued to pay his suppliers on time and to impress his customers with the quality of his workmanship. Inevitably, the camper units they drove away far exceeded their expectations.

WITH HILDA AND his stepdaughters, Don arrived at the Drover residence shortly after seven o'clock p.m. He had obviously hurried out of the shower to offer his help, as his thinning hair was still damp and he remained unshaven. Although Ruth didn't know her neighbours too well, Kathleen and Robyn were friends of the Hay children, and watched as Don, wringing his sinewy hands, explained how he had fixed Abby's rock tumbler for her only the night before. "We sure hope nothing's happened to her," he said.

Sitting beside her common-law husband, Hilda Hay seemed small and timid but equally concerned. Hilda described how she'd found out that Abby was late after she herself had returned home from her job in the stockroom at Sears.

After his stepchildren had gone to school, Don added, he had gone into town that morning to get them tickets for an upcoming basketball exhibition by the Harlem Globetrotters. "The kids are really looking forward to it," he said. "When we find Abby, maybe I can get her a ticket too."

"I don't even know where you could begin looking for her," said Ruth, deep fear showing in her eyes.

"Don't worry," said Don. In addition to his own stepdaughters, he suggested, he could also squeeze Abby's sisters into his truck and all five of them could go searching for her. "We can check all the shopping centres," he proposed. Furthermore, he explained, their son Brent had been instructed to stay home in case Abby called there in the meantime.

While the search party set out, Hilda remained with Ruth to offer comfort and support. "Abby's a lovely little girl," she said. "Don and I are both very fond of her. It's my daughter Wendy's fifteenth birthday on the weekend. We hope Abby can come to her party."

Scarcely conscious that Hilda remained with her, Ruth again paced the floors, still occasionally peering through the living room window into the gloom outside. It was two hours before the search party returned, and a downcast Ruth could tell from the looks on their faces that they had been unsuccessful.

Wendy, pert and curvaceous in her skin-tight jeans, was the first to speak. "We went down the highway looking for her school books, but we couldn't find anything of Abby's," she said.

Her sister Jackie shared the family's deepening concern. Plainer and more studious than her sister, Jackie had found some discarded school supplies at the side of Barnet Highway, including a damp exercise book. She hadn't known Abby well but was confident that the smudged writing was definitely not that of Abby Drover.

The makeshift search party also quizzed a young student who thought he had seen Abby on St. John's Street after school. The student must have been mistaken, however, because Abby's teachers had already reported that the girl had not been seen at school throughout the day. Abby, it seemed, had disappeared without a trace. There was no sign of her at all.

Abby's sisters reported how Don had even thought to have the missing girl paged over the loudspeaker system in the K-Mart store at Westwood Mall. Obtaining no response, they had headed hopefully to the perfume counter, but this time Abby had not been there either. Afterwards, Don had waited in the truck while all four girls scoured the grounds of Moody Senior Secondary School.

As Ruth made them coffee, Don and Hilda continued to show empathy and support. "Remember, we're just up the street," said Don. "If there's anything else we can do, anything at all, just give us a call."

No sooner had the neighbours left the Drover residence than Ruth began to get replies to various calls she had made to friends and relatives. None of the calls was from her daughter, however, and each time she answered, Ruth's heart sank. "I've got to hang up in case Abby calls," she would explain to each caller.

The distraught mother was somewhat encouraged when she received a call from her younger sister Del and brother-in-law Doug. Because the young couple lived across the Fraser River in Surrey, it would take them a while to get there, but Ruth eagerly anticipated their arrival.

Tall and brunette, Del was similar to Ruth in looks and personality, and each of the sisters seemed instinctively to know what the other was thinking. Not only had Del and her husband always taken a great interest in their nieces, they also had three daughters of their own. Both she and Doug were quick to agree that Abby was not the kind of girl who would run away from home.

Del hugged Ruth Drover as soon as she arrived. As both of them tried to hold back their tears, Ruth explained how she had contacted the neighbours as well as other friends and relatives. "I don't know what else I can do," she said.

Ruth buried her head in her hands. Although she knew better, she found herself hoping that the runaway theory might be correct. At least that way Abby might be safe — but then she and her daughter had never had any serious arguments. There were the occasional disagreements over what Abby could wear to school, but surely that couldn't be a factor? They were an essentially happy family.

"It's a real mystery," said Ruth. "She wouldn't run away. Either she's hurt and can't get home or something even worse has happened. It's all my fault because I was at work."

"No," said Del. "You've done everything you can for those kids. You mustn't blame yourself."

Kathleen and Robyn looked expectantly at Doug. Surely their favourite uncle could do something? Standing just under six feet, Doug was a good-looking dark-haired man, decked out in immaculately pressed clothes as usual; like Don Hay, he was self-employed, but Doug appeared much more successful as a businessman. Still in his mid-thirties, he already managed his own trucking company and no longer had to do any of the driving himself. He was a take-charge, problem-solving, energetic entrepreneur, and quick-tempered if anyone stood in his way.

Scratching his head for a moment, Doug finally hit on an idea. Perhaps the general public could be of help, he reasoned, if he could persuade local television and radio stations to broadcast a description of Abby, along with the details of her disappearance.

"You'd better check with the police," Del told her husband. Such information, she thought, would probably have already been released, but Doug wasn't about to take anything for granted. He still wanted to confirm that the authorities were doing all they could.

He immediately dialled the police number listed beside Ruth's phone. Doug was quickly connected with a duty officer at the Port Moody Police Department but was angered by the response. In accordance with standard policy, the officer told him, the police didn't plan to go public for at least twenty-four hours. "The majority of these cases turn out to be false alarms," the policeman explained.

"We keep telling you Abby doesn't fit the profile of a runaway child," Doug argued. His voice was rising, but he calmed down as the duty officer showed sympathy and concern. It might not be immediately apparent to the general public, the policeman added, but there were good reasons for procedures that had been tried and tested over a good many years. The officer could well understand, however, that the family wanted immediate action. "I can't see how we'd have any objection," he proposed, "if you want to contact the media yourselves."

"Okay," said Doug, looking at his watch. He appreciated the suggestion but it was getting late. "We'll try to get it on the late night news."

The late BCTV news aired at 11:30 p.m. The newscast would air in most parts of the province, and get picked up by local radio stations.

Initially when Doug called the television studios, someone at BCTV told him much the same thing as the police. If the family waited a day or two, the child would probably show up. Doug, however, insisted on being put through to the newsroom, where he was able to convince a night editor that Abby was not the kind of girl to run away from home.

"We'll be on the air in just over an hour," the night editor said. "If you can bring us a picture of her before then, we can run it with the story."

"Let's go!" Doug said impatiently to his wife. "We might still make it in time." Jumping into their car, he and Del paid little attention to the speed limit as they raced through the night to the BCTV studios. Ushered into the newsroom, they were pleased to learn that their story was already being typed up, and their photograph of Abby was quickly cropped for broadcast. By sheer persistence, Doug and his wife had made the last minute deadline, enabling the story and picture of Abby to be aired that evening.

As a day shift reporter, I must have retired early and missed it, but Ruth and her children were watching the local BCTV newscast at their home and, for the first time that evening, they felt at least a slight glimmer of hope. Among thousands of viewers, perhaps Abby — or someone who knew where she was — might see the broadcast and give them or the police a call.

5 CECIL DROVER

ALTHOUGH it had begun to rain again and the wind had started to blow, the little house at 1617 Barnet Highway shone like a beacon on the dark, remote street. Every light was on, as though to beckon Abby home from the gathering nightfall. Inside the house, gloom and despair usurped the usual sounds of happy family activities, and the familiar, comforting smell of cakes baking in the oven was conspicuously absent.

Ruth Drover went to bed, resisting the temptation of a cigarette, despite having quit rolling as many as fifty cigarettes a day only two years previously. The stress had knocked her right out and she slept soundly. Nothing could have been gained by staying up and pacing the floors anyway, for it wasn't until the next morning that the phone rang, abruptly bringing Ruth back to the awful reality of her daughter's disappearance.

Trembling, Ruth picked up the receiver. It was Corporal Roy Stevens from the Port Moody police department. "You've found Abby?" Ruth said, almost holding her breath.

"No, Mrs. Drover," the officer said sympathetically. "I'm just calling to let you know that we've been able to locate Abby's father. We found him in Calgary. He seems very concerned. He's driving out here right away."

For the past several years, Cecil Drover had been selling cars and working in the southern Alberta city as a painter and decorator. Over the phone, the long-lost father told the police he had never heard from Abby, and he seemed genuinely shocked by her disappearance.

Beyond that, Ruth was told, an officer had been looking for Abby throughout the night. The search had been unsuccessful, but inquiries would continue during the day at known youth hangouts in downtown Vancouver. Abby had recently made a casual remark to a friend that she would like to visit the old revamped Gastown area on the Vancouver waterfront.

"Sometimes these kids stay out overnight and show up in Gastown or at Granville Mall," Corporal Stevens suggested.

"I know she'd never go there by herself," Ruth insisted. She realized police felt it was still too early to discard the runaway theory, but she was eager for the authorities to start viewing her daughter's disappearance as something more sinister. "Abby isn't at all streetwise or tough," said her mother. "She's still very much just a child."

Before Ruth hung up, her older daughters had gathered around the phone trying to overhear bits and pieces of their mother's conversation. It had been ten years since they'd last seen their father. They still vaguely remembered him, but had no idea he was living in the neighbouring province. Calgary, six hundred miles away, was about a twelve-hour drive through the Rocky Mountains. Their father might still arrive in time for supper. Kathleen and Robyn were curious and excited.

Ruth had mixed feelings, however. She wasn't too proud to admit that she was feeling terribly alone. She still felt angry that Cecil had left her with three young children those dozen years ago. Nonetheless, Ruth found herself momentarily looking forward to Cecil's impending return. At least she and her ex-husband could share some mutual concern over their missing daughter.

Ruth made breakfast in a daze, going through the motions of running the household like an automaton. She even did the dishes before leaving a telephone message for her boss to let him know she wouldn't be coming in to work. Although Ruth didn't know it yet, her employers would soon be assisting in the search as though Abby were one of their own. In addition to messages of concern from complete strangers, there would be outpourings of support among Ruth's friends and relatives, as well as former colleagues at places where she had previously worked.

At Shell Canada, where Ruth had recently toiled as a bookkeeper in the oil company's heating services branch, shocked employees hearing radio reports of Abby's disappearance could scarcely believe what had happened. "It was so unexpected," former colleague Doug Larson told Ruth later. "It was so close to home." Aware that Ruth had recently been the victim of an oil theft, the Shell employees collected enough money to pay off her outstanding oil bill for $83.57. "We wanted to let you know that we are thinking of you," said a note accompanying the cancelled invoice. "Your friends at Shell."

MEANWHILE, KATHLEEN and Robyn walked to the house at the end of Gore Street to tell Donald Hay that Abby still hadn't come home. The handyman appeared unshaven but was already working in his shop. "Can Wendy, Jackie and Brent come with us to search for Abby before school?" they asked. As usual, Hay was considerate, sympathetic and helpful. He put down his tools, bowed his head and looked at Abby's sisters with compassion. "Sure, that's okay," he said, starting up his truck. "Call the kids from the house. We'll all go looking for her at Rocky Point Park."

Members of the search party looked up and down Barnet Highway as they drove toward Port Moody. There, Hay waited in his truck while the five children scoured the park without success. After searching through bushes behind the elementary school, the girls inquired at stores and gas stations but found no trace of Abby. "We walked all over Port Moody," Wendy told Ruth when they returned. "We didn't find anything of hers. Don said that it was too bad that she was the one to go missing." Ruth was too distracted to ponder Hay's strange way of putting it.

After Hay drove them home, the children set out for their respective schools. Other kids, they noticed, headed for their classes either with their parents or in large groups. The previous night's newscast about Abby's disappearance had rippled through the small community, setting off a wave of fear.

At the Port Moody elementary school, Principal Ed Parkachin was stunned by the disappearance of one of his pupils. Some schools had begun contacting parents at home (or at work) if their children failed to show up for classes without notification, but such a policy had not yet been instituted at Moody Elementary. Parkachin was aware that Abby had transferred to the school from Burnaby only four months previously, but he doubted she was a runaway, because it seemed to him that she had adapted well to her new surroundings. "She's already made lots of friends," he told a local reporter. "I would never think of her as stubborn or headstrong. She's just a run-of-the-mill kid."

Parkachin and his staff did their best to comfort Abby's classmates. "We want you to be cautious and not to talk to strangers," the principal said gently. He wanted to warn the schoolchildren without causing them undue alarm; it was a difficult balance to strike.

During recess, several teachers kept an eye on the children as they played on the swings and other equipment outside. The playground was partially fenced but precariously located in front of the school, immediately adjacent to the street. Concerned teachers nervously scanned the general surroundings for anything suspicious.

Throughout Greater Vancouver, many others had seen the previous night's newscast about Abby's disappearance, including Dr. Mitchell Rubin, the Drovers' much beloved family physician. Arriving at his office near the Oakridge shopping centre in Vancouver, Rubin pondered what to do. He had attended at the births of each of the Drover children and made house calls to their residence over the years. When Abby had chicken pox, Ruth had calmed the girl by telling her what a wonderful, kind and gentle practitioner Dr. Rubin was. The news of Abby's disappearance had moved the doctor to tears, and he was eager to help the Drover family. Finally the grey-haired family physician put on his half-glasses and wrote out a prescription.

Ruth felt no obvious need for medication, but the doctor's receptionist phoned to suggest otherwise. The doctor, she informed Ruth, had paid for a prescription that was now on its way to the house by courier. "Dr. Rubin is very upset," the receptionist told Ruth. "He thinks you should have some sedatives. You don't need an appointment. You can come in any time if you want to see him. In any case, he wants you to call him the moment you have any news."

Reluctantly, Ruth took one of the sedatives that afternoon. She wanted to be alert in case there was anything more she could do. She and the kids had already scoured Abby's bedroom, as well as the rest of the house, in case they might find a note explaining her absence. There was nothing; no explanation, no clues, just an overwhelming sense of helplessness and frustration.

Now, as she entered Abby's room for another look, Ruth no longer cared that it wasn't the tidiest part of the house. Her eyes fell upon a broken doll that Abby had had since she was a baby, and it brought back a flood of memories. Ruth found herself again regretting she hadn't always had as much time for Abby as she would have wished. For the second time since Abby had first disappeared, Ruth broke down and cried.

There was still no news of Abby as darkness fell over Port Moody and seemed to gather over members of the Drover family as they gazed at Abby's empty chair. They had just finished picking at a makeshift dinner when they heard the rumble of a car engine shutting down outside on Gore Street. With the sound of footsteps approaching the house, a hopeful Ruth descended the staircase to open the front door.

Dressed in a suit and tie, the tall man standing on the porch outside looked sheepish and uncomfortable. His dark hair hadn't greyed at all, but he'd gained a lot of weight since the last time Ruth had seen him. Even so, she recognized him immediately, and there was a moment of awkward silence as they beheld each other for the first time in ten years. "Wow, you were really skinny the last time I saw you!" said Ruth.

"I know," Cecil Drover replied. Obviously tired after his long drive from Calgary, he nevertheless endeavoured to project some energy. "Ruth," he said, "I wish I could have seen the kids growing up. I can't tell you how sad I feel about this whole thing."

Ruth's eldest daughters still vaguely remembered their father, and Robyn especially hit it off with him as they pored over family photo albums, bringing Cecil up to date on the family from which he'd been so long estranged.

Meanwhile, Ruth informed her ex-husband of the efforts that had been made to find Abby so far. There was nothing he could really do, they agreed, other than to help in the full-scale search that was being organized by the police and volunteers for the upcoming weekend.

Admitting he didn't have any other suggestions, Cecil agreed to help in the search. It was getting late when he prepared to leave for the night, and he declined an invitation of something to eat. He didn't say where he would be staying, but confirmed he would drop by each day before returning to Calgary. Even though he now had a second family, all of the girls, he said, would be welcome to visit him there — and hopefully that would include Abby as soon as she was found.

The next morning, Friday, March 12, the decision was made at the Port Moody police station to record Abby's description and details of her case in the computer data bank operated by CPIC, the Canadian Police Information Centre. Overseeing the investigation, Chief McCabe also decided it was time to seek public assistance. Now that forty-eight hours had elapsed since Abby's disappearance, both Vancouver's daily newspapers — the *Sun* and the *Province* — were afforded full police cooperation.

"We checked every kid in the school in case she was staying with a friend," Corporal Roy Stevens told the newspapers. "We are really concerned. She's a quiet girl who never hitchhikes and there are no problems with her family we know of. She isn't the type of girl to just disappear."

Stevens added that there were several runaway children in Port Moody at any given time despite the fact that it was a relatively small town. But Abby's disappearance did not fit any of the usual patterns. The girl had apparently left home without any money. While she may have been carrying her schoolbooks, she didn't even have a purse. Nothing appeared to have been taken from her home except the clothes she was wearing when last seen by members of her family. "There are several aspects of this case that concern us very much," Stevens said. Repeating Abby's description, he appealed to the public to contact the Port Moody Police Department with any pertinent information.

By now, police had searched through some old horse barns on Oakmount Drive and checked out a remote Bible camp on Ioco Road. But as the search expanded to the wilderness areas north of town, another chilling possibility arose. Since moving to Port Moody, Ruth Drover had seen deer in the area, but was also aware of occasional sightings of bears and cougars. Abby's mother preferred not to think about it, but the fact remained that bears had just finished hibernating through the winter and would be emerging from their dens with their cubs. Weighing upwards of four hundred pounds, a hungry black bear could easily outrun and maul a human to death. And the possibility of a cougar attack was even more frightening. Nationally, only a half-dozen fatal cougar attacks had been recorded during the past hundred years — all of them so far involving children. If undisturbed, the big cats would eat the majority of their prey, and bury the remainder where the victim would likely never be found.

The police hadn't ruled out *any* possibilities, but were pre-occupied with arranging a full-scale search to begin on Saturday morning. Through local hockey teams, word had been cir-culated that volunteers would be welcome to gather at Port Moody Elementary School. When Saturday morning arrived, members of the Drover family were heartened and surprised by the turnout. Almost three hundred people had shown up at the makeshift command post to offer their assistance. Port Moody, it seemed, was a community that cared.

In addition to the large numbers of people on foot, several volunteers had arrived in four-wheel-drive vehicles, and seven dirt bikes were available to traverse even the most difficult ter-rain. As promised, two machines from Transwest Helicopters, the company for which Ruth Drover then worked, waited in the schoolgrounds to take off for an aerial search, while a boat was positioned in the nearby harbour ready to scour the waters of Burrard Inlet. There was no practical way to drag the inlet, however. As one police officer explained, "It is too deep, too wide and has too many obstacles."

The same officer persuaded Abby's mother to stay at home while the search took place, assuring Ruth she'd be the first to know of any developments.

Dividing the volunteers into eighteen teams, police advised the searchers they hoped to cover as much of the thirteen-square-mile municipality as possible before nightfall. Each team, consisting of eight to fourteen members, was assigned a specific area. Unless they found Abby in the meantime, they would meet back at the command post at dusk to discuss anything promising they'd found.

After receiving instructions from the police coordinators, the volunteers fanned out to search the city as well as the thick bushland north of town and on nearby Burnaby Mountain. There, they found several unoccupied "camps". Searcher George Zubak, clad in boots, jeans and a warm jacket, picked up a rain soaked, one-man tent that he found in a mossy clearing, but the canvas shelter had obviously been abandoned months before.

At least two of the police officers taking part in the search were doing so on their own time. Constable Wayne Smith, a family man, had given up his Saturday off to take his first-ever helicopter ride. "We searched just above the trees and we also seemed to be in close proximity to the power lines across Burrard Inlet," he would later recall. "Basically we were looking for anything out of the ordinary. We found an old still but not much else."

Meanwhile, as they scoured and prodded through the woods below, several of the searchers called out Abby's name. But no response came, except the occasional birdcall or the whir of the helicopters fluttering overhead.

In the end, it was a frustrating day and the searchers had to admit they were stumped. Abby Drover, it seemed, had disappeared without a trace. By now, she — or her remains — could be miles away. Certainly, it was unlikely that the searchers could have overlooked some kind of clues if the young girl still languished anywhere close to home.

For now, at least, it was over. Cecil Drover dropped by for a last visit at the gloomy house at 1617 Barnet Highway before climbing into his car, bidding everyone a sad farewell and setting out for his return to Calgary.

6 WITHOUT A TRACE

LISTENING TO YET another radio newscast, a terrified Abby Drover felt increasingly desperate knowing that everyone had been looking for her without success. Despite their efforts, they were still no closer to finding her than they had been from the start. Throughout, she had remained trapped in the same cramped surroundings, her heart sinking in utter frustration at being unable to communicate her dreadful plight. In constant fear, the child was hungry and cold. She was losing her strength with each passing day, but she refused to give up hope. Unless he killed her, she had to come up with some way to survive.

Until her voice had become hoarse and faded, Abby had screamed for help at the top of her lungs. She had heard muffled sounds from the outside world but, after a day or two, had realized with a sinking heart that no one could hear her.

The girl trembled as she picked up the ball-point pen from her school supplies and made yet another mark on the palm of her hand. There were seven ink marks now. It had been exactly that many days since she'd been forced into the damp, filthy cell, where she had been repeatedly raped and defiled. The solid walls around her precluded any hope of escape, but she still prayed for a miracle.

As she looked at her dark, dismal, surroundings, Abby could taste the tears that streamed constantly down her face. She wondered what her family must be thinking. Would they ever see her again? She had realized the danger at the very last moment, but it had been much too late. She should never have trusted the man to give her a ride. She should have known better. Her mother, she suspected, would be angry with her. If only she hadn't dawdled and been late for school, this might never have happened.

Abby had tried to run away when Donald Hay started to force her into the dungeon, but she had only taken a couple of steps when he grabbed her. Helpless in his vise-like grip, she'd felt her heart pounding wildly as he dragged her roughly into the cell. Then he had kicked shut the heavy door behind them with a flick of his foot. With no handle inside the door, she was completely trapped.

It was obvious now that no one had seen the abduction. Although she was in constant fear for her life, Abby was so lonely she could scream. She had begged her captor to bring her a dog or a cat for company, but her request had been denied. The cell had been dusty and dry at first, but now water was beginning to seep in. The child's only comfort was an old radio beside her bed — a damp mattress atop a rickety bed frame, which was beginning to make her stiff and sore.

Hay had ordered her to be quiet, warning her not to turn up the volume on the radio. "If you do," he said, "I might have to strangle you." Numb with fright, the child sat transfixed as the man coldly explained how he might have to dispose of her body in the ocean.

But nobody outside would have heard the radio anyway. The heavy plank door to the cell was insulated with thick foam rubber as well as a piece of old carpet. At first the child had felt slightly encouraged by the radio reports that the police did not believe she was a runaway. Every hour, immediately after the familiar news tone, she had listened eagerly for new developments. With the broadcasts saying that people had searched everywhere without a lead, however, Abby began to lose hope. Was anyone still looking for her? The reports of her disappearance were fading with each passing day.

The child could still listen to music and weather reports but, since the fan had broken down, the atmosphere in the cell had become suffocating and stagnant. In one corner opposite the bed was a portable chemical toilet. There seemed to be an air vent, but there were no windows. The only source of light was a bare 60-watt bulb in the low, acoustic-tile ceiling above her. Abby hoped it wouldn't burn out.

There was a wash basin with cold running water on the opposite wall. Filling a glass with water, Abby looked with despair at the almost totally bare shelves above the sink. She had been unable to stomach the canned sardines or most of the other meagre food supplies that her captor had left for her.

Without help, the child realized, escape would be impossible. Trapped in the cell, which measured about five by seven feet, she was effectively entombed. Perhaps if she tried to befriend Hay, thought Abby, she might be able to persuade him to release her. In time, she thought, perhaps she could outsmart him.

Abby replayed that first day in her mind, as she had done countless times already. She had struggled, but Hay was far too strong for her to fight him back. She had immediately realized she was in his control. Then, as now, she had thought her life was over. Thinking back, sheer terror wouldn't even begin to describe it. There wasn't a word in the dictionary that would have explained her fear and helplessness.

She recalled vividly each word of their conversation as it had unfolded during those first, almost surreal, moments in captivity.

"Don't scream," Hay had hissed. "I don't want to hurt you."

"What do you want?" asked Abby, crying.

"Sit down on the bed," he ordered. "I want to play house. I'm the dad and you're the mom."

Abby was still a virgin but she knew what he meant. She froze as the man pushed up her sweater, placing his hands on her slender waist and quickly pulling down her pants. Naked except for her socks and boots, the child shrieked with fear and embarrassment as Hay attempted to rape her. Up close, she could smell him; it was a strange mix of alcohol and fuel oil. Abby went limp. Shock intervened as she began to mentally block him out, but she gained a temporary respite: frustrated in his attempts to penetrate her, the man gave up and allowed her to get dressed.

"Quit crying!" he snapped, as the child sobbed uncontrollably. "I'm going to let you go before school gets out, anyway."

Praying she could believe him, Abby stopped struggling before she realized that he was only just beginning. She froze

in horror as he slapped her tightly in handcuffs, which he secured to the wall above the bed. Then he chained her feet to
the bed's footboard before leaving. Returning a few moments
later with Abby's schoolbooks and lunch supplies, the man seemed
to be having second thoughts. "Don't think you're the only one
who's frightened," he said, "I'm pretty damn scared myself."

"Please let me go!" Abby begged. "My mom would be mad
if she knew I was late for school. I can still make it in time. I'll
be your friend. I promise I won't tell anybody."

Hay could see she was lying. If he let her go, obviously she
would tell the whole world what had happened to her. Briefly,
he equivocated, but he had spent far too long creating this
scenario to let her go now. Abby's eyes widened with fear as
the man stuffed a dusty rag in her mouth, securing the gag
with duct tape. Ignoring her panic, he leered at her with satisfaction as he rose to leave.

"I've got to work for a while," he said. "Don't move till I
get back or the chains will just get tighter and hurt."

The rag in her mouth tasted of rust. Frantic, recalling her
childhood allergies, Abby was suffocating. Momentarily, though,
she stopped panicking as she remembered how she had always
been able to escape when her sisters had playfully tied her up.
Moistening the dirty blue cloth with her tongue, she managed
to push it out of her mouth. Taking in a deep gulp of air, the
child wriggled out of her boots to release her feet. Removing
the chains, she then slipped her boots back on, hoping that might
confuse her captor as to how she had gotten partially free.

In the midst of trying to get the handcuffs off her wrists,
Abby heard the door being unlocked. He was coming back.

"How the hell did you get untied?" Hay barked. He seemed
disappointed and angry. If he had intended to rape a completely
restrained victim, the young girl had at least partially thwarted his
plans. "I had this all planned and now you've gone and ruined it,"
he said. It was as if his fantasies had suddenly evaporated and it
would take time for him to recharge his libido.

Despite her tender years, Abby was quickly able to sense her captor's flaws and weaknesses. It would be a calculated risk but, from now on, she would try to frustrate his plans at every opportunity. She still hoped that the man was about to release her but was unable to reason with him for the time being. "I can't let you go yet," he said. "I'm scared you might tell somebody. I just want to think about it a little while. I'll let you go after supper."

This time, instead of the chains, Hay tied her to the bed with rope. As he fumbled with the dirty blue cloth, the child pleaded with him not to gag her again. "I couldn't breathe with that in my mouth," Abby told him. "That's why I had to take it out."

For once, the man heeded her pleas. "The place is sound-proof anyway," he confirmed. "It doesn't matter whether you scream or not."

If that were the case, Abby thought, why had he threatened to strangle her if she screamed? Although he hadn't beaten her, he was obviously deriving pleasure from inflicting psychological pain; he was even sicker than she had first thought.

What Hay hadn't bargained for, though, was the child's determination. This time, after he left, she struggled to undo the rope with her teeth, managing to get free but deeply scraping her face in the process.

"How the hell did you get untied again?" Hay asked upon his return. Abby ignored him as she rubbed her swollen wrists. Tying her up, he seemed to realize, was futile. He promised not to shackle her again. Suddenly he seemed concerned about the child's bruises, and his tone became softer.

"I love you," he said.

Abby looked at him with astonishment. "I'm just a kid," she replied, as though she had to explain that to him. "What kind of love?"

"I want to protect you," Hay replied. "I have to keep you here for a while. I'm not going to be able to let you go tonight."

"Why?" asked Abby. "You promised you would. I still won't tell anybody."

Sitting on an old chair at the end of the bed, Hay sighed as he held his head in his hands. "People are starting to look for you," he explained. "I'll wait till morning when everybody has gone to school and I'll let you go then."

Abby would soon realize the futility of hoping for release, but as he left that night, she believed him. There was a tattered red and brown sleeping bag on the bed, but the stuffing was coming out and it would have afforded little warmth; despite the cold air, she couldn't bring herself to climb into it. Like everything else in the cell, the sleeping bag was musty. It was as though all the furnishings her captor had provided had come from a junkyard.

The first night, Abby had stood on the bed and pounded on the ceiling. Outside, she could hear voices and traffic. "Help, help, let me out!" she cried, but there was no response. It was the same when she screamed into the air vent. She called for her mother repeatedly, but her pleas had gone unheeded throughout the night. The child couldn't figure out why no one could hear her. She tried but was unable to budge the door. Again, Abby froze as she began to comprehend her predicament. What if there was a fire or he never came back?

Abby checked each of the few items on the shelves. There were some dry crackers, canned peaches, some Laura Secord pudding, a jar of marmalade, and some sardines. For the first time, she noticed there was also a small hotplate, but it brought her little comfort. It was just one more indication that her captor had equipped the cell to imprison somebody for a long time. He'd obviously gone to the utmost lengths to build the place.

Spurning the food he'd left her, Abby suddenly realized she still had her lunchbox. She had packed the lunch herself before leaving for school. Hungrily, she drank the milk and devoured the sandwich and cookies inside.

Abby hadn't eaten much since then. She had always been slender, but now she was getting even thinner and could see the bones beginning to protrude from her arms. The cell was so small that there was scarcely enough room to turn around. Sitting on a bed for a week hadn't required much energy, but she had also lost her appetite and slept little on account of the things Hay had done to her. "If I come in and find you sleeping, I'll take advantage of you," he had warned. Since then, Abby had remained almost constantly awake. She had never been caught asleep when he visited.

When she did occasionally doze off in his absence, she dreamt that there were two windows in the cell. She planned to climb through one of them, but the window overlooked a cliff. The other window was too high to reach. Even in her dreams, escape was impossible.

Though her head ached, the child stayed awake all night listening to the radio, which she left on twenty-four hours a day. Apart from newscasts about the efforts to find her, Abby listened to old drama programs hosted by CKNW broadcast personality Jack Cullen. Although some of them were horror stories, they were tame by comparison to her own plight.

Abby was fascinated, her imagination supplying visual images in the absence of the TV pictures to which she was accustomed. At least it was an escape of sorts, and the child hoped fervently that the radio wouldn't stop working. It was the only friend she had, and the only way she could keep track of time.

Hay returned the following day just after she should normally have left for school. He admitted then that he'd designed the room specifically to hold a young girl hostage. He shocked Abby by admitting he had originally planned the cell for his own stepdaughter Wendy, but he had felt it too risky and had changed his mind when he first saw Abby. As he sat talking to her, the man drank some liquor out of a mug.

"Have a drink with me," he offered.

"No, I don't drink," said Abby. "It tastes terrible. I already told you, I'm just a kid."

"Well, what can I get you?" her neighbour asked, as though suddenly motivated by generosity.

"I want some proper food," the girl replied. "I can't eat all this canned food and stale crackers."

Hay said he would consider Abby's request, but first she would have to do something for him. It was obvious to the child that things were going to get worse. For now, she was completely at his mercy. Sitting on the chair at the end of the bed, the man forced her to kneel in front of him. Too afraid to resist, Abby shuddered as he unzipped his pants and forced her head down to his groin. She had heard of this from her abused schoolfriend Sandra, but nothing had prepared her for the revulsion and fear she felt as she pleaded with him to stop.

"No, no, please don't," she begged, but the man threatened her and held her down until he ejaculated in her mouth. Seeing the child's reaction, he moaned and then laughed, "Don't you like Hay's cough mixture?"

Abby heaved so violently that the man tried to push her away, but the room was too small for him to back off. The only other time the girl could remember feeling so sick was when her mother had washed out her mouth with soap for using bad language. She decided that in the future she would eat some soap when she could hear him coming; if she were gagging whenever he came into the cell, it might deter him from a re-peat performance.

She hadn't seen the man throughout the first weekend. On Monday, while using the hotplate to warm some food, Abby heard him coming back. It was too late to eat any soap, but her jailer seemed a little more friendly. "I still love you," he repeated. "I want to protect you." The man had brought more books for her, but they were beyond her reading comprehension. One of them was a volume entitled, *You Can Change Your Life Through Psychic Power*. Again, Abby reminded him: "I am just a kid."

If she pretended to be his friend, Abby reasoned, maybe he would be more sympathetic. Obviously, if he thought he loved her, he must be mentally unbalanced. "Maybe if I can get him to trust me, I can live," thought Abby.

But how could she go on pretending to be his friend? At first the man had been unable to rape her, but he had kept on trying until he had succeeded. She would have preferred to have defied him openly at every opportunity but now realized that subtle resistance might be safer and more effective. Several times, finding the child constantly crying, Hay left without molesting her.

Apparently his fantasy wasn't working out the way he had hoped, but his disappointment would not be without retribution. In retaliation, the man returned to the cell to show Abby one of her missing posters. He taunted the child with speculation about how her mother and sisters might be reacting. The child cried, knowing how worried they must be. They would attempt to draw on their religion, she suspected, but in reality their faith was not as strong as hers. For his part, the man could see that Abby became upset whenever he talked about her family. Perhaps he could make her compliant yet.

Furthermore, he wanted to know if the child had any rich relatives from whom he might be able to extort a ransom. Both of them knew from the radio that her father had taken part in the search, but Hay seemed to believe the child when she told him that none of her relatives had any money. If that were the case, he retorted, she was going to have to do things to earn her keep. "You either work for a living, or I won't bring you any food," he told her.

As she lay on the bed, Abby spent hours imagining herself in a different life, with make-believe friends. She felt as if she were watching herself from a distance. Living in her dream world, she fantasized about being grown up with her own family, living a happy life with a perfect husband and a dozen kids.

But too often she was jolted back to reality. As part of his sick game, Hay had told her always to take off her clothes when she heard him coming, so that she would be ready for him when he entered the room. After the first few days, she had defied him.

Abby could tell that the man had been drinking, though he was still coherent. "Take your clothes off," he ordered. Silently,

Abby complied, removing everything except her socks. He never made her take her socks off. But again he forced the child to fellate him before he entered her. Abby felt the man climax inside her. After getting off her, he sat on his chair at the end of the bed. Refusing to let the child get dressed, he fondled her small breasts, drinking and smoking as he sat there with his pants off. "I'm still trying to think of some way of letting you go," he said, but Abby was convinced that he was lying. Never once had he allowed her past that heavy plank door. One way or another, it now seemed certain that she would die inside this cell.

Abby prayed. God had helped her so far, she thought, but somehow she had to figure out a way to escape. Perhaps, she thought, there might be some way of hiding a note and getting it to the outside world.

7 NEWSROOM

City Editor Don MacLachlan arrived for work as usual at the newsroom of the *Province* in Vancouver at 9 a.m. on Monday morning. Located on the south shore of False Creek, the Pacific Press Building had a spectacular view of the downtown peninsula but was cut off from the bustle of the city by the six-lane Granville Street Bridge. Occasionally, some of the reporters grumbled about it, but the city editor had no time for complainers. He ran a tight ship.

An avid sailor, MacLachlan sported a full mustache and beard but was otherwise conservative in his mannerisms, dress and views. The bespectacled editor was an average-sized man in his mid-thirties, who could be curt and abrasive with his cityside staff if they failed to meet his expectations. Generally, though, he had their respect for his ability to judge what was newsworthy and for not sending them on trivial assignments or wild goose chases.

Against the incessant background clatter of teletype machines, MacLachlan scanned the weekend papers and then thumbed through his files, updating the memos that he would divide up and assign to his reporters. Behind him, a large wall map with five clocks showing different time zones around the world gave the cavernous newsroom a feeling of relevance and importance, though it was more for show than practical use. At least it seemed to impress the schoolchildren who occasionally came on field trips to the big-city newspaper.

Like their contemporaries at many other North American dailies, reporters at the *Province* were currently caught up in the midst of technological change. Typewriters were finally being replaced in 1976 by first-generation video display terminals, eliminating the need for stories to be reset on the old linotypes that had been a fixture of modern newspapers since their inception. The old image of the hard drinking reporter with a bottle of whisky in his desk had become virtually a thing of the past, but most of the desks still had heavy black ashtrays, their contents filling the air with ever more cigarette smoke as the nightly deadlines approached.

As he scanned his files, the city editor decided the Abby Drover story wasn't yet a priority. There was no indication that the girl might not show up safe and sound, but the search of Burrard Inlet caught the nautical man's attention. He scanned the newsroom deciding who would be the reporter to follow it up.

I was one of those *Province* reporters, but I must have been working on other stories. I had passed through Port Moody on my way to Vancouver ten years earlier, but neither the city nor the Abby Drover disappearance meant much to me at the time. Eventually, however, the part of the story I did cover would haunt me forever.

Instead, MacLachlan approached the desk of Georgina Hammond, a thin, serious, dark-haired woman who had only recently joined the paper but had already proved herself to be a conscientious and reliable member of the staff. "We've still got this missing girl in Port Moody," said MacLachlan, handing her the file. "See if you can find out if there are any new angles."

Georgina took a sip of her coffee and nodded, although it was not a task she relished. Looking through the earlier stories, it was obvious she would have to call Abby's mother. Contrary to public perception, newspaper reporters are no more heartless than anyone else when it comes to intruding on family at a time of tragedy, but it was a job that had to be done. After researching the limited information at hand, Georgina began to assemble what few details she could find for next morning's issue of the paper.

Among the loose ends were persistent reports that police wanted to talk to a twenty-six-year-old man in connection with Abby's disappearance. Following the full-scale search on Saturday, a Vancouver citizen had phoned to report that a man in a beer parlour had shown him a photograph of a twelve-year-old girl who he claimed was his daughter. The informant had thought it odd that such a young man might have a daughter of that age, and his suspicions had been further aroused on seeing the man leave the beer parlour in a gold coloured Oldsmobile with front-end damage.

Upon phoning the Port Moody police station, however, Georgina drew a blank. Apparently, it was just the first of what would turn out to be hundreds of false leads. "We've determined the man was older than we first thought," Corporal Rick Nelson explained to the reporter. "We might want to find out if his car damage resulted from a possible hit and run, but we've pretty much ruled him out as being involved in Abby's disappearance."

With trepidation, Georgina now phoned the Drover residence and found Abby's mother remarkably helpful and coherent under the circumstances. Ruth Drover cooperatively recounted the details of her daughter's disappearance.

"Is there any chance she could have run away?" Georgina asked nervously.

"No," Ruth said emphatically. Despite having been asked the same question over and over again she remained patient. "She's a good kid. She's very respectful. She wouldn't go anywhere without telling me first."

Ruth added that Abby regularly attended church services in New Westminster and got on well with her sisters. "She normally walks to school with a group of friends, but on Wednesday she dawdled taking out the garbage and missed them. One of her friends offered her a dime to take the bus, but she refused, and said she'd walk."

"Is there anything else that I can put in my report?" Georgina asked.

Ruth Drover remained convinced that her daughter had not run away, but told the reporter she could quote a mother's appeal. "Please tell Abby she has nothing to fear by coming home," said Ruth. "We just want to see her alive and healthy."

The story ran in the next day's issue of the *Province*, appearing on page 10 under the heading: "Abby's mother seeks help." At her home on Barnet Highway, Ruth Drover read the article believing the more publicity she could generate, the better the chance that someone might come forward with some pertinent information.

Ruth clipped out the article and placed it in a file with everything else she could get her hands on concerning Abby's disappearance. Her work training had made her well organized and she wanted to keep all the newspaper accounts, phone numbers, police records — anything remotely to do with the case — in the event such information might ever be needed.

Being a strong woman, she had reported back to work, believing some routine in her life would make her more effective at dealing with her feelings of helplessness and frustration. "I was on automatic," she recalled, "but everybody at work was so helpful and concerned. Wherever the Transwest pilots went throughout the province, they put up the missing posters. Some of them even got circulated as far away as Alaska."

Still, it was hard to remain optimistic. Following Georgina Hammond's article in the *Province*, a more ominous story struck fear in Ruth's heart as she thumbed through the next day's edition of the local weekly *Enterprise*. There, her eyes focused on the large block letters of a headline:

MOODY GIRL MAY BE DEAD.

Ruth felt pangs of fear as she sat down to read the accompanying article. According to the report, hope that Abby might still be alive had begun to diminish in light of the unsuccessful weekend search. Because the girl had not been at school on the day of her disappearance, the report added, evidence now indicated she had "mysteriously vanished" in the morning, and not in the afternoon as first believed.

After reading the article at her kitchen table, Ruth stoically managed to clip it out and place it with the rest of her files. No sooner had she done so than the doorbell rang. Who could it be this time? Despite the headline, Ruth felt strongly that Abby was still alive and rushed to the front entrance in anticipation of good news.

Folding his umbrella, Pastor Bill Tucker stood on the doorstep looking glum. A tall man in his mid-thirties, the minister from the Seventh-Day Adventist Church in New Westminster had no news of Abby but had called to lend the family his support. Ruth invited the pastor in. She poured him a glass of fruit juice, knowing that his religion precluded anything more stimulating, including even tea or coffee.

Immaculate in his suit and tie, the crease in his trousers as sharp as a knife, Pastor Tucker sat down to drink his juice and inform Ruth that members of the congregation had been sending up prayers to the church rafters and beyond for Abby's safe return. "We have sent up so many prayers," he said comfortingly. "I am sure God is listening." When they felt the time was nigh, the pastor suggested, the Drover girls could together fulfill their wishes to be baptized. If there was anything else he could do, he told Ruth, she could call him at any hour, day or night.

It was crucial to Ruth Drover and her family that they keep the faith — as it would soon be sorely tested by the many twists, turns and mysterious events yet to take place.

8 REWARDS

IT WAS STILL ONLY midday, but Norm Patterson, a friendly, gregarious man in his early forties, looked at the gathering black clouds above him and turned on his headlights. The fastest speed of his windshield wipers seemed scarcely adequate against the increasing downpour, but the weekday commute was a ritual to which he'd become accustomed. Since becoming mayor of Port Moody, Patterson had been leaving his downtown stockbroker job every lunchtime and driving back to his city hall office to spend his afternoons and evenings working in his role as a civic politician.

Leaving Vancouver, Patterson turned east onto Hastings Street, which eventually threaded through Burnaby and turned into Barnet Highway. At least it was an easy drive, the mayor reflected — just one thoroughfare paralleling Burrard Inlet and the Canadian Pacific Railway — but his two full-time jobs meant he never had time to stop for lunch.

In keeping with his routine, Patterson juggled a sandwich and coffee between himself and the steering wheel, one thought uppermost on his mind as he drove through the rain. Today, he reflected, had marked one week since the mysterious disappearance of Abby Drover, and the mayor wanted to get back to his municipal office to see if there was something he could do. His hectic pace might have caused an ulcer in some people, but the forty-two-year-old was a big, easy-going man able to take things in his stride.

Upon leaving school, Patterson had joined the Dominion Bank. Transferred to the west coast, he and his wife Dorothy had no sooner returned with a baby girl to their new home in Port Moody than they were again transferred to one of the bank's existing branches on Vancouver Island.

After renting their property for the next twenty-four months, the Pattersons had finally returned to the mainland. Deciding

Port Moody was a good, safe place to put down roots, Patterson chose to avoid the constant spectre of transfers by quitting the bank altogether. In 1963, the young family man decided to become a stockbroker.

It was a strange year, a time when things suddenly seemed less secure. Less than a month after the assassination of President John F. Kennedy, Patterson and others of his generation were jolted again when singer Frank Sinatra's son was kidnapped near Lake Tahoe and held two and a half days for $240,000 ransom. Patterson and others would find the events of special significance later, but such things for the time being, at least, seemed far removed from the quiet backwater of Port Moody.

Over the next twelve years, Patterson got to know numerous Port Moody residents."You know, Norm, a lot of us would like to see you run for council," local salesman Harvey Cook proposed one day. "We think you'd do a good job."

The popular Patterson was reluctant to get involved in municipal politics. He agreed, however, that he would run for council "if for some reason one of your team of candidates has to drop out." Relaxing at home not long afterwards, Patterson and his wife were enjoying a cold drink when they spotted Harvey Cook walking up their driveway. "I have a funny feeling here comes trouble," Patterson groaned.

Sure enough, just as he feared, one of the nominees had pulled out of the race and Patterson felt obligated to keep his promise. He did, however, lay down certain conditions. "Okay, Harvey," he smiled, "now that you've got me to run, you'd better make sure you get me elected. Furthermore, you can darn well be my campaign manager."

After being duly sworn in as a member of council, Patterson successfully spearheaded the construction of several new community facilities and easily won re-election for a second term. Four years later, running as a free-enterprise candidate, he had become mayor when the incumbent stepped down on account of poor health.

Now, after parking outside the old city hall building on St. John's Street, Patterson walked into his office, tossed his sandwich wrapper and paper coffee cup into a wastebasket and gazed out across the grey expanse of Burrard Inlet. The two-storey heritage structure did at least have a partial view, overlooking the whitecaps now forming on the wind-whipped inlet, but the building was so small that the council chambers themselves were located down the street in the almost equally old police building.

Underneath the glad-handing political facade, Patterson remained very much an unassuming man with traditional tastes and family values. Abby Drover had vanished right here in his city, and it was almost as if this child had been one of his own. The mayor didn't hesitate long before he picked up the phone to call Police Chief McCabe. "Len," he said informally, "it's Norm Patterson calling about this Abby Drover case."

At the other end of the line, the chief seemed a bit on edge too, perhaps wondering if the mayor might be critical about the lack of results from the police efforts so far. "Yeah, Norm," he replied, trying not to sound too despondent. "I guess you know we had the big search on the weekend. We've had scads of calls from people who think they've spotted Abby after seeing her picture in the paper, but nothing concrete so far." Warily, the chief continued with his account of the investigation. Another lead, he advised, had sounded quite promising. A man had been observed taking pictures of children outside Port Moody Elementary School, but he had vanished and had not returned. "Did you have anything particular in mind?" McCabe asked.

"I was wondering," said Patterson, "if the council put up a reward, whether you think that might help?"

"Hmmm," McCabe pondered. "I can't see that it would hurt. How much were you thinking?"

"No particular amount at the moment," said Patterson. "Within reason, whatever I can get the council to agree on. If it's okay with you, I'll go ahead and see if I can get it on the agenda for our next meeting."

At the police station, the switchboard continued to light up. Over the next few days, almost one hundred calls flooded in from communities all across Canada. In addition, several people called to say they thought they had seen Abby in various locations in the United States.

On March 16, police thought they had a hot new lead when a man acting suspiciously with a large blue trunk in the back of his car was detained for questioning by the Royal Canadian Mounted Police in the small B.C. mountain community of Sparwood, not far from the Alberta border.

Chief McCabe quickly attempted to have two of his members fly up to the mountain town, only to be thwarted by a late winter blizzard that would have precluded their landing. The RCMP advised they were releasing the man because they could only detain him for twenty-four hours without charge. "I've done nothing wrong," the suspect insisted. "I'll go to Port Moody voluntarily to talk with them."

But the man and his trunk disappeared. Despite reports he'd been seen at a motel in the Fraser Valley on the way back to Greater Vancouver, neither he nor his trunk was ever located, even though McCabe asked police officers to check every Fraser Valley motel between Vancouver and Hope.

The next day, one week after Abby's disappearance, there seemed to be another promising lead. Members of the Vancouver Police Department announced they had found a pair of child's size ten boots under the Second Narrows Bridge, which would have been en route from Port Moody if an abductor had been heading to any of the remote areas surrounding the North Shore and beyond.

Police showed the boots to Abby's family but they did not belong to the missing child. Ruth Drover sighed with relief.

Later in the week, Mayor Patterson was pleased when he was able to get unanimous approval from Port Moody council for a $1,000 reward for Abby's safe return. The mayor's satisfaction quickly turned to anger, however, when he learned that a flamboyant Vancouver businessman by the name of Alexander Di Cimbriani had phoned Chief McCabe to criticize the council for not being more generous.

Di Cimbriani had recently been taking out newspaper advertisements, proclaiming himself Vancouver's "mayor of a city within a city" on account of his mysteriously large holdings in downtown real estate. Now running as a Vancouver mayoralty candidate himself, the millionaire had offered numerous other rewards during the preceding months.

Patterson was skeptical of the millionaire's claims that he wanted to help the authorities because a policeman had paid for him to have cleft palate surgery while he was a poor orphan growing up in eastern Canada. Only recently, Di Cimbriani had thrown a lavish party for retiring Vancouver Police Chief John Fisk.

Patterson, however, was troubled by allegations that Di Cimbriani had occasionally directed abusive comments at some of his elderly tenants, and questions were also being raised about relationships between Di Cimbriani and some of the teenaged boys who worked for him.

"This guy seems to be some kind of blowhard," Patterson told the police chief. "If he's trying to make a political issue out of this, I find it rather offensive."

Despite his reservations, the mayor sat down to write Di Cimbriani a letter challenging the businessman to post a higher reward of his own. On March 19, Chief McCabe informed the media of the reward offers — and the mayor's challenge appeared to have worked. In addition to the $1,000 posted by the City of Port Moody, the police chief announced, Di Cimbriani was offering a $2,500 reward for information leading to Abby's whereabouts — and a further $5,000 for any information resulting in the arrest and conviction of anyone responsible for the little girl's disappearance.

Some people had their doubts whether Di Cimbriani's rewards would ever be paid, but details were announced in the weekend newspapers, while posters advertising the total of $8,500 were quickly distributed throughout the region. At her home on Gore Street, Ruth Drover was encouraged by these latest developments, and heartened by the fact that members of the Port Moody Police Department were calling to visit her almost every day. "If you see anything suspicious," Corporal Rick Nelson told her, "we'll be at the house right away."

It wasn't long before she felt it necessary to take up the policeman's offer. Home from work that weekend, Ruth eagerly responded to yet another knock on the door. Instead of a familiar friendly face, the person standing at the porch was an unknown, scruffy young man with a disconcertingly wild look in his eyes.

As he babbled something about trying to solve Abby's disappearance, the phone rang inside the house and Ruth turned back to answer it. Since Abby's disappearance, both Kathleen and Robyn had made a point of keeping their mother informed as to their whereabouts. Kathleen was frantically calling to say she'd been on her way to play tennis with a friend when a "really weird guy" had stopped to ask them if they knew where the Drovers lived.

"Why do you want to know?" Kathleen had asked.

"I'm working on the case," the man told her.

Kathleen had run to a nearby property to alert her mother that the man was on his way to the house at that very moment. As Ruth hung up, intending to return to the front door, she turned around to notice that the scruffy young man had already followed her into the house and was standing in the kitchen almost immediately behind her.

"Just what the hell do you want!?" she exclaimed, almost jumping out of her skin. "What do you think you're doing in here?"

"I'd like a drink of water," said the young man. He seemed virtually incoherent. "I'm working on the case. I'm just looking to see where Abby lived."

When Ruth informed the unwelcome visitor that Kathleen

had called the police, the stranger abruptly turned and bolted from the rear of the house, sliding in a small avalanche of rocks and debris down the steep embankment to Barnet Highway. Ruth's heart was palpitating. For some inexplicable reason, she observed, the man was pressing a dirty white rag to his mouth while running off in the direction of Port Moody.

The police arrived almost immediately in response to Kathleen's call and, shortly afterwards, informed Ruth that they had picked up the man for questioning. Contrary to hopes of a break in the case, however, he did not seem to know anything about Abby's whereabouts. "Apparently his brains were fried from sniffing glue," Corporal Nelson told Ruth. "We told him to get the hell out of Port Moody."

For Abby's mother, life had become an emotional roller coaster. Often, the exhilaration of a fresh tip would evaporate into despair as each new lead turned out to be false. Meanwhile, though, Ruth was able to draw some comfort from the flurry of letters and cards that had begun to arrive each day from relatives, friends — even total strangers — offering their condolences and support.

Occasionally, tears fell from Ruth's eyes as she read the numerous messages of kindness. Despite the gloom and apparent hopelessness of the situation, several of the letters ended with expressions of optimism and faith.

"Dear Mrs. Drover," began one of the letters from another Port Moody mother, "I just felt that I had to write to you. I lost a six-year-old daughter sixteen months ago in a traffic accident. I know the anxiety that you are feeling and, while there is nothing that can be done until you find Abby, I just wanted you to know that we and many others are praying for you. God bless you, Joyce Taylor."

Among the other messages was a March 19 letter from one of Ruth's aunts in the British Columbia interior. "Dearest Ruth and Girls," it began, "It is with a heavy heart that I write this letter. My heart truly aches for you. We've been listening to every newscast, radio or TV, for any word of Abby, but for the last few days there has been no word at all. Abby is in my prayers and mind constantly. I wake up often during the night and Abby is first on my mind. I pray that she will be returned to you in good health. I wish I was closer to be of some help and comfort to you. Perhaps when this is over, you and the girls, or just the girls (just as you wish), can come and spend a week or two with us by the lake. We would enjoy getting to know the girls better. The last time I saw them, they seemed such lovely girls. You've done a good job in bringing them up alone. All credit to you. We send our heartfelt sorrow and concern."

The message ended with words of such optimism that Ruth pressed the letter tightly to her chest as she sobbed. "Keep your chin up," the letter concluded. "She'll return to you. With love, Uncle John and Aunt Hazel."

Just down the street, close neighbours were filled with apparently similar heartache and concern. Hilda Hay especially remembered how she and her common-law husband Donald shared this time of grief and anguish over Abby's disappearance.

"I wonder where she is," Don Hay said frequently as he spoke with his wife. "It's terrible that a thing like this had to happen to such a nice family."

Hilda still wanted to help, even after the full-scale search failed to yield any trace of the missing girl, but she had to agree with her husband that there was nothing more that could be done. "I feel so bad," her husband concurred. "Let's not talk about this anymore — it's just too upsetting."

9 SUSPECTS

IF MEMBERS OF the public knew how many sex offenders could be found living within a few blocks in a typical North American neighbourhood, they might be quite concerned for the safety of their sisters and wives — and even more protective of their children. Certainly, officers at the Port Moody Police Department were surprised by the high number of rapists, pedophiles and the like that cropped up in their records as they continued their investigation into the mysterious disappearance of Abby Drover.

Even within a short distance of the Drover residence, Constable Wayne Smith noted, there were several residents with prior convictions for sexual offences. Constable Smith, a plain-clothes detective, had been placed in charge of the case, following the initial investigation by Constable Paul Adams, who had resumed his more uneventful duties as a uniformed patrolman. Methodically, Smith included each of the local sex offenders' names in his list of suspects.

As file coordinator, Smith would be responsible for recording and updating all facets of the case so the department could avoid duplication of efforts and focus its limited manpower on the most urgent priorities. Progress, or lack of it, would be monitored by Corporal Archie Connell, but Smith was regarded as an efficient investigator, in whom the department had the utmost confidence.

Smith, a dark-haired, clean-shaven man, had started his police career in 1964 as an eighteen-year-old rookie cop in Edmonton, one of the continent's coldest population centres, three hundred miles north of the U.S. border. Apart from its often inhospitable climate, the Alberta capital also had some tough working-class neighbourhoods, where Smith had once been shot at — narrowly escaping injury — while investigating a disturbance at the Exhibition Grounds.

Smith had transferred to the Port Moody Police Department in 1973 — a welcome respite after having been on the front lines in a big city. The Abby Drover case was an exception to the relatively tranquil police work in a small town. "I don't think this girl is a runaway," the detective told his colleagues from the outset. "She just doesn't fit the profile."

Now, as he pored over his files, Smith found himself especially interested in the criminal record of the family's close neighbour Donald Alexander Hay. Hay had first come to the department's attention on October 2, 1974, when he threatened to shoot his common-law wife and her three children.

According to the police files, Smith noted, the woman and her children had managed to run out of the house before officers arrived to find the man still inside and armed with a revolver. While at the scene, Smith read, the police officers felt it unsafe to jump the gunman until several hours later, arresting him as he walked out of the house at eight o'clock the following morning with the weapon still in his jacket. Despite the serious nature of the incident, Hay had some-how managed to escape with probation.

Already curious, the policeman found himself raising his other eyebrow as he noticed that Donald Hay also had a conviction for attempted rape, although it had been in Brandon, Manitoba, eighteen years earlier. More recently there had been allegations that Hay had indecently assaulted a young girl named Faith in the neighbouring municipality of Coquitlam.

Hay had been acquitted of the most recent charges, but the policeman felt that Hay's dubious record, as well as his proximity to the Drover residence, clearly put him at the top of any list of potential suspects. Although terms of his proba-tion had prohibited Hay from possessing any more weapons, the order had expired. Conceivably, the man may have bought himself another weapon, raising the possibility that he might have abducted the Drover girl at gunpoint.

Shortly after eight o'clock on the evening of March 19, Smith and Corporal Archie Connell climbed into their unmarked police car to drive the one and a half miles to Gore Street to pay Donald Alexander Hay a visit. As a precaution, each of the plainclothesmen carried a .38 revolver in shoulder holsters under their jackets.

Smith shut off the car's headlights as he parked outside the Hay residence, which was barely discernible through the bushes at the top of Gore Street. Hearing the sound of a power saw, Smith and Connell warily descended to the large detached garage beside the house to attract the attention of the balding man with sideburns who was working inside. "Donald Hay?" the policeman inquired. "Constable Smith with the Port Moody police."

Hay put down his saw, nodding as though he were not surprised by the officers' visit. "Hi," he said nonchalantly. "What can I do for you?"

Smith and Connell peered past him into the workshop, its air heavy with the smell of paints, sawdust and solvents. It was now 8:30 p.m. As the two policemen scanned the surroundings, they could see that Hay was in the process of completing a camper unit in the centre of the shop. It looked so well constructed it could have been built in a factory. Obviously, the policemen thought, this guy is quite a craftsman.

Smith and Connell were in no hurry to begin their questions. Smith, in particular, was the type of cop who could make people nervous just by the air he projected. Some members of the department had likened him to Lieutenant Columbo, the rumpled television detective who could rattle his quarry through his unremitting persistence. There was no doubt that Smith was a "make 'em sweat" type of investigator who had perfected his skeptical approach to a fine art.

Despite that, Hay was eager to be of assistance. He didn't seem ruffled at all as Smith confirmed that the reason for their visit was to investigate the disappearance of Abby Drover.

"It's terrible," Hay said. "She used to come here and play with the kids. We've all been out looking for her."

In fact, Hay added, he had probably done more trying to find the girl than all the other neighbours combined. He explained how he had taken Abby's sisters and his own stepchildren looking through all the malls, as well as searching the bushes around Rocky Point Park.

Although Smith and Connell suspected that Abby had met with foul play, there was no body and therefore no proof that the girl had indeed been kidnapped or murdered. Apparently convinced otherwise, Hay snarled though his tobacco-stained teeth, "I hope when they catch the bastard they hang him high!"

Smith and Connell showed no reaction, despite Hay's vociferous outburst. "Mind if I look around?" the detective inquired.

Hay seemed disappointed that the policemen hadn't immediately responded as his friends, but he appeared to understand why he had to be ruled out as a suspect. "No, of course not," he replied. "I'm doing whatever I can to help."

The handyman lit another cigarette. Inhaling deeply, he stood aside as Smith circled around him to peer inside the camper under construction. Finding nothing suspicious, the detective and his colleague surveyed the remainder of the garage. With its open rafters and no attic, the only other places to look were in the cupboards surrounding the far wall. Opening and closing each of the blue painted doors in turn, Smith found only tools, hardware and cans of paint.

Hay was fully cooperative as the search took place. If he had anything to hide, he didn't seem at all rattled. It looked as if Smith had been wrong in his suspicions after all. Like Columbo, he might unexpectedly return for another visit but, for the time being, the detective would have to focus his investigation elsewhere. "If you see anything suspicious," he said, straightening to leave, "be sure to let us know."

After returning with Connell to the police station, Smith took another look at the file on the suspicious glue sniffer, the man who had recently barged uninvited into the Drover's kitchen. Although it seemed unlikely that the incident merited further investigation, the man oddly enough had given Ruth Drover his name, which had enabled the police to find an address for him through the post office. With few other leads to go on, Smith decided to make further inquiries about the glue sniffer that afternoon. It proved to be yet another dead-end. The man had a perfect alibi: at the time of Abby's disappearance, he had been serving time in a prison forestry camp.

Taking his suspicions a step further, Smith picked up the phone to contact officials at the British Columbia Penitentiary, seeking records of yet more sex offenders who might have been at large when Abby dropped from sight. The Pen was located not far away in New Westminster, raising the chilling possibility that someone set free could easily have travelled the few miles to Port Moody to commit yet another heinous crime.

Receiving the names of five possible suspects, Smith checked the activities of each of them, only to conclude the same thing — none of them was in the area at the time of Abby's disappearance.

Before leaving that day, Smith decided to check out one more prison lead. He was aware, of course, that convicts didn't normally snitch on each other, but they hated sex offenders. Several prisoners told Smith of their concern about a fearsomely violent inmate who had recently been paroled. The convicts considered the man quite capable of murdering children but Smith quickly was able to establish that he too had a perfect alibi. Smith, however, wasn't about to give up on what seemed the most likely explanation for the child's disappearance. It was always possible, he realized, that Abby may have been abducted by a paroled sex offender from an institution outside the province. Thoroughly checking out all of them, however, would be an impossible task for the twenty-one members of the Port Moody Police Department. To do that, each of his colleagues would have needed several lifetimes.

Instead, Smith decided, he would seek the help of the Royal Canadian Mounted Police. A description of the missing child had already been entered into the national computer bank operated by CPIC (the Canadian Police Information Centre). The RCMP, being a national force, might be aware of other possible suspects.

Contacting RCMP headquarters the next day, Smith was given the name of Staff Sergeant Jim Steenson. Though Steenson worked at the RCMP detachment in Surrey, across the Fraser River, he had compiled a list of unsolved cases known as the "highway murders" in which the bodies of young women had been found in ditches throughout British Columbia, Alberta and the northern United States.

After receiving a copy of Steenson's files, Smith took them home to read after dinner. Although the policeman was tired from the long hours, the case of the missing child still occupied most of his time. While his wife and children watched television, Smith resisted the urge to nap, so that he could review each of the twenty cases in the files. Again, however, it was always the same thing. He was unable to find a common denominator linking any of the cases to the disappearance of Abby Drover.

From past experience, Smith knew he might be facing a long, methodical investigation. Each passing day would mean increasing public scrutiny. Impatient for developments in such cases, members of the public would inevitably question the competence of their police force and express skepticism and concern about whether their investigators were doing enough.

Already, people on Gore Street and elsewhere were becoming increasingly edgy. It was still chilly, despite the arrival of spring, and with the possibility of a child murderer in the neighbourhood, some residents had begun to speculate on whether it might be safer to move away. Ruth Drover also wanted to leave the neighbourhood, but felt that the police were doing all they could. She vowed to stay until they could establish what had happened to her daughter.

Faced with the awful reality of a missing child, Smith resolved from the outset that he would examine each and every piece of information in his efforts to solve the case. No matter how insignificant a lead might seem, the police officer decided, he would either follow it up personally or ask for assistance from fellow members of the department.

Despite periodic meetings with Chief McCabe and other members of the department, Smith found himself alone with his thoughts much of the time, as he devoted himself to all aspects of the investigation. While others may have thought him crazy, Smith resolutely followed up each scrap of information. Apart from the predictable false confessions of crackpots, the detective also found himself analyzing a flood of tips from would-be psychics, water diviners, dowsers and the like, who all claimed to have supernatural knowledge of Abby's final resting place.

Although Smith was aware of the occasional unexplained miracle, in reality he was just as skeptical of such phenomena as his colleagues were. But there was always the possibility, he knew, that a murderer might pose as a psychic as an ex-cuse to help the police find his or her victim. Regardless of underlying motives, Smith felt such leads might at least rule out possible body disposal sites. Whenever practical, he would check out each of the psychic tips. Sometimes, he realized, there was nothing else he could do in any event.

It seemed unlikely but there remained a slim possibility that Abby was still alive. Arriving for work on the morning of March 20, Smith found the police station abuzz with excite-ment; Chief McCabe received at least two insistent telephone calls from an anonymous male saying he had found Abby and would bring her into Port Moody. The calls were too brief to trace, but four patrol cars were dispatched to stake out St. John's Street. On the pretext of routine traffic stops, officers pulled over several cars containing young female passengers, but none of them was Abby. Finally, the anonymous male called back, his voice barely a whisper as Smith picked up the phone.

"I'll bring her in if I get the rewards first," he said. Before Smith could arrange a cash drop, however, the man hung up. The detective cursed under his breath but it seemed in retrospect that it was either a hoax or an extortion bid — just one of many false leads that would consume valuable police resources.

It was amazing, Smith thought, how mercenary some people could be in times of tragedy. Several other tipsters would also make unjustifiable claims for the reward, but the anonymous male caller was never heard from again.

10 A VOICE FROM ABOVE

ALTHOUGH RUTH DROVER clung stubbornly to the hope that her daughter was still alive, I would have shared the opinion of most Port Moody residents by that point: the little girl had most likely been kidnapped and murdered. Nonetheless, as a reporter at the Vancouver *Province*, I had covered enough missing-child stories to know that even the most apparently straightforward cases could occasionally end in something unexpected.

If a newborn disappeared, for example, the culprit might well be a distraught mother who had lost her own child — and such cases usually, though not always, ended with the child being found. Abby Drover had obviously not been in that category, nor did it seem at all plausible that she might have been snatched by her non-custodial parent. Abby hadn't seen her father for twelve years, and Cecil Drover had willingly taken part in the search for her.

But several other possibilities — however unlikely — still remained. One of my newspaper reports had concerned a young Jehovah's Witness kidnapped from hospital by both her parents to prevent a court-ordered blood transfusion. While authorities raced against the clock to find her, the little girl had died. The Drovers also belonged to a nonconformist denomination — but surely there was nothing so extreme about their religious views as members of the Seventh-Day Adventists.

According to the best available information, Abby had been happy at home—but could she have run away on account of something that everyone might have overlooked? An unexpected pregnancy, for example, would surely have inspired her mother's wrath, but that also seemed unlikely. As far as Ruth knew, her twelve-year-old daughter was not yet pubescent.

There was always the possibility that Abby had gotten lost exploring some unfamiliar territory on her way to school, but no one, including the police, seemed to give much credence to that idea, or to the even more remote scenario that Abby might have been the victim of an animal attack. Although dangerous animals showed up at certain times, no one had reported seeing bears or cougars in the neighbourhood recently.

Ruth Drover believed she loved each of her children equally, but it was virtually impossible for her to be a stable, level-headed parent when her youngest was missing. Under excruciating stress, she found herself snapping at Kathleen and Robyn so often that the normally happy household was beginning to crack. Ruth had returned to work in hopes of keeping the family together. At least the office provided some semblance of routine, but there was just too much tension at home to carry on with the status quo.

Abby's mother needed a break from her day-to-day responsibilities, and finally admitted after dinner one night what was on her mind. "It's really hard for me to be a good mom right now," Ruth conceded, as she put away the dishes. "Maybe it *would* be a good idea after all if both of you took up your father's offer to visit him in Calgary."

In her heart, Abby's mother hated to send her daughters to someone she felt hadn't shown any interest in them for so many years. Admittedly, Cecil had come to see them in their crisis. He still claimed he would have liked to have had his daughters visit over the years if only Ruth had let him. Perhaps it wasn't such a bad idea for now, Ruth conceded, if the older girls were to stay with him during the forthcoming Easter break.

The girls seemed pleased by the suggestion as they helped tidy up. Kathleen and Robyn welcomed the opportunity to escape for a while, and wasted no time making the arrangements to visit their father. Easter was still almost a month away but nonetheless was something they could look forward to. Cecil seemed genuinely to have wanted the reunion.

While she tried her best, Ruth's heart ached for her youngest child, tears welling in her eyes as she remembered how the baby she'd fed, changed and clothed as a single mother had grown into such a sweet girl. "I just can't accept that she may be dead," she insisted to her sister Del. Although there had been painfully few promising developments, Ruth tried to draw solace from the fact that some people were doing everything possible to keep the search alive.

HOWEVER FAR-FETCHED it may have seemed, Constable Smith again found himself actively considering the runaway theory when a bus driver contacted him to report that he had picked up a passenger fitting Abby's description in Vancouver. "I dropped her off at the Jericho youth hostel," the driver reported over the phone.

Meeting with the man that afternoon, Smith showed him photographs of several young girls, the policeman's heart skipping a beat in anticipation as the driver positively identified Abby's photo. Well aware that the Jericho hostel was a known hangout for hippies and disaffected youth, Smith decided to follow up on what surely seemed one of the most hopeful tips since the investigation began.

Parking his car outside, Smith ignored the occasional waft of marijuana smoke as he looked for Abby among the long-haired flower children prowling the hostel grounds. Please, he hoped, let me spot the missing little girl among them. But there was no sign of her as he crisscrossed the grassy knolls. Initially suspicious of the police, the hostel residents quickly became concerned and cooperative as they learned the frightening circumstances of the young girl's disappearance. It soon became apparent, however, that they had nothing to offer, and a dejected Constable Smith returned once more, empty-handed, to Port Moody.

With so many disappointments, Smith welcomed the high degree of support that the police continued to receive from members of the public. When a child disappeared, it was heart-warming to observe how complete strangers would often go to extraordinary lengths to help. Unknown to Smith, one of these concerned citizens wasn't much older than the teenagers he'd just interviewed at the youth hostel.

Still only twenty-two years of age, Roy Bentley from Surrey had recently obtained his pilot's licence. Although Bentley was aware of the previous helicopter search, he wondered if there was anything more that could be done. Bentley was no stranger to tragedy. He had been only nine years old when his teenage sister Dorothy had drowned in the Fraser River. He and his family had found themselves in agony during the subsequent two days that it took to find her body.

Although licensed only for fixed-wing aircraft, Bentley was intrigued by the idea that helicopters were usually equipped with undercarriage speakers to facilitate air-to-ground communication. If it was possible to adapt the technology, he suggested to his engineering friend Jocko, he might then be able to make wide ranging aerial announcements about Abby's disappearance. "I'm just curious if we can figure out a way to do it," he said to Jocko.

Together, the two young men borrowed a stadium loudspeaker, which they fastened to a wing strut of Bentley's rented Cessna 150. After Jocko helped him wire the speaker into the plane's power supply, they took off from Pitt Meadows Airport for a day of trials. At first, the young pilot was disappointed. Helicopters could hover while making aerial announcements, but people on the ground listening to Bentley's experiment informed him that his messages were fading away as his plane passed overhead.

Bentley refused to give up. It was a sunny spring day for once, with barely a cloud in the sky. "I've got an idea," he told Jocko. "Let's keep the message short and sweet and I'll fly into the wind."

After a few minutes, Jocko looked out the passenger window to see people on the ground giving them thumbs up. "It's working!" he shouted excitedly above the drone of the engine. By keeping their ground speed down to sixty knots, their message was coming through loud and clear—and in its entirety.

Bentley's stubborn determination had paid off. He was now ready to put his plan into action. Ten minutes after taking off from Pitt Meadows the following day, he observed the railway tracks and Burrard Inlet coming into view as he maneuvered the Cessna over the top of Burnaby Mountain, carefully watching for power lines and any other dangerous obstacles as he descended.

Unaware of Bentley's mission, Constable Smith was driving in Port Moody when he was startled by a thunderous voice from the sky: "Anyone with information about Abby Drover, please contact Port Moody Police Department." The message boomed so loud and clear that Smith wondered for a moment if he could be hearing the voice of God. Then he spotted the plane and realized it was yet another good Samaritan.

Crisscrossing the inlet, Bentley continued his high-decibel broadcasts for the next two days, and Smith had to agree that the young man's efforts were at least a partial success. If any residents had been unaware of Abby's disappearance *before* Bentley's goodwill flights, they certainly knew about her case by the time he'd finished. At the police station, switchboard operators found themselves inundated with new tips.

Before he could investigate them, however, Constable Smith still had several other leads to pursue, among them the various tips from psychics telling him where to look for Abby's body. For now, though, he would follow up on the more mundane, such as reports that a man in the adjoining municipality of Coquitlam had been observed going in and out of the bush with a shovel. After receiving help from the Coquitlam RCMP, Smith ascertained that the man indeed was breaking the law—but merely had been stealing trees for a backyard nursery.

Unable to find any similar Port Moody missing-child cases in recent memory, Smith began to wonder if a newcomer to the city might have been responsible for her disappearance. Told that a stranger had been living on a fishboat at the Rocky Point downtown launching ramp, the policeman decided to investigate.

Driving up to the water's edge, he spotted the fishboat immediately. "G'day, mate," said the friendly sailor as Smith approached and identified himself, explaining that he was visiting from Australia. "Nobody was using this here skiff so I just converted it into a houseboat."

Smith learned that the bearded young Australian had been staying on the boat for the past two and a half weeks—which would have put him in Port Moody at the time of Abby's disappearance—but the man apparently seemed concerned only about whether he might be evicted as an illegal squatter. It seemed clear he had nothing to hide. For a variety of reasons, Smith ruled him out as a suspect. The policeman had bigger fish to fry. It was a pleasant, warm day and he didn't much care whether the Australian was illegally living on the boat or not. "Hope you're enjoying your visit," Smith smiled. "Have a good day yourself."

The daily grind continued, Smith painstakingly filing each new lead as it came across his desk—examining even what seemed to be insignificant scraps of information on the chance that one of them might hold the key to solving the case. Learning that RCMP in nearby Haney had detained someone who had allegedly assaulted a young girl, Smith interviewed that suspect too, only to verify that he couldn't have been in Port Moody on March 10.

Smith was especially interested in reports that a Port Moody resident had suddenly left town after bragging of plans to imprison a girl and subject her to his sexual fantasies. It had seemed a promising lead and Smith enlisted the help of the Royal Canadian Mounted Police. Thumbing through his telephone messages a few days later, Smith discovered the RCMP had called back to report that the man had moved clear across the country to Nova Scotia. Under almost constant surveillance since his departure, he had not been observed in the company of any young women during his cross-country travels.

Meanwhile, Smith was intrigued to learn that his colleagues had arrested a known sex offender for trespassing at night. After the man was questioned, however, that suspect too had a foolproof alibi. Later that day, an anonymous individual phoned to say he would give police the name of Abby's abductor in exchange for $500. Smith learned that his police colleagues had obtained the name without paying, only to ascertain that the alleged "abductor" was the innocent victim of a revenge hoax.

None of the leads so far, it seemed, had come close. Perhaps finally the time had come to check out the supernatural abilities of the psychics.

WHILE THEY COUNTED the days until they could visit their father in Calgary, Abby's sisters continued to get out of the house by visiting the Hay children up the street. At least members of the Hay family continued to be very understanding, although the stress was obviously gnawing at their stepfather. Don had been like a father to Abby, as well as to his own stepchildren, and he remained too upset to discuss her disappearance.

With the approaching dusk, Brent was busy helping his stepfather, putting tools away and sweeping out the workshop as Abby's sisters arrived for a visit. Entering the garage, the girls could tell that Hay had started drinking again from the way he had exploded over some insignificant disagreement with his stepdaughter Jackie. During the ensuing row, he even became exasperated with Abby's sisters and made a rude gesture at Kathleen Drover.

"Just get the hell home and don't come back!" he snapped.

Perhaps his stress was understandable, they all felt. Abby Drover had brightened the lives of just about everyone who had known her. The thought that her own short life might be over was just too much to bear. Elsewhere, there may have been a lot of weird people at large, but it was amazing that something so terrible could happen in such a quiet residential neighbourhood.

Later, Donald Hay told Jackie he wanted to apologize to Kathleen for his behaviour. He'd been very drunk and upset because Abby was still missing. He was also mad with everybody, he explained, because Hilda had been nagging him and giving him ultimatums on account of his renewed drinking.

Hay wished Hilda wouldn't complain so much. He wasn't a bad provider and he'd always appeared sober to his customers even if he had been drinking. Hilda's brother-in-law Dieter, approximately eight years Hay's junior, agreed with him. Don handled his liquor well. When it came to nagging wives, men had to stick together. Dieter had confirmed he could never detect much change in his brother-in-law even if he were intoxicated. Not only that, Hay had proved himself a good neighbour through his concern for Abby Drover. "I've done more than anyone else around here trying to find her," he told Dieter.

Finally, however, the stress proved just too much. On the afternoon of March 30, Hilda had a nasty shock when she came home from working in the Sears stockroom to find her common-law husband sprawled unconscious on the floor, an empty prescription vial beside him. After calling an ambulance for the short trip to Royal Columbian Hospital in New Westminster, she waited tensely in a corridor while medical staff pumped out his stomach. Hilda had probably saved him just in time; Donald Hay had indeed taken a near-fatal overdose.

The Hay's family physician, Dr. Korchendorfer, visited his patient at Royal Columbian the following day. Donald, running a hand through his thinning, uncombed hair, admitted he had tried to end his life by taking an overdose of Amitriptolene, the antidepressant drug that he had been given for his alcoholism. "My business is going down the tubes," Hay explained. After examining his patient, Korchendorfer suggested that Hay should remain in hospital. The patient had been chronically depressed and withdrawn throughout the time that the doctor had known him. "We'd like to keep you here for a while for observation," the doctor advised him.

It was not until a week later, on April 6, that Constable Smith learned Hay was in hospital. The policeman was intrigued by reports that the Drovers' neighbour had attempted to commit suicide. The detective slid into his unmarked police car and drove to Royal Columbian Hospital to visit the man who had originally been his number one suspect.

Arriving at the hospital just before noon, Smith was guided by white-coated medical staff to Hay's recovery ward, where the handyman seemed pleased to have a visitor. After asking about his condition, Smith got straight to the point. "Has this got anything to do with the Drover girl?" he asked. Sitting on his hospital bed in his pajamas, Hay showed no apparent discomfort at the question, though he appeared upset that Abby still hadn't been found. "No," he replied, shaking his head. "I wish there was more I could do to help find her. Like I explained to the doctor, it was because of my financial problems."

Smith still had his doubts, but there were many other leads that needed to be pursued. The next day, Hay's condition seemed to improve. Although his nurses thought he might have stayed a bit longer, Hay seemed suddenly full of energy and inexplicably anxious to be discharged. "I'm fine," he told them. "I have to get back to work. Just let me go home."

11 PSYCHICS

STILL TRAPPED IN HER concrete tomb despite the passage of almost a month, Abby Drover pricked up her ears as she detected the sound of objects being moved outside. She had not seen anyone for the past week, nor had she had anything to eat. Could someone at last be coming to rescue her? Her heart pounding wildly, the child turned down the radio. Immediately, though, her hopes evaporated as Donald Hay reappeared in the doorway.

"I've brought you some food," Hay said gruffly. He looked pale and tired, and Abby tried to appear grateful as he put down his grocery bag beside the sink. As usual, he kicked the door shut behind him.

Although weak from starvation, Abby raised herself from the bed to open a can of spaghetti, hungrily devouring its contents with a slice of stale bread. She still hoped she might receive some pity if she pretended to remain his friend. "Thanks," she said. "I ran out of food. Why haven't you been coming to see me?"

The man snapped in response to her question. At first, he had emptied the chemical toilet and taken out the garbage regularly, but the air in the cell was now becoming heavy and putrid. "I told you to keep the place clean," he scowled.

Secretly, despite her fears, Abby felt a glimmer of satisfaction. Frustrating him through passive resistance was exactly what she had hoped for. Alone for a week, she'd been panic-stricken that something might have happened to him. If he died, she realized, it meant she would probably die too. Was it possible, however, that her psychological retaliation might be paying off?

Despite the terror that was her constant companion, Abby had tried to keep up her strength by doing physical exercises, but it was hard to be motivated. She ached to get out of the cell. As time dragged on, the walls closing in even more, she grew extremely worried that she had missed so much school. Concerned that she would fail Grade 7, the child desperately wanted to get back to her classes. All she could do for now, though, was to keep reading and re-reading the schoolbooks she had, as well as the few magazines he'd left for her.

In a recent issue of the *Reader's Digest*, Abby had read stories called "Moonraker's Bride" and "Wherever Lynn Goes" at least twelve times. Apart from that, by listening to the radio, she had memorized the lyrics to dozens of new songs. Looking at the acoustic tiles on the ceiling, she imagined being in her own recording studio. No one could hear her outside. She could sing as loudly as she wanted, and as the hours ticked by, there was little else to do. When she didn't know the time, she'd try to guess whether it was day or night. Other than that, she spent hours trying to think of ways to escape.

"Things just aren't working out," Hay finally said, oblivious to her thoughts. "You cry too much. I'm still trying to figure a way of letting you go."

Before explaining it, he insisted she would have to take off her clothes once more, and this time he wanted her to lie on her stomach. Abby complied, tears welling in her eyes. It seemed to take an eternity before he finally grunted, concluding his assault. Sick bastard! she thought, as he rolled off the bed. How could he do this to a child? As though it was not enough that he had stolen her innocence, Hay had now degraded her in almost every possible way.

Allowing the child to get dressed after her sobbing subsided, the man was ready to discuss his plans. Although he claimed he loved her, it was obvious he had no compassion for her. "I've got something to show you," he said nonchalantly, as though nothing unusual had just happened. Sitting on the chair at the end of the bed, he carefully unfolded a sheet of paper from his pocket and straightened out the creases to show it to the young girl.

Although there had been no mention of it recently, Abby had heard about the $8,500 in rewards on the radio. Hay was now showing her one of the posters, confirming the $1,000 being offered by the city and the $7,500 being offered by Alexander Di Cimbriani. The poster was headed with large block letters:

REWARD
MISSING FEMALE
ABBY DROVER

Encouraged that they were still searching for her, the child reached for a tissue and dabbed her eyes, attempting to focus on the black-and-white photograph of herself on the poster. Apart from her description, the poster spelled out the details of what she had been wearing when last seen. After all this time, Abby realized she was still wearing the same clothes, although she had been able to wash her underwear in the sink. Other than hearing about him on the radio, Abby had no idea who Alexander Di Cimbriani was. She didn't even know what he looked like or what would motivate a complete stranger to post such a large reward. Why was he so interested in her? What exactly did he know about her case? Did he have any reason to suspect she was still alive? Even her captor seemed to be having difficulty pronouncing his name. Or was he just trying to torment her by making light of it?

"Maybe we can get the money from this Cepperoni guy or whatever his name is," Donald Hay was saying. "If you cooperate with me, I'll give you some of the money. Or you can write a story about it and sell it."

Despite her incredulity, Abby pretended it was a good idea. As she looked at her neighbour, he seemed to be smiling, as though relishing the thought of pulling off yet another perfect crime. Even if she could help him, the child suspected, he would probably take the money and split.

Cooperation, however, seemed her best hope. It was amazing,

she thought, that a grown man would be seeking the advice of a twelve-year-old as his partner in crime, but Abby took only a moment before responding.

"I think I know how we could do it," she said softly.

"Well, spit it out, girl!" the man said impatiently. "Think of a way to raise the money, and I'll think of the place."

"Okay," Abby said. "If you make a tape recording of my voice, you could deliver the tape and pick up the money."

Hay pondered the idea for a moment, but it seemed too risky. It might be possible to get the money in unmarked bills but, unless he had the help of an intermediary, how could he possibly pick it up without being the subject of a massive police stakeout? "I'll have to think about it," he said. "Meanwhile, if you want to eat, you're going to have to work for your food."

Reaching into his grocery bag as he got up to leave, Hay handed the child some wool and a woodframed cloth sketched with the proposed needlepoint outline of a sailboat on water. "I know a lady downtown who'll pay $65 for it," he said. "I'm not going to let you go until you've finished it."

WHILE THE DISAPPEARANCE of Abby Drover had begun to fade from the airwaves and the news pages, it remained the uppermost concern at the Port Moody Police Department. Chief McCabe doubted there had ever been a more serious case in the city's history, and his colleagues could see that it weighed heavily on his shoulders. He knew, however, that it continued to be the top priority for Constable Wayne Smith.

Smith informed the chief he still had a number of leads to pursue, but the initial deluge of tips was beginning to dwindle as the investigation dragged on.

On April 9, Smith learned about a man who had left his Port Moody home in a great hurry. For a variety of reasons, Smith wanted permission to look through the man's house, but the suspect refused, raving with indignation. Undeterred, the policeman obtained a search warrant. Although police spent hours combing every nook and cranny, officers on the premises found nothing to indicate that Abby or any other young girls had ever been there.

Constable Smith received another tip three days later that seemed more promising. A hitchhiker phoned to say he'd recently been picked up near Port Moody by a driver who claimed to have found a body. The driver had told him he was too afraid to report the matter to the police and hadn't fully explained where the body was located. Smith was frustrated that the hitchhiker hadn't made a note of the licence plate number. He didn't even have a good description of the car.

Of greater interest was an April 17 report that someone had found clothing in a ditch beside a remote area of Belcarra Road. The location was just outside the city, but several miles from Abby's home, skirting the eastern fringes of Burrard Inlet. Leaving the police station in the company of Sergeant Bob Irving, Smith went to the scene to investigate, anticipating that finally he might have a break in the case.

It was strange, all right. Just off the picturesque, winding road, the two policemen found a red jacket with several .22-calibre bullets in one of its pockets. Even more odd was what they found nearby — a strange dummy consisting of scrunched up papers attired in adolescent clothing. More clothes were found in nearby bushes beside a stand of alder. The clothing, damp but not faded, might have been there since about the time Abby disappeared, but closer examination proved there was nothing to link any of the items to the missing schoolgirl.

The time had come to probe some of the more unusual material being proffered by psychics, water diviners, dowsers and others claiming to have some degree or another of supernatural insight.

One of the first was a phone call from a woman saying she'd had a dream that Abby could be located at a specific phone number. Smith checked it out but no such number existed. Shortly afterwards, another would-be psychic telephoned from miles away in Boonville, Indiana, to say that Abby was dead, and that her body could be found near some pine trees within five miles of her home. Smith was amazed that people from halfway across the continent could know about the child's disappearance, though they'd probably heard about the case from friends or relatives in the Greater Vancouver area. Although he wanted to check out the American psychic's tip, the description was too vague to be pursued. He couldn't think where he'd find the pine trees anyway. Most of the conifers in the area were fir, cedar or hemlock.

Still early on in the investigation, an elderly man with a dowsing rod led Smith and other police officers to neighbouring Port Coquitlam. As Smith and his colleagues followed the eccentric old man through a garbage dump, the dowser came to an abrupt stop. In his gnarled hands, the stick seemed suddenly to twitch and shake involuntarily in front of him. "She's here," the man insisted. "She's buried here. There's no doubt about it."

The police officers started digging and, almost immediately, their shovels unearthed some books and papers. Could they be schoolbooks? It was hard to tell. The books were decomposed. Frantically, the police officers continued digging, pausing only briefly to catch their breath. After they'd dug until they were knee-deep, the dowser admitted he'd made a mistake. "Sorry," he conceded. "It must've been those books."

"Sure," one of the officers said, trying to hold back a touch of a sarcasm. "Thanks anyway. Better luck next time." Wearily, the officers, muddied and sore, put away their shovels and abandoned the search.

Upon his return to the office, Smith picked up the phone and called Abby's mother. "We've been following up every lead," Smith confirmed. He wanted to keep the family informed and wondered in the meantime if they themselves knew of any further developments. "Thanks," Ruth Drover replied. She knew the constable was doing everything possible and assured him of the family's gratitude. The degree of police concern was a source of great comfort for the Drovers. Despite her doubt about psychic phenomena, Ruth had nothing else to offer, either. "I've got the name of some card reader who claims he could help," she added. "Here, I'll give you his name."

Still doggedly determined, Smith called the card reader that night but found the man had nothing of value to add to the investigation. Neither did five more psychics who claimed to be experts in "dowsing and adiethesia". About the same time, Smith began to spend hours with a Simon Fraser University student who led him with elaborate dowsing equipment on a tortuous series of hopeless expeditions. After an exhausting trek up Burnaby Mountain, the student led Smith the next day to a potato farm below the flight path to Vancouver International Airport. After checking a nearby strawberry patch, they found nothing except a dead dog and a dead coyote. It started to rain and they finally gave up.

Another psychic told Smith they could find Abby's body in some water at the bottom of a mud slide in Port Moody. "I could see a bone from the top of the slide so we scrambled down to the water," Smith would later recall. "The bones turned out to be the skeleton of a horse, and the place was full of snakes. I never got out of anywhere so fast in my life.

"Other members of the police department were beginning to think I must be crazy," Smith smiled when I interviewed him years later. "You don't have to believe in these kind of tips but, like I said, a murderer could pose as a psychic and lead you to the victim."

Around the same time, Mayor Norm Patterson phoned to say he'd received a letter from a mental patient claiming to know something about Abby's disappearance, but Smith ascertained it was yet another false lead. He racked his brain to think of an angle he hadn't explored.

Despite Vancouver's pre-eminence in west coast shipping, several ocean-going freighters still called at Port Moody, and Smith received a tip that Abby may have been picked up by the wife of a ship's captain. Was it plausible that the child had somehow — either voluntarily or involuntarily — become a stowaway? With the help of records from maritime employers, the policeman ascertained that two vessels, with a total of thirty-one foreign crew members, had indeed left Port Moody on the day Abby had disappeared.

Strange as it seemed, the investigation was now taking on global proportions. Smith had the names and registry of the two ships involved and, after conferring with Chief McCabe, the policeman sent inquiries to Interpol — the international police agency headquartered in Paris. Interpol responded that two of the listed crew members had come to the attention of the police in the past, but neither of them had anything to do with sex offences.

There was one more lead from a psychic that Smith found interesting. A sixty-year-old man from the semi-desert town of Oliver, in the British Columbia interior, had mailed a sketch, along with numerous maps and other drawings, to the police shortly after Abby's disappearance. The psychic, from two hundred and fifty miles away, had predicted that Abby would be found under the floor at the back of an old garage. In red ink, one of the man's drawings showed a piece of wood covering some earth beneath the left side of a workbench.

Later, Smith and even the most hardened disbelievers, myself included, would end up shaking their heads over just how accurate the drawings had been. While they may have been totally skeptical about psychic phenomena, none of them would ever be quite so sure again.

12 HOLIDAYS

WITH NO DEFINITE leads in Abby's disappearance, just about everyone became a suspect — even members of the Drover family.

Upon his return home, Cecil Drover found himself under police scrutiny after phoning the mother of a missing Calgary girl to offer his condolences. Despite being a family man with three additional children by his second marriage, Abby's father received a visit the next day from Alberta police officers wanting to know why he had called a complete stranger.

"How do we know you're not retaliating because someone kidnapped your own daughter?" one of the officers suggested skeptically.

Cecil was stunned. "That's absurd," he replied, leaping from his chair. "I thought I could offer some comfort because I'm going through the same thing."

It was an unnerving experience even though the police officers hadn't directly accused him. Later, they found the body of the missing Calgary girl, aged fifteen, and it was quite apparent that her murder had nothing to do with Cecil.

With each passing day, as far as Cecil was concerned, it seemed more and more likely that his own daughter was dead, too.

In Port Moody, Ruth remained convinced otherwise. Could it be maternal instinct that led her to believe Abby was still alive, or was she merely clinging to empty and unrealistic hopes? Ruth's sister Del and husband visited often, bringing some degree of comfort, but the tension in her home was becoming unbearable. As far as Robyn was concerned, her mother seemed to be blaming her and Kathleen for Abby's disappearance. "Because there was nothing to indicate that Abby had been kidnapped," Robyn told me later, "it was as though Kathy and I must have had something to do with it."

Feeling they had always taken special care of Abby while Ruth was at work, both girls failed to comprehend the full extent of their mother's grief or the fact that the tranquillizers may have been affecting her judgment.

"We both loved Abby so much," Robyn insisted. "Because she was the youngest, we were really very close."

Their happy days as a cake-making team were long since gone, but Robyn desperately clung to the reports that Abby might somehow have gotten aboard one of the ships that had left Port Moody around the time of her disappearance. "Maybe these psychics know more than we think," she told Kathy.

In the meantime, she and Kathleen were desperate to get out of the house. Feeling that Ruth no longer wanted them at home, they telephoned their father, imploring Cecil Drover to come and fetch them.

Only five years old when her parents divorced, Robyn had longed to see her father again and had been thrilled when he'd visited Port Moody following Abby's disappearance. Although he was distraught, she realized, her father had been a calm, reassuring presence. "He was my knight in shining armour," Robyn later recalled.

At Easter, Cecil Drover heeded the call and returned with a friend to drive Robyn and Kathleen to his home in Calgary. There the girls were greeted by their father's second wife and, for the first time, met their two half-brothers and a half-sister, aged five, seven and nine.

As a Calgary car salesman, Cecil was doing well. The oil capital of Canada was enjoying boom times on account of high energy prices; inflation was rampant elsewhere, but just about everyone in Calgary seemed prosperous. It may have seemed a bit antiseptic, but the city was clean and modern, and as far as Robyn was concerned, she intended to enrol in school there after the Easter break and never go back to Port Moody again.

It was simply too depressing.

DOWN THE STREET from their mother's house, the Hay family also thought it would be a good time to get away. Hilda had remained close friends with Ruth, and Don Hay had been especially vigilant since Abby's disappearance, urging the children in the neighbourhood to make sure they always had a ride to school and to be on the lookout for any suspicious strangers.

Reciprocating their help and generosity, Ruth had taken one of the engineers from work to the Hay residence to check out prices on various types of camper units. Although the two men never actually struck a deal, Ruth was impressed by the quality of her neighbour's workmanship as she looked around his garage. Hay continued to show his concern over Abby's disappearance. "If you ever need me just call," he repeated. "I will come and help."

Ruth would be alone for several days now, however, because the Hays, as well as her own eldest daughters, would be away for Easter. Don Hay, who had made a quick recovery after his release from hospital, was apparently on the wagon again, well aware that Hilda would take a bus home with the children if he ruined their five-day holiday by getting drunk.

Hilda had only recently laid down the law, after becoming suspicious that her husband was drinking again. Although her husband could appear sober while drinking as many as three bottles of vodka a day, Hilda was concerned about his pale, grey complexion, as well as his depression and impotence. While looking for some paint and brushes to redecorate the living room, she had found some empty bottles in the workshop. Although she hadn't actually been able to find any liquor among the maze of tools and equipment, she had still suspected the worst.

Contacting her husband's probation officer to no avail, Hilda confronted Don herself. "If you've decided to start drinking again, that's up to you," she told him. "But you can get the hell out of here because I don't want you drinking around me." Although her husband accepted the ultimatum, Hilda had become perturbed by reports that he had been seen drinking in the company of various other women at a cheap downtown hotel. After Don promised her lasting sobriety, Hilda had relented by driving into Vancouver to retrieve him.

IT WAS A PLEASANT spring day as the Hays set out in their camper truck, stopping only for gas at the Shell service station in Keremeos, on their way to the semi-desert wonderland south of the Okanagan Lakes.

On April 17, the family checked into a campground at Oliver, unaware it was the hometown of the psychic who had sent his red ink drawings about Abby to Constable Wayne Smith at the Port Moody Police Department. If the psychic had met the missing girl's neighbours, might he have been able to divine some telepathic energy from their visit? Apparently he had no knowledge that Abby's neighbours were in his bailiwick.

The Hays travelled on, enjoying their holiday as they visited relatives in Kamloops. Immediately upon returning home, however, they experienced an unpleasant encounter back on Gore Street. As he unpacked his truck, Don Hay noticed that some concrete had spilled onto his property from a retaining wall that neighbour Ken Woodward had built during his absence. With his wife and two children, the unemployed glazier had only recently moved back in the house next door after renting it out for the past several years.

"I thought you'd be glad of the wall," said Woodward, trying to smooth things over.

"Oh, sure!" Hay said angrily. "Why should I have to clean up this mess?"

Hay was in the midst of gesturing with his finger when his neighbour knocked him down. "He was a very violent type," Woodward later told others, attempting to justify his action.

Still upset by the incident after supper, Hay suddenly felt thirsty and told Hilda he'd be staying for a while at the Blackstone Hotel in Vancouver. Having stayed dry for the family vacation, he couldn't be expected to come home to such problems and remain sober forever.

ALTHOUGH ROBYN DROVER wanted to remain in Calgary, Ruth insisted that she and Kathleen would have to return home after their Easter break, unless Cecil was prepared for a protracted custody battle. Obediently, the girls boarded a plane for the flight back to Vancouver. Once in the air, they enviously eyed the other passengers, who were gazing out the windows at the majestic Rocky Mountains below, unaware of the dark tragedy shared by the two girls in row fourteen.

Still depressed when their plane touched down just over an hour later at Vancouver International Airport, the girls hurried through the terminal building to meet their mother. "Have you heard any more about Abby?" Robyn asked expectantly, as they waited beside the baggage carousel.

Both girls could see from their mother's expression that there'd been no new developments. "Not a thing," Ruth lamented. Although she claimed she always slept well, her physical appearance indicated otherwise. There were dark circles under her eyes. "The police have been checking every lead. It's still a complete mystery."

Ruth was trying her best but finding it difficult to remain patient as she grappled with the passing of each day. What should have been a happy reunion for all three of them turned out to be an agonizing, silent trip back to Port Moody.

Soon after getting home, Kathleen and Robyn left the house to visit with the Hays. Being close in age to the Drover girls, Jackie and Wendy Hay were their best friends, so Kathleen and Robyn visited them whenever they could to escape their mother's depression.

April 26 was Robyn's sixteenth birthday. Her sister Abby, if she were still alive, would be thirteen in exactly one week.

Wanting to be in the company of friends on what should have been a special day, Robyn visited the Hay residence, sharing a meal with Jackie, Wendy and Brent. Hilda always made Abby's sisters feel welcome, but was annoyed that her own children were procrastinating with cleaning up after dinner on account of wanting to stay at the table with their birthday guest.

"Don might be in the garage," Hilda suggested to Robyn. "Why don't you go out and see him for a while, while the kids do the dishes?"

108 — John Griffiths

Having retrieved her husband from the hotel after his latest four-day bender, Hilda seemed to have forgiven him again. He was a good husband when he was sober, even though he was never intimate and hadn't been for several years. "There's still no news of Abby," Hilda had informed him after they got home. "I wonder where she is," her husband had replied.

Now, as she went out to the garage, Robyn wondered if the handyman would let her in. Until recently, the girls had always been able to see through the garage window by cupping their hands beside their eyes and standing close to the glass. Just a few days ago, however, Don had covered the inside of the window with a piece of cardboard. He had also put up a sign saying "Beware of the Dog". The family had had to put down their previous dog but had replaced it with a new Doberman. The animal was reasonably tame, but its size and fierce bark kept strangers at bay. Hay had named it Ripper.

Also — perhaps on account of recent thefts — the handyman had begun locking the garage, which in the past had almost always been open. What was he doing in there? Robyn wondered. Drinking again, she assumed.

Crossing the yard from the house, Robyn felt some apprehension as she knocked on the workshop door. Since returning from his trip to the interior, the handyman had seemed angry at everybody, and generally in a bad mood. As he opened the door, he looked unshaven and hungover, but smiled and let the girl in when she told him that it was her birthday.

Soon after she was inside, Robyn was taken completely by surprise. As she turned her back on the handyman to look at one of his campers, she suddenly found herself being swept off her feet. The breath was knocked out of her as her neighbour silently hurled her to the concrete floor. There wasn't time to be frightened. The attack was so sudden that Robyn had no idea what to expect. She was looking at his expressionless face, her own eyes wide in astonishment, when both of them heard approaching footsteps and saw Hay's younger stepdaughter standing in the doorway.

"Oh, hi, Wendy," Hay said without missing a beat. "It's Robyn's birthday. We've got to give her the bumps!"

Still shaken, Robyn wasn't convinced it had all been in fun. If Wendy hadn't disturbed them at that moment, she wondered what might have happened next but went along with the horseplay. Grateful that Hay had possibly saved her life during the recent dog attack, she still felt a certain loyalty to him. He'd also been helpful in taking everyone out looking for Abby. After his strange behaviour, however, Robyn would always look at him with some degree of wariness.

Don Hay got back to business as usual. After his vacation and drinking spree, he had a lot of catching up to do. There were advertisements to place in the *Buy and Sell* for new customers, and stores to visit to pick up lumber and hardware. Whatever doubts Hilda may have had about him, Donald's business associates always found he was sober and friendly, and they appreciated the fact that he always paid his bills on time.

Life on Gore Street would never be the same, but everyone was carrying on as best they could. Faced with an unsolvable mystery, they had no other choice.

13 BIRTHDAYS

SIX WEEKS HAD GONE by since Abby had disappeared, but no one, other than her captor, seemed to have any clue that she might still be struggling for her survival. Desperate for her freedom, Abby tried to loosen one of the acoustic tiles above her, only to realize that the ceiling — just like the rest of the cell — was built of concrete. Hay frequently left her alone for days at a time. With the hours ticking by so slowly, the child found herself trying to figure out different ways to escape.

Once again, Donald Hay came into the cell. He was drunk as usual and seemed to pass out after he assaulted her. It was late at night, thought Abby. Had he really fallen asleep or was he just pretending?

If only she could sneak past him to her freedom! Abby held her breath as her captor began to snore. When she stirred, however, he woke up before she could slip out from beneath him.

"Don't even think about it," the man said. "I've got a gun outside. If necessary, I'll use it."

"I was just getting up for a glass of water," Abby lied.

If she was going to escape, she realized, she'd have to think of some other way. Would it be possible, she speculated, to pin a note to the back of his shirt — or even slip a note into one of his pockets — identifying him as her kidnapper? It was tempting, but surely he'd kill her if he discovered what she'd done.

Abby was also concerned that such plans might endanger other people's lives. If anyone saw such a note and confronted him, she feared, he'd surely dispose of them, too, before any of them could report him to the police.

Obviously, she was unable to struggle with the man. He was much bigger than she was, and he had her under his complete control. She had always been taught to respect her elders, too; if she survived, how could she ever trust adults again?

The physical pain of being raped as a child was excruciating, but the mental anguish, she imagined, would be the same even if she were grown up. It was best to comply with his demands. He was always much crueller if she tried to resist. She made no attempt to hold back her tears, however. God, how he hated her crying!

Passive resistance still seemed to be the most effective way to survive. Abby craved a hot shower, but seldom heated the cold water even for a sponge bath. She never drank the liquor he left, but secretly used it to dab her cuts and scrapes to prevent infection. If she avoided washing herself, she reasoned, the man might be less inclined to continue with his assaults.

The strategy may have worked to some extent, but it also incited Hay's ire. Furious upon finding the floor of the cell covered in debris, he shouted at her.

"Why don't you keep the place clean?"

"There's no place to put anything," Abby replied meekly. "I tried to put the garbage in paper bags, but they just broke apart 'cause the floor was wet."

In retaliation, Hay announced he would no longer clean the chemical toilet, and the air became increasingly putrid. Abby already feared the huge spiders that crawled around her, and now other bugs started to infest the cell too.

Barricaded within, the child heard the man starting up what sounded like a vacuum cleaner outside. He must have been reversing the air flow because a cloud of dust suddenly emanated from the vent above the sink.

"What are you doing?" she screamed. Frantically, as she felt the air swirling about the cell, she plugged the vent to the cell with dishcloths, fearing that the man was trying to gas her.

Abby could still feel her heartbeat for several minutes after the vacuum stopped. Otherwise, silence filled the cell, and the atmosphere was becoming increasingly stuffy and oppressive. Perhaps, she thought, he'd only been blowing in air, but she was afraid to open up the vent again in case Hay tried to gas her while she drifted in and out of fitful sleep.

When the man came into the cell, he was puzzled at first that his matches kept going out, each time he tried to light a cigarette dangling from the corner of his mouth. Momentarily, it dawned upon him that the matches wouldn't burn because the air in the cell was almost completely without oxygen. "Just what the hell are you doing?" he said, discovering the plugged-up vent. "You could have died. The place has to have air flow."

Abby felt a tightness in her chest, but it wasn't only from lack of air. Although the remainder of her body was pathetically thin, her training bra was squeezing her tiny but growing breasts. Feeling cramps below her stomach, she realized now that she was about to have her first ever period.

As soon as he discovered that the girl was menstruating, he abruptly turned on his heel and departed. At last, the girl prayed, maybe he would let her go. Wasn't he, after all, simply a sick man who would no longer be interested in her now that she was turning into a woman?

Abby's hopes for freedom were thwarted once more as the man returned to the cell with some aspirin for her pain — and a supply of sanitary napkins. Despite all his talk to the contrary, he still obviously had no intention of letting her go. In fact, he seemed excited by the changes occurring in her body. By way of celebration, he feted her with more nourishing food: bread, apples and wieners and beans.

Again and again, Hay wanted sex, but Abby begged for some kind of reassurance. "What if anything happens to you while I'm down here?" she asked. "How would anybody ever find me? If you die, then I die."

"I've left a note in my safety deposit box," he claimed. He was probably lying, the child realized, but there was no way of disproving him.

As the days turned into weeks, Abby was becoming increasingly stiff and sore from lying on the damp bed, her body sore and battered from the continual abuse. Seeking momentary diversion, she counted the ink marks on the palm of her hand.

There were over fifty of them. According to the marks, it had been exactly fifty-four days, in fact, since she'd been kidnapped. That meant today must be May 3. Abby hadn't heard the date on the radio but she assumed she had counted correctly.

It was her thirteenth birthday!

Birthdays had always been so special at home, and Abby remembered how her mother, throughout the years, had often baked her a cake. She could still visualize the photograph of herself holding a doll cake that her mother had lovingly made for her on her seventh birthday. Blissfully lost in her thoughts, Abby almost forgot her surroundings for a moment as she recalled how she'd always helped Kathleen and Robyn as the fourth member of the Drover cake-making team.

Despite being entombed in a concrete cell, the child simply had to make a cake. Jumping to her feet with a sudden burst of energy, she looked in the cupboard beside the sink. There was nothing. The cupboard was bare. As she looked further, however, her eyes lit up. On one of the shelves, there was a stale loaf and some peanut butter.

Abby hummed softly along with the radio as she made her "cake". It was easy, really. Apart from using the peanut butter as a filling, all she had to do was spread some more peanut butter on top to make the icing. The child was preoccupied now, putting her creation aside for a moment as she looked for ways to enhance her special day.

Noticing a can of paint, Abby pried off the lid and cleared the table. Ignoring the fumes as she loaded up the brush, she painted a special greeting to herself on top of the table. Thinking her captor would be pleased by her creativity, she stood back to admire her work: "Happy 13th Birthday" in broad, careful strokes.

Abby even tried to save a piece of "cake" for her captor, but eventually she was unable to stand the hunger any longer. Although she ate the extra slice, she still thought he'd be pleased that she'd tried to make everything seem like home.

It was ironic, she realized, that she looked forward to seeing Donald Hay, but he was the only person in her life, and he brought her news of friends and family, while the radio provided her only other link to the outside world.

Confused by her ambivalent feelings, the girl was pleased when she heard him opening the cell door, but her "happiness" quickly evaporated as Hay flew into a rage. Abby recoiled in fear as her captor banged his fist on the table. "Just what the hell is all this?" he snarled. "You can damn well paint over it right now."

Because he was furious, Abby did as she was told. Unable to speak, she sobbed uncontrollably as Hay forced her to obliterate the only thing she'd been able to do that might have lessened the pain. Tears streamed down her cheeks as she made the message disappear.

It was so unfair, she thought. Just a week and a half ago — after a lengthy absence — he'd come into the cell explaining he'd been indisposed, but wanting favours from her because it had been his own birthday the day before.

Thinking he might be more sympathetic if she were nice to him, she had made him a birthday present by carving a sailboat and fish from a bar of blue soap. She had even made a card for him, which read:

Happy days are always here. Have a happy year all throughout, until your next birthday anyway.

> *Abby Drover*
> *P.S. Get out there and do your best.*

The man had left the card in the cell, as well as a flower she'd drawn and a note she'd given him on a piece of pink paper. Obviously, Abby reasoned, he wouldn't have wanted anybody to find such items in his possession. As she re-read her note, Abby realized she'd made several spelling mistakes and felt foolish that she'd tried to be nice to him. The letter read as follows:

> *I know you think I'm stupid. Like you say, everybody is entitled to their own thoughts, but I do believe in God and I believe in friends and I just wish you would be my friend. I also know that I will get out of here so I'm not worried. God has helped me so far and he'll help me to the finish. God works in mysterious ways but what he does is right —*
>
> *Abby Drover*
> *I know you don't believe in God, but I'll just say that God will be with you.*

The man is so screwed up, she thought. At first she had hoped to gain his trust so that she might live. Initially, she must even have had some sympathy for him, but now, now that he'd so cruelly destroyed her birthday, she began to see him differently. She really hated him.

Hay was even cruel to her about her family. Abby could see that he enjoyed tormenting her with news of what her mother and sisters were doing in the outside world. "Your Mom's bought a new truck," he told her. "I guess she doesn't care about you as much as you think."

She realized now that the man was completely evil. But why did he hate families so much, she wondered. What had happened to him as a child that might have caused such inner rage? Had his own parents neglected or humiliated him? And why had he needed to torment *her* to sate his own depravity?

The questions were endless, but Abby was more concerned that Hay had made no further mention of attempting to collect the reward money. Had he been in touch with Di Cimbriani, or had he temporarily shelved the idea so that he could continue using the child as his slave?

Sensing that he had no intention of letting her go, Abby handed him back his needlepoint sailboat. She had worked hard on it at first, but it was only partially completed. "The scissors are too blunt," she said. Secretly, she was doing everything possible to thwart him.

Reluctantly, her captor took away the needlepoint, but ordered the child to refinish the "furniture" in the cell with the remainder of the paint. "Like I told you," he growled, "you're gonna have to earn your keep." If she didn't comply, he warned, he would shoot her — then dump her body in the ocean and fill the cell with earth.

For the first time since being kidnapped, the child found herself agonizing over ways to end her short life. There was no way to escape, but killing herself would certainly thwart his plans.

It wouldn't even matter then if she failed Grade 7.

Before carrying out her plan, she decided to hide a note on herself to ensure that at least Hay wouldn't get away with it. He never made her take off her socks, so maybe she could hide some notes there, she thought. But the paper would probably disintegrate there, so she took off her right boot. Weak, her hands trembling, she deliberately slit the lining. Her mother would be so angry with her, she thought, if she destroyed her perfectly good footwear — but there was no other choice.

The child slipped the note inside the lining of her boot:

> *To who ever this may concern: If I Abby Drover ever live through this, I will try to donate my life to Christ, and if I don't live through this, I will go to heaven to serve Christ. If I don't live through this I would like my body to be cremated and the ashes poured all over my house on 1617 Barnet Highway.*
> *Abby Drover*

P.S If you find me dead, my killer was Donald Hay of 1601 Gore Street. He kidnapped me on the morning of March 10, 1976. I also died (if so) after my 13th birthday.

Abby wondered what her mother and sisters were doing. None of them, she thought, would ever know what she had gone through. Having written the note, she turned on the cold water tap and prepared to immerse her face in the sink. Knowing that she'd want to come up for air, she tied a sheet under the drain to hold down her head while she drowned.

14 A NEWSPAPER SCOOP

WHILE THE NEWSPAPER I worked for, the *Province*, was published
in the mornings, the only real competition in Vancouver at the
time was the *Sun*, which came out in the afternoons. Both daily
newspapers shared the same printing facilities in the Pacific
Press Building at 2250 Granville Street, but maintained separate
departments when it came to advertising, circulation and news.

Of the two, the *Sun* had the larger circulation, but both
newspapers prided themselves on their responsible, non-tab-
loid approach, and enjoyed a reasonable measure of respect as
influential beacons of Canadian journalism.

Reporters, however, tended to be a critical breed by nature —
and a good number of them at Pacific Press often complained that
their editors were too obsessed with often boring political coverage
at the expense of hard news and human interest. Neither newspaper had printed much detail about Abby Drover, who had now
been missing for more than two months.

Not that there was much to report on anyway.

Without mentioning the missing Port Moody girl, the *Sun*
did come out with a story that was certainly of interest to anyone following the case: a damaging exposé of Alexander Di
Cimbriani, the millionaire property tycoon who had affronted
Port Moody Mayor Norm Patterson with his ostentatious
$7,500 reward offer for the apprehension of the person re-
sponsible for Abby's disappearance.

Prominently displayed at the top of Page 1, the story was
written by Paul Musgrove, a reporter like myself who prided
himself on his reputation for hard-hitting news. Studious and
intense behind his gold-rimmed spectacles, Musgrove was a
large, sandy-haired man in his early thirties, who had spurned
joining his family's successful Vancouver car dealership in fa-
vour of becoming a career journalist.

Already immersed in my own plans for a career change, I

wasn't particularly concerned about the competition, but the *Province* editors were chagrined when they were scooped by Musgrove's exclusive disclosure that Di Cimbriani was not exactly the orphaned rags-to-riches political hopeful that he claimed to be. While Di Cimbriani had always portrayed himself as a hardworking Christian who had overcome substantial personal adversity in his meteoric rise to success, Musgrove had found otherwise.

Suddenly, Di Cimbriani was being forced to shelve his hopes of becoming the mayor of Vancouver. Citing ill health as the reason for his withdrawal from the mayoral race, his surprise announcement came on the eve of Musgrove's story, which appeared in the *Sun* on Wednesday, May 12, 1976:

WOULD-BE MAYOR DI CIMBRIANI HAS SECRET PAST.

ACCORDING TO THE article, Di Cimbriani had shelved his political ambitions "within hours" of learning that the *Sun* had been talking with the father and siblings he claimed he never had, on the opposite side of the country.

Musgrove also disclosed that the millionaire had in fact been born Ralph Di Cimbriani and was later renamed "Ralph Sims". Contrary to Di Cimbriani's claims, Musgrove reported, he was not raised in an orphanage at all, nor had a policeman paid for his cleft palate operation. He had paid for it himself. Neither, said the newspaper, did the businessman have the university degrees of which he boasted; and furthermore, he was twelve years older than he claimed.

According to the *Sun*, the businessman's brother Alex Sims had advised the property tycoon to drop out of the campaign because the newspaper knew his true background. "I told him I didn't think it would be a good idea," Sims stated. "I said 'Ralph, you're not that clever, and there are a lot of problems.'"

Musgrove cited the total of $185,000 that Di Cimbriani had recently offered in various rewards — including the $7,500 for Abby Drover. Noting that Di Cimbriani had also hosted several lavish parties for the Vancouver police, the newspaper questioned the source of his wealth. Family members of the businessman were quoted as saying Di Cimbriani had somehow managed to accumulate mysteriously large amounts of cash from various insignificant jobs — even before he had severed his connections with family more than twenty years before.

Concluding his story, Musgrove reported that Di Cimbriani was unavailable for further comment. The blinds were drawn on his office windows, the journalist noted, while the telephone company reported that his phone number was out of order.

In Port Moody, police and municipal officials found Musgrove's report fascinating. They had no reason to doubt Di Cimbriani's motives in posting the Abby Drover reward, but the disclosures indicated that Mayor Norm Patterson's initial reservations about the millionaire landlord had not been unfounded. Sitting in his office as he read the newspaper, the mayor couldn't help feeling intrigued. There wasn't even an orphanage in the town where Di Cimbriani claimed he had been raised by Catholic nuns. Why would anyone bother to fabricate such apparently meaningless details, especially when they could so easily be disproved?

Patterson found it all very strange. When they talked about the article, neither the mayor nor Police Chief Len McCabe knew exactly what to make of it.

ON GORE STREET, Ruth Drover discussed the article with friends and neighbours but none of them seemed to think it was of any significance either. Despite Di Cimbriani's reward, they agreed, no one seemed any closer to finding Abby than they had been since the fateful day of her disappearance.

Winter had turned into spring, and Abby's birthday had come and gone. Unable to make her a cake, Ruth had cried all day long. There were so many reminders in the house of her youngest child. But something — call it mother's instinct — always convinced Ruth that Abby was still alive. So many people, including the Vancouver bus driver, were positive they had seen her. Could they all be wrong?

Others, however, gently tried their best to prepare her for the worst. Her older sister Dorothy from Toronto was concerned that Ruth was not doing at all well.

"You've got to accept reality," insisted Dorothy. "Isn't it time you had a funeral for her?"

"That's a stupid suggestion!" Ruth snapped. "How can you have a funeral without a body? Abby isn't dead. I just won't accept it."

Ruth scowled as she put down the phone. Her sister meant well, she knew that, but a thousand thoughts were swirling in her head. She couldn't prove it, of course, but something told her Abby would eventually turn up. She also had a strong premonition: when they did find her missing daughter, she believed, it would be some time in the middle of the night.

Things looked bleak, however. They still hadn't found any trace of her, but then, neither had they located any of her belongings. If they had unearthed any of her clothing, Ruth knew, it would have been very ominous indeed, but they hadn't even so much as discovered an abandoned lunchbox or a page from a schoolbook.

Chief McCabe told the family he was thinking of assigning a whole new squad of officers to the case, in case there was something the original investigators might have missed. At the back of his mind, however, he felt quite sure that Smith and his colleagues had left nothing unexplored in their efforts to solve the mystery.

Smith was still hard at work, following up a tip from a Vancouver prostitute. "I met this kinky customer who wanted to be lined up with a girl between ten and twelve years old," the concerned woman had told him.

Smith made further inquiries but once again found the information had no bearing on the disappearance of Abby Drover.

FOUR DOORS AWAY from the Drover residence, the Hays had just received a bill for Donald's recent treatment at Royal Columbian Hospital, but the camper manufacturer was feeling better. On May 17, there was a spring in his step as he took his propane tank into Port Moody to get it repaired in preparation for the barbecue season.

It was time to get back to work, the handyman realized. He had to pick up supplies from lumber yards and upholstery shops. Despite his financial worries, business wasn't too bad. At least there were always a reasonable number of people visiting his garage to inquire about campers. Some of them were only shopping for quotations, but always there were enough customers admiring his workmanship to keep him in business.

Smiling, Hilda watched from the house as Donald unloaded yet more supplies. Her heart still ached for the Drover family, but the weather had warmed up and it looked like it was going to be a good year. The children helped Don keep the workshop clean and tidy, locking it for him whenever he had to go into town for more supplies.

She knew such periods of stability never lasted, however. Brent thought his stepfather was working in the shop one day but found the door locked. He knocked several times but there was no answer. Hilda believed her husband remained depressed that Abby still hadn't been found and sensed that he was drinking again. Predictably, Hay left yet again in July for another week-long binge. He stayed for three days at the Blackstone Hotel in Vancouver and a further two nights at the Cariboo Trails Hotel in Coquitlam.

Fortunately, Don sobered up in time so that all of them could leave together for their planned summer vacation to California. It was only the booze that made Donald so depressed, Hilda thought. If he could just stay sober, there was so much they could look forward to.

After catching up with his telephone and utility bills, Hay took Ripper to the nearest boarding kennel and loaded his vehicle for the trip. Although the family would be gone for more than a week, it wouldn't cost too much because they could save money by sleeping in his yellow GMC pickup truck with its white, canopy-type camper.

After setting out on August 1, the Hays crossed the United States border at Blaine, Washington, passing through Seattle on their way to Klamath Falls and the spectacularly rugged Oregon coast. With Hilda beside him, Hay knew better than to spoil the holiday by drinking, and the family all seemed to be having a good time. Staying at various campgrounds, they enjoyed the scenery, and the children especially were awed by the giant sequoias as they drove through Redwood National Park and the Trees of Mystery in northern California.

Before returning home, the Hays swung back to the coast to visit the Sea Lion Caves, San Francisco and a place by the name of Deer Park. It was a fabulous time, but Hilda noticed that Don was becoming irritable as the vacation drew to a close. The kids were fighting, but she suspected her husband was more frustrated by not being able to pick up his quota of duty-free vodka as they crossed back through Canada Customs. Hilda noticed he was still in a bad mood as they arrived home on Gore Street. Dropping them off at the front door, Hay departed to get the dog from the kennel. At least an hour and a half ticked by as she unpacked and made dinner.

Finally, the dog bounded in happily after his week in the kennel, but Don was drunk. Once again, thought Hilda, he obviously couldn't wait to get their holidays over with. It was clear as he left that he was heading straight for the liquor store, and another extended stay at one of his downtown hotels.

Hay checked into Granville Street's Austin Hotel, an old building with metal fire escapes, where desk clerk Noreen Olafson observed him in the company of an unknown woman. Late the following morning, August 12, the clerk knocked on the door of room 611 to ask if Hay wanted to sign for another night, but he refused her entry.

He stayed for another week, seldom leaving his room except when staff had to transfer him to 601 to make way for another guest. If they did catch a glimpse of him, employees noticed that he appeared drunk at all times. When Hilda finally found him, she was fuming. "You'd better come home and pay up your bills," she said. "Then you might as well leave. I can't go on living this way."

Hay pleaded with Hilda for another chance. He filled his truck at the Port Moody Shell station and returned home to pay his bills as requested. To calm his nerves, he stayed off the booze for a while and took Valium instead. While Hilda may not have noticed, her son Brent saw him getting so high on the tranquillizers that he almost fell on his stepdaughter Jackie as he got up and staggered to the table for his dinner.

Brent also noticed a bottle of vodka stashed under his stepfather's desk, but Donald had gotten back to work despite his addictions. Once again, he was frequently in the garage starting up his power saw, putting the finishing touches to yet another camper.

Wendy went out to see her stepfather one day but Don wasn't there and the workshop was locked. Normally, she would have waited until he got back, but she wanted to get some closet doorknobs for Abby's mother. She thought for a moment, then remembered a gap above the porch of a new addition, which she was able to climb through.

She knew Don was depressed but still found it odd that there were no campers under construction. A customer from Vancouver had recently placed an order in response to one of Hay's advertisements in the *Buy and Sell* newspaper, and just a few days earlier, she had held off Ripper while another customer came up to the house. What had Don been doing in his workshop all that time?

She found the doorknobs and left.

15 CRISIS

ON SUNDAY, September 5, 1976, mother of three Kathleen Selfridge set out from home for her evening shift at Life Line Coquitlam. It should have been a quiet night at the crisis centre, she thought. It was the day before Labour Day, the last day of summer vacations for schoolchildren but certainly not the kind of occasion, like Christmas, that would prompt a flood of calls from emotionally distraught people.

The pert, forty-year-old redhead had been with the centre on King Edward Street for two years. As an unpaid volunteer, she worked only part-time, but felt more than a small amount of satisfaction, knowing that she and her colleagues could sometimes mean the difference between life and death.

It was hard, in fact, to imagine a more worthwhile cause than sharing a few kind words with people who phoned in on the verge of suicide. Selfridge was a department store cosmetician by day, but at the crisis centre she and her colleagues were on the front lines — even if their contribution wasn't always fully appreciated. It was, after all, altruistic work, and they weren't in it for the recognition.

As she expected, though, the phones this night were generally quiet. It was becoming a long and boring night and, for the most part, Kathleen Selfridge was able to catch up on reading her files. With no one phoning in for help, she looked forward to the end of her four-hour shift so that she could get home to her family.

Being the only volunteer on duty, she couldn't leave the one-room office until her replacement came in at the end of her shift. Just as she was thinking about leaving, however, the telephone rang.

Selfridge had been required over the past twenty-four months to attend numerous training sessions with police and health care professionals, and it was obvious as soon as she picked up the phone that the caller was distraught. "I need somebody to talk to," he said. "I'm very depressed." The man's voice implied utter dejection.

Selfridge looked at the clock on the wall. It was 9:30 p.m. She wrote down the time on her notepad as she responded to the call. "What's the problem?" she asked. Her tone was kind and caring as she inquired if the caller would like to give her his name.

The man immediately picked up on Selfridge's Scottish accent. "Your voice reminds me of my family," he digressed. "My mother was Scottish. It's Don. I'm very depressed. If I had a gun, I'd shoot myself, but they won't let me have one."

Selfridge asked the man more about his family background before continuing with the immediate problem. "What do you mean?" she asked. "Who won't let you have a gun?" It was an odd question, but Selfridge was anxious to keep the conversation going.

"I can't say," the man said warily. "I'm losing my wife and family because of my heavy drinking. I run my own business and it's being badly affected, too. I just want to end it all. I've got so many problems."

The volunteer wrote down the information as the caller unburdened himself. At least she'd been able to keep him on the phone long enough to get his first name. Because of the Scottish connection, she realized, she'd been able to build up more than a usual degree of rapport.

Suddenly, though, the man sounded leery and it seemed as though he was about to hang up. "There's somebody at the door," he said nervously. "Have you sent somebody to my house?"

"No," Selfridge reassured him. "I don't even know where you live. Do you want to tell me what your problems are?"

"It'd take hours to relate all that," the caller sighed. "I won't go into that now."

Selfridge could tell that the man was absolutely desperate. She felt compassion for him as she listened to his voice, filled with despair. "You're going to read about me tomorrow on the front pages of the newspaper," he said.

"No, Don," the volunteer replied. "If you think that, you're wasting your time. It'd probably be somewhere in the back of the paper, and they won't even spell your name right. Why don't you tell me about your drinking problem?"

"Yeah, okay," the man agreed, as Selfridge sighed with relief. At least he was willing to talk about that. The volunteer was good at her job but, until now, the conversation had been more than usually tense. "I was a patient in Riverview for eighteen months," the man explained. "They were treating me for alcoholism."

"Who was your doctor?" Selfridge asked. It might defuse the crisis, she thought, if the caller would allow her to contact his physician.

"Dr. Wood," the man replied. "But she didn't do much for me except getting me in there. I don't want to go back. I may be an alcoholic but I wouldn't be able to stand drying out again. It was a terrible experience."

The caller didn't sound drunk right now, and Selfridge tried to reassure him that she might be able to find help for him as an outpatient. The man reiterated that he was quite definite on his plan to kill himself. "I love my wife and children," he said, emotionally. "I had a first wife, too, and I've got a kid that I haven't even seen."

"Maybe I could tell them how much you care about them," said the volunteer. She realized that the caller was still depressed but at least she had talked him down from the initial crisis. The man was beginning to sound quite rational. Obviously, he felt better for talking to her, and was even ready to identify himself.

"Would you like to talk to my dog?" he joked. "I'm sitting here with my Doberman."

Finally, thought Selfridge, he's in a better mood. "No, that's okay," she chuckled. "So who've I been talking with?"

"It's Don Hay," said the caller. "I'm going to have a vodka." Selfridge looked again at the clock. It was 10:15 p.m. She had talked with the man for three quarters of an hour and he didn't even thank her as he hung up.

Selfridge told the replacement worker about the call as she left for home. "I'm really worried about this guy," she told her colleague. "I have an awful feeling he's going to call back."

Selfridge was right. Not long after she left, the man called back and asked to discuss something else with the Scottish worker he'd just spoken to. There was something he'd desperately forgotten to tell her, and he pleaded for her home number.

Unsuccessfully, the replacement worker tried to step into the breach. Even though Donald Hay called back three times, she couldn't put him in touch with Selfridge. Giving out home numbers, she explained, was completely against office policy.

Although she was unaware of his call to the crisis centre, Hilda Hay could also see that her common-law husband was extremely depressed. He was often like that, but now he tossed and turned throughout the night like someone running a high fever. Hilda just knew that things were getting worse.

Having the next day off, Hilda was able to go out to the workshop to talk to him. As she expected, he was very low and intoxicated. Hilda tried not to sound judgmental or nagging as she spoke her mind. "You've got to do something about the drinking," she told him. "I'm going to try and have you committed."

Hilda returned to the house to do some domestic chores. She realized, however, that she needed to shop for some dinner fixings. As she stood outside in the driveway, she asked her son to get some money from his stepfather in the workshop. Brent tried getting in but his stepfather refused to open the door.

"Go away!" Hay called from inside. "I'm on holidays."

"Sorry," Brent said meekly. "Mom just needs to ask you something."

"Yes, I need $20 to get some groceries," Hilda confirmed. She was growing impatient, but her husband momentarily appeared at the garage window to give her the money.

Hilda finished her shopping and returned home to make dinner. She wasn't especially surprised when Don didn't come in to eat with the rest of the family — his appetite was gener-

ally depressed when he was into the booze. Besides, she sur-
mised, he often bought snacks for himself. One day her daughter
Wendy had found a grocery bag in the garage containing some
fruit and crackers, as well as some toilet paper, and now some
potato chips that Aunt Adeline had brought and left on the
kitchen counter had mysteriously disappeared from the house.
"I guess Don must have taken them," said Wendy. She imagined
he'd filched them wanting a snack while he worked on a camper.

Hilda did begin to worry, however, when Don didn't show up
as it started to turn dark. About 9.30 p.m., Hilda felt something
was definitely wrong. She returned once more to the garage —
but the door was locked.

Unable to get any response when she knocked, she assumed
that her husband must have fallen asleep. She hammered on
the door — first with her fists and then with a rock — but
there was still no answer. She was really worried now. What if
he had tried to kill himself yet again? Maybe he was lying unconscious on the cold, concrete floor inside. After pausing a
few moments to collect her thoughts, Hilda rushed back into
the house and called the Port Moody police.

Police officers throughout Canada and the United States know
only too well that domestic disputes often pose the deadliest
risks of all. If alcohol is involved, such situations can often
become a powder keg of passion and violence. Even in a small
jurisdiction such as Port Moody, circumspection was called for,
and it was general policy to have at least two members respond
to such calls.

The first officer assigned to investigate Hilda Hay's complaint
was Constable Paul Adams, the same policeman who had visited Gore Street six months before to investigate the disappearance of Abby Drover.

Adams was well aware that Donald Hay had held his family
at gunpoint only two years previously. This call, Adams realized, demanded the utmost of caution. Instead of pointing his
cruiser in the direction of Gore Street, he would drive first to

police headquarters to pick up one of his colleagues and a second shotgun.

As he hurried into the police station, Constable Bill Reed was already waiting to go with him. Reed was a slightly pudgy officer, clean-shaven with sideburns, about the same age as Adams but somewhat more withdrawn in personality. He was a sincere man, and Adams had always liked him. If there were going to be any trouble, he couldn't have wished for a more reliable partner.

The two men obtained a key to the gun cabinet, situated in the report-writing room. Silently, they exchanged glances as Reed reached for his 12-gauge Winchester. Neither officer had ever had to fire his shotgun in the course of duty and probably never would. The pump-action Winchester was a menacing looking weapon. With its 00 buckshot, it could easily blow a baseball-sized hole in any human target.

Both weapons were loaded and ready for action as Constables Adams and Reed pulled out of the parking lot.

It was 10:17 p.m. as they arrived outside 1601 Gore Street and descended the steep driveway. In accordance with safety rules, they carried their shotguns in port position, pointing skywards over the shoulder.

Hilda Hay, with her hair scraped back into a bun, looked coarse and dishevelled as she met them in the darkness outside the garage. "My husband has locked himself inside," she said, shaking nervously. "He's been drinking heavily. I can't raise him. I'm afraid he might have killed himself!"

The woman fidgeted as she confirmed that she didn't have a key to get into the outbuilding.

Circling the garage, the policemen confirmed for themselves that both entrances were locked. "Open up, Don," said Adams, knocking on the front door. "Port Moody police. There's no problem. We just want to talk to you." Adams waited for a moment after his loud pronouncement but there was no response.

"I know he's in there," said Hilda, becoming even more agitated.

"How do you know for sure?" asked Reed.

"Because his truck's still here," Hilda replied. "He hasn't come out since he went in there. He could have killed himself. He took an overdose once before."

Both officers were still extremely cautious. "Has he got any firearms in there?" asked Adams.

"Not that I know of," said Hilda.

It wasn't very reassuring, and the police officers could see no way of opening the front door. This time Hilda accompanied them as they walked once more to the rear of the building, where the policemen asked if she wanted them to kick in the back door.

"We can't just break in," said Adams. "Not unless you give us permission."

Hilda nodded in agreement, and Reed kicked open the door on his second attempt. Ordering the woman to remain outside, Adams felt his heart pounding as he and Reed warily entered the building and fumbled for a light switch.

There was no way of knowing what they were getting into. Was the woman's husband really dead? Or was he waiting for them in the dark, out of range of their flashlights? Both policemen were apprehensive. Reed could feel the hair rising on the back of his neck, as they fumbled for the lights.

In the middle of the garage there was a camper under construction but no sign of Donald Hay. Cautiously, both officers searched the building, looking under the camper as well as in all the cupboards around the perimeter, including the rafters and every conceivable nook and cranny.

Leaving the lights on, the officers emerged to give Hilda the news that her husband had not killed himself. It should have assuaged her fears, they thought, but the woman clung to her vociferous denial.

"He's in there," she insisted, wringing her hands. "I just know he is."

"Look, lady," said a frustrated Adams. "He isn't there. We can absolutely guarantee it. He's probably out on a bender somewhere.

When he gets home, if you're scared that he's too drunk, you can call us back."

Despite their thorough search of the premises, the woman continued to argue. Finally, the policemen cut it short. "Okay," Reed suggested. "We'll put it down as a missing person."

Having other things to do, the policemen walked back up the driveway and carefully placed their shotguns in the back seat of their car.

It was nearly eleven o'clock on a warm summer night, and the officers rolled down their windows as they prepared to drive away. After smelling all the paints and chemicals in the garage, they welcomed the breath of fresh air. Suddenly, a message over the car radio and the incessant, outdoor chorus of frogs and crickets was replaced by a bloodcurdling sound that split the night air.

It was a scream — the most terrifying, spine-tingling scream either of them had ever heard.

16 LOSING HOPE

PACKING THEIR PENS and exercise books at their home on Gore Street, Kathleen and Robyn Drover were considerably more nervous than usual. The night before the first day back at school would cause butterflies in the stomachs of any child; for Ruth's older daughters, it was even more daunting than usual. Not only would they be in a new grade, they would also be switching from old teachers and friends in Burnaby to new, unfamiliar surroundings at the senior secondary school in Port Moody. Other students were bound to know about their plight, so it would probably be even more difficult to slip into new friendships.

It was especially stressful, too, because Abby would have finished elementary school and should have been packing with them, ready to start her first day of Grade 8 at Port Moody Junior Secondary. Everyone in the family had hoped at first for some kind of miracle, but it had been six months now since Abby seemed to have vanished from the face of the earth. At least confirmation of her death would have brought some kind of closure, but this had been half a year of uncertainty and despair, the worst frustration, anguish and torment any family could imagine.

Everyone had done all they could: police, pilots, psychics and all manner of good Samaritans, including the three hundred or so volunteers who had combed what seemed like every square inch of the municipality. It was time to admit the obvious. None of them was likely to see Abby ever again, although Ruth had bitterly resisted any such suggestions all summer long.

Unconsciously, Ruth had been snapping at her eldest daughters for even the slightest of transgressions. Her mind had been programmed for denial from the outset. No one, not even her own sister, had been able to get her to face reality. She would have to reach that saddest of conclusions by herself.

Finally, earlier that night, she seemed to have come to terms with the situation for the very first time. The transformation had been gradual, starting with her decision, only as recently as the previous week, to take in a lodger. It was perhaps the first indication that she was ready to carry on with her life as normally as possible.

"I've got a room for rent," she told a student at nearby Simon Fraser University. "I wonder if you could advertise it for me on your bulletin board." With Abby missing, the family had the space and could always use the extra income. Ruth specified that she would rent her basement to a suitable female student. It was not a complete suite, but it did include a bed, sitting room, kitchen facilities and a washroom with a shower. Robyn had moved back upstairs into Abby's bedroom, so it didn't seem as if the family would really need the basement anymore.

The rent was reasonable, and a pleasant young Victoria woman, aged about twenty, gave Ruth a deposit. She seemed to be a studious sort of girl, so it was doubtful she'd be any trouble or cause any kind of disruption. "It's just what I was looking for," the prospective tenant said immediately. "I'll take it." The university student came back with her belongings and had just settled in as Kathy and Robyn got ready for school. Although the girls were looking forward to meeting her, there hadn't yet been time for them to get to know the new lodger, and the young woman was not yet aware that Ruth's youngest child was missing.

Other indications that Ruth might be prepared to accept the worst had also been accumulating. Perhaps it was because it had been so long, or maybe because it was the start of the new school year — whatever the reason, Ruth Drover seemed ready to concede that her youngest daughter wouldn't be coming back.

The final admission came almost by accident. Ruth's Aunt Margaret, an experienced seamstress, had offered to make her a new dress during a visit to the house on Gore Street for a roast beef supper. After the children washed and dried the dishes, Margaret peered through her spectacles into Ruth's closet, to see what her niece might be needing for the fall. Ruth was an accomplished dressmaker, too, but found it harder to make outfits for herself than for others.

With a vacant expression, Ruth seemed oddly uninterested as, one by one, she rejected each of her aunt's suggestions.

"Maybe you could make me a black dress," she finally said. "I guess I might be needing it after all."

Kindly, Margaret reached out, not knowing whether to nod her head, or shake it in disagreement. Instead, she held her niece as Ruth sobbed in her arms. "Whatever you want, Ruthie, dear," she said. "Whatever you want."

O**N THE OTHER** side of town, other people also felt indescribable sadness that Abby had still not been found. Among them were church youth leaders Bob and Donna Kantymir. Bob, a horticulturist, had grown up in a Seventh-Day Adventist family, and his attractive, soft-spoken young wife had joined him as a member of the church when they got married.

The church was quite fundamental, but Donna still found it a worthwhile experience. "We were at that stage where we were both searching for the meaning of life," the agriculture department secretary explained to me later.

The Kantymirs had met Abby through the church and immediately liked her. Both of them trusted her implicitly as she cradled their recently adopted baby son in her slender arms. It was obvious that she adored him. "She was a very special girl," Donna recalled. "She had some very special qualities."

Donna felt, however, that Abby — despite her apparently placid nature — had begun to resist her mother's authority and might be at the age where she was beginning to have some problems at home. Shocked when Abby disappeared, she and her husband had not hesitated to join the massive search. Even though the searchers had come up empty-handed, both Kantymirs had had the overwhelming feeling that she was still alive.

"Abby was very resilient," Donna Kantymir would later re-call. "We honestly felt that we'd find her." She desperately hoped that no harm had come to the child, and still felt she may simply have run away from home. But when the summer holidays ended with no further news of her, even the most stalwart of the church faithful had begun to give up hope.

"By that time," recalled Donna, "we were pretty heartbroken. I'm ashamed to say I honestly didn't think we'd ever see her again."

THE KANTYMIRS AND Ruth Drover weren't the only ones preparing for the worst. Abby herself no longer had any hopes for a miraculous discovery or escape. The child had been unable to drown herself, but her captor had left her so malnourished that it was surely only a matter of time until she perished.

In the dank, dismal cell, the man had left her alone for as long as a month with only two chocolate bars and a can of sardines. Although the child tried as hard as she could to eat the sardines after removing the parts that repulsed her, she hated the way they smelled and was unable to swallow them. Sealing the remnants of the fish in a glass jar, she realized she didn't need much food anyway. It wouldn't consume too many calories to lie on her back staring at the ceiling.

But the child was starving, and had lost about a quarter of her body weight. Even worse, the light in the damp prison had finally burned out, leaving the girl trapped in terrifying total darkness for almost five days.

Abby shivered in the pitch-black cell. Occasionally she recoiled as she felt unseen insects crawling on her skin. Her eyes played tricks on her; she began to see shapes that weren't even there.

Finally, when Hay did replace the light, her eyes hurt from the unshaded glare. When her captor departed for another extended period, Abby again tried to think of ways to thwart him. Though she couldn't fight him off, she could make it clear to him that she had a mind of her own.

The man had installed a peephole in the door, apparently to

satisfy his voyeuristic perversions by spying on the child from outside the cell. During one of his lengthy absences, Abby was able to loosen the fish-eye lens and remove it. The man was frustrated by her continuing passive resistance but apparently realized it would be futile to reinstall the peephole, even if he could bully the child into revealing where she'd hidden it.

He lost his temper, however, when the child asked him for food. "I've got two handguns and a rifle," he threatened again. "If it's necessary, I'll use them." As though to break her will further, Hay now left the child with absolutely no food except some powdered milk. Abby used six tablespoons to make a glass of milk. Thinking he might never return, she gradually cut the portions to five spoons; then four spoons; then two.

Just as the milk disappeared, Abby heard Hay coming back and unlocking the door. All he brought with him, however, was a bottle of liquor. "Didn't you bring me any food?" the child asked plaintively. "I haven't got anything left to eat."

"I don't give a hoot!" he told her as he poured himself a drink. Apparently, he was angry that she still resisted his orders to take off her clothes whenever she heard him preparing to come in. She never did *anything* willingly. It just wasn't working out. Her constant crying was driving him crazy. He had to find a way to get rid of her.

Hay disappeared for several more weeks but finally returned with some Kentucky Fried Chicken. "How is it?" he asked as the child hungrily devoured everything except the bones.

"It's fine," said Abby thanking him. "It's really good, except it's cold."

The child's strength — the resilience that Donna Kantymir had spoken of — surprised even the captor himself. "Yeah, I know," he replied. "I didn't hurry back with it. Quite honestly, I didn't think you'd still be alive."

Hay added that he had finally come up with a definite plan to release her. "It'll be on Friday," he said. "I told everybody I'm going camping. I'm going to tie you up. It'll take you a couple of hours to get free and by then I'll be gone."

Abby knew better than to believe him. He had made similar promises throughout the summer and hadn't kept any of them. Although he said he had booked a taxi to set his plan in motion, the child was quite sure that he was lying. *This is the end of it,* she thought. He would probably shoot her, fill in the hole and commit suicide.

Hay poured himself a drink and ordered Abby to take off her clothes. Roughly, he shoved one of his fingers into her, then four fingers, then two.

He still wanted her, even though her body ached and she was little more than a moving skeleton. He lay down beside her, but suddenly froze. He could hear something outside. The sounds were muffled, but Abby held her breath and could hear them, too. The girl didn't know what to expect at first. She was weak, dehydrated and almost delirious, but then it became unmistakable. She was hearing the sound of footsteps and voices! Hay placed one hand on Abby's neck, holding the other over her nose and mouth so forcefully that he almost choked her.

"Keep quiet!" the child heard him whispering. "Make the slightest noise and you're dead."

17 DEAD MAN WALKING

CONSTABLES PAUL ADAMS and Bill Reed had driven no more than halfway down the block when they received the message over their car radio advising them to return immediately to 1601 Gore Street. Believing, as they headed back downtown, that Donald Hay was out drinking, the policemen had half expected that they might pass him in an approaching vehicle being driven home, bleary-eyed, by one of his friends.

The 10:45 p.m. message from the Port Moody police station, however, disclosed some surprising news to the contrary. "The complainant has found her husband and believes he's dead," said the dispatcher in his ever present monotone.

Without turning their car around, the policemen backed up the hill in the darkness. Immediately, they realized the scream had come from Wendy Hay, who was clinging to her mother at the foot of the driveway — peering with trepidation through the open front door of the garage.

Forgetting their shotguns in the back seat, the policemen leapt out of their car and hurtled down the driveway. Adams' feet barely seemed to touch the ground as he raced to the garage, Reed puffing close behind him. Neither officer knew what they were getting into this time either — but Adams was about to make a split-second decision that may have saved their lives.

As the policemen rushed in, they were presented with an apparition that should have stopped them dead in their tracks.

It was like a scene out of a horror movie.

Donald Hay was supposed to be dead. How, therefore, could he be crawling — his face as white as a ghost — out of one of the lower cabinets that the policemen had searched only minutes before? Unfolding in the far corner of the garage was the eeriest scene that Adams had ever witnessed in life: a supposed suicide victim emerging from what may as well have been his own coffin. For that moment,

Constable Adams and Donald Hay stared at each other in mutual amazement.

Sidestepping an assortment of hammers and chisels, Hay scrambled onto the workbench in a desperate attempt to reach some object atop the upper cabinets. Call it instinct, an infusion of adrenaline, a gut reaction or just total shock — whatever the reason, Adams reacted immediately. Breaking into a sprint, he tackled the man and hauled him down. In the dim light of the garage, bottles of varnish and paint cans flew in all directions as the policeman wrestled Hay to the ground. By the time Constable Reed ran up beside them, Adams already had the man in a headlock. Both policemen noticed Hay's belt was unfastened and that his pants and underwear were down around his ankles.

Despite the shock that had just reverberated through the garage, everything seemed under control. After heeding Hay's pleas to have his pants pulled up, Adams advised the man he was in violation of his probation order. Attempting to catch his breath, the officer explained that authorities might also detain him under mental health legislation as a suicide risk.

Marching Hay towards the front door of the workshop, Adams looked back as Reed returned to the cabinet to see where Hay had come from. In that instant, both policemen saw a second apparition, a sight that would be forever seared in their memories: a young female, her face gaunt and pale as she slowly struggled to claw her way to freedom.

"That's Abby Drover!" Adams exclaimed. Reed pulled the young girl out, whereupon she immediately collapsed, like a rag doll, to the concrete floor.

IN SOILED, LOOSE-FITTING clothes, the pathetically thin child whimpered as Reed found some old coats to cover her, attempting to keep her warm and to reduce the effects of shock. Adams observed that the child was still wearing the same blue slacks, black socks and beige turtle-neck sweater he'd noted when he had reported her missing, an eternity ago.

As Adams handcuffed the suspect and frogmarched him to a separate room in the northeast corner of the garage, both policemen realized they had an audience. Frozen near the garage door, a speechless Hilda and her daughters had witnessed the entire drama.

After the officers had returned to their car, she explained to the police, her daughters had reminded her about the existence in the garage of an underground pit. Her husband had told her he'd constructed it to work under his vehicle but that it had subsequently caved in. She'd had no reason to doubt him — until that night, when the policemen had searched the garage without success.

"The girls mentioned the hole," said Hilda. Noticing that several bottles of gasoline and glue appeared to have been moved aside from one of the cabinets, she had opened the cupboard doors and knelt beside the floor of the cabinet. "I lifted the board and could see his feet. I thought he was dead, and Wendy called the police again. I left the board off the hole and we waited by the door. That's when you came in and saw him crawling out."

The heavy plywood floor that Hilda had described was painted the same inconspicuous blue as the rest of the cabinets. It was easy to see how it blended in. Adams gestured emphatically for the woman and her daughters to leave the garage. "I want you back in the house right now," he ordered. "Don't phone anyone or open the door for anybody unless it's one of us."

Inside the house, Hilda struggled to catch her breath, gasping through a whirlwind of emotions. If she and her daughters hadn't been so transfixed by what they'd seen, they surely would have fainted. It was all so clear now: the missing potato chips; the bag of apples that Wendy had found in the garage; the hours on end that her husband had been spending out there alone.

Hilda was overcome. She shuddered as she realized she'd been living with a man who may well have posed a threat to her own children. Despite her fear and guilt, however, the woman felt incredible relief that little Abby Drover had survived. She yearned to call Ruth, but the policeman's explicit instructions were still ringing in her ears, and she didn't dare pick up the phone.

Returning to the garage, Adams peered into the cabinet. With its doors still open, both policemen could see that the entire cupboard floor had been moved aside to reveal a crude wooden stepladder leading down a concrete shaft.

Adams went back to Hay. "What's down there!?" he asked. The handyman made no intelligible response. It would be no use asking the same question of Abby. Crying continuously, the child was hysterical and incoherent.

"Bill, you've got to go down and check it out!" Adams called out. Unsure of what might be lurking below, Reed was nervous. None of it seemed real. He had been out with a police dogmaster looking for Abby the first night the girl disappeared, but now he was being asked to delve into a nightmare. Adams, however, did something to reassure him. Taking his revolver from its holster, he cocked the gun and jammed its barrel into the suspect's mouth.

"If anything happens to Bill, I am going to kill you," Adams said.

Being careful to touch as little as possible, Reed descended nearly eight feet into what seemed to be the bowels of the earth. Adams guessed he was gone less than two minutes, but it seemed like hours before his partner climbed back to the top of the shaft. Reed also now looked white as a ghost. "God, you wouldn't believe it!" he exclaimed, as he crawled back into the garage. "But there's nobody else down there."

Having secured the crime scene, Adams and Reed turned their attention to the victim. Abby was still lying in a fetal position, sobbing uncontrollably on the floor of the garage.

Still trying their best to comfort the thin, pathetic child as they knelt beside her, Reed and his colleague briefly discussed plans for a specific course of action. It would take all their professional training, under the circumstances, to steady their nerves and come up with a logical plan.

Both policemen felt sure the girl realized they were there to

MISSING

ABBY DROVER

WHITE FEMALE
AGE 12
HEIGHT 5'3"
WEIGHT 90 LBS
BROWN HAIR
BLUE EYES

wearing orange nylon ski jacket,
white turtle neck sweater,
blue button vest,
blue slacks,
brown boots.

PORT MOODY POLICE DEPARTMENT

Abby's missing poster was circulated
all over British Columbia.

photograph courtesy *The Vancouver Province*

Donald Hay's workshop

Moody Elementary, where Abby failed to appear for school on March 10, 1976.

photograph by John Griffiths

The six-by-five-foot cell where Abby was imprisoned for 181 days.

photograph courtesy *The Vancouver Province*

photograph courtesy *The Vancouver Province*

Port Moody police constables Reed (left) and Adams at the opening of the cell.

photograph courtesy *The Vancouver Province*

Donald Hay hides his face as he is driven away by police.

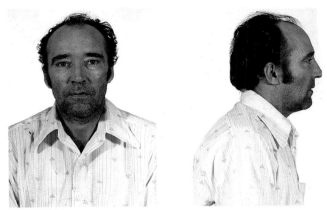

Donald Hay's 1976 mug shot.

Donald Hay in prison today; in late 1999, he will stand trial on three new charges of sex offences which allegedly occurred between 1970 and 1976.

Abby looking cheerful at Disneyland a few months after her rescue.

Abby (left) relaxes on a California beach with sister Kathleen.

Frank Sinatra, whose son Frank Jr. was once abducted, signed this album cover: "To Abby and Family, a very Merry Christmas and peaceful New Year— Love, Frank Sinatra."

photograph courtesy Ruth Drover

photograph courtesy Ruth Drover

Christmas 1976: Abby receives a hug from Police Chief Len McCabe.

photograph courtesy Abby Drover

"The day my son was born," Abby has said,
"was the happiest day of my life."

photograph by John Griffiths

The author (left) recalls the case with former Port
Moody mayor Norm Patterson in 1997.

rescue her. At all costs, however, they wanted to avoid any action that might compound her anguish and shock. The last thing they needed was to trigger an avalanche of media attention. The sobbing child had to be kept calm, well away from the glare of television lights and untimely questions from prying reporters.

Exchanging a nod of agreement with his colleague, Reed pressed the squelch button on his portable radio, advising his dispatcher that he was calling from the garage at 1601 Gore Street. "We need an ambulance," he said. "It's an emergency but we don't want a Code 3."

"No sirens or lights?" the dispatcher replied.

"Ten-four," confirmed Reed, relieved to get the message out. "We don't want any attention. Just tell them to get here as fast as they can."

At the police station, the dispatcher feared something dreadful must have happened. Either one of the policemen or a member of the Hay family must be down. Experience told him not to question the officer's request, but it was obvious that something serious was afoot, especially when Reed asked for two of his colleagues. "We need Corporal Connell and Constable Smith here right away," the policeman concluded.

CORPORAL ARCHIE CONNELL arrived at the garage at exactly 11 o'clock, followed three minutes later by Constable Wayne Smith. It was crystal clear but still seemingly unreal confirmation of what they'd always believed. They had never seriously thought that Abby was a runaway, and Hay had been their number one suspect all along. Adams admitted both of his colleagues to the workshop, but his brief explanation seemed almost unnecessary as they observed Abby, still lying in a fetal position, being comforted by Constable Reed.

For Smith, it was perhaps the most heartwrenching moment of his life. After all the hours — days, weeks and months — that he had spent searching throughout the Lower Mainland and beyond, the girl had been imprisoned no more than half a block away from her own house all along.

It was incredible, he reflected, that he had looked under the workbench almost six months ago, when he had questioned Hay soon after Abby's disappearance. Smith remembered how he'd noticed an unusual notch at the base of the cabinet, and could see now that the reason it had been cut away was to hold the top of the ladder.

But the false floor was so inconspicuous that Reed and Adams had also overlooked it as they had searched for the missing man. It was the only cabinet on the premises that was completely empty, yet the floor had appeared to be a completely normal part of the woodwork. Hay's common-law wife and stepchildren had known about the underground chamber all along, but they, too, had been fooled by his subterfuge. Not only had Donald Hay deceived the police and the Drover family, he had also been able to avoid detection by the very people who lived with him and knew him best.

It was almost too much to believe. Corporal Connell immediately got on his radio to call for a police photographer. As soon as Abby could be removed by ambulance, Connell wanted the evidence recorded in full colour, so that the courts could witness the horror that the officers had seen. Outside the garage, Identification Officer K.G.A. Lylack loaded his camera, ready to take dozens of pictures of the workshop interior, as well as the cabinet and the underground cell.

As Constable Adams prepared to escort Hay to the Port Moody police station, the ambulance silently pulled up at 11:13 p.m.

Crouching beside the victim, paramedics Robert Thompson and David Sheffley found that Abby was unable to stand by herself. They were amazed that the girl was still alive. Constable Reed had been comforting her and would accompany all of them to Royal Columbian Hospital. The child squealed with pain as they lifted her onto a stretcher but spoke her first clear words since being rescued.

"I want my mom," Abby sobbed. "I want my mom."

18 HOSPITAL

RUTH DROVER HAD just retired for the night when the front doorbell rang. Although it was late, the call didn't seem too unusual. In their quest for information, the police had come back to the house numerous times over the past six months. Wearily, she got out of bed, put on her navy blue housecoat and switched on the lights. Conditioned to disappointment, she plodded down the hall and peered through one of the glass panels beside the front door.

She recognized the police officers standing on the porch but froze at the foot of the stairs for a few moments before she was able to open the door. Constable Smith and Corporal Connell needn't have said anything. She could tell just by the looks on their faces that the case had been solved.

"We've found Abby," Constable Smith blurted out, almost choking on his words, "and she's alive!"

Standing beside his colleague, Corporal Archie Connell shared the moment of ecstasy. All too frequently, the officers were messengers of tragedy; it was a rare thrill to tell an incredulous mother her missing daughter had been found alive.

Abby had been taken to hospital, they explained, but it appeared she would be okay. It was news that, after six long months, seemed nothing short of a miracle.

"They've found her!" Ruth screamed as she ran back upstairs. "They've found Abby!" In their nightgowns, Kathy and Robyn raced out of their bedrooms, their feet barely touching the floor as they jumped up and down, hugging each other and squealing with delight.

Smith and Connell stood back as Ruth picked up the phone to rouse her sister Del with the news. For members of the family, there was no doubt it was the best day of their lives. Only recently — for the first time in six months — had Del been able to mention Abby's name without watching Ruth break down.

"We'll be right there!" said Del. Imparting the good news to her own children, she slid into the passenger seat of the family's Mercury station wagon beside her husband Doug, who hurriedly backed out of the driveway at their home in Surrey.

Speeding over the Port Mann Bridge, the couple arrived in Port Moody, where Ruth jumped into the back seat of the station wagon. "Abby's alive, Abby's alive!" she repeated over and over again as they set off for the hospital.

Flying across a set of railway tracks at nearly one hundred miles an hour, Doug heard a siren and spotted a police car in his rear-view mirror. Pulling over, he leapt out of his station wagon and ran back to the officer who was pulling out his ticket book.

"Abby Drover!" Doug yelled.

"I'll give you an escort!" said the officer. "Just follow me to the hospital!"

With the police car's red lights flashing, it was only a matter of minutes before they reached the hospital. Ushered into a brightly lit waiting-room, Ruth was met by Constable Reed.

"They'll be examining her in a few minutes but I think she's going to be all right," he said. The policeman told them he had already asked the girl several questions and was amazed by her courage.

Reed had just come from Emergency Room 1, where nurse Colleen Nelson had handed him the girl's clothes. The policeman was fully aware that everything would have to be clearly labelled and properly documented. Even though the suspect had been caught, literally, with his pants down, one of the perpetual concerns of police officers was that the justice system might not always back them up in obtaining a conviction. It was important to keep a precise record of the evidence.

Noting that the girl had not been wearing a brassiere, the policeman carefully bagged her clothing and numbered each item in his notebook:

1 Navy blue, woolen, buttoned vest
2 Beige, cord, turtle neck sweater
3 One pair, black socks
4 One pair, blue slacks
5 One pair, ultra-violet coloured, female underpants

Covered with blankets, Abby had perked up as the police-man went about his work, although her first comments had seemed confused. "Any girl that told you they saw me down at Vancouver was lying," she said.

"Who told you that?" Reed responded.

"That bloke fluke that kidnapped me did."

Reed glanced over at Nurse Nelson, apparently wanting her to witness the strange conversation. Then he turned back to Abby. "Did you know the man you were with?" he asked.

"Yes," the girl replied, her voice becoming stronger. "I thought he was a friend of mine."

"Do you know his name?" Reed asked softly.

"Yeah."

"What is it?"

"Donald Hay," said the girl contemptuously. "He's a fruit, if you ask me. Did you get that bloke's pants up? You should have arrested him for indecent exposure!"

At six minutes past midnight, Ruth Drover was finally allowed to see her daughter. Rushing over to hold Abby in her arms, she was shocked by her daughter's foul-smelling, emaciated condition. Despite their mutual sobs, however, Ruth was sure that the child was now safe and was strong enough to survive.

"I haven't had anything to eat in six weeks," said Abby.

"How long?" Ruth asked incredulously, brushing away each of their tears.

"Six weeks," Abby repeated. "Just two chocolate bars and some milk to drink."

As Ruth took a cloth to wash Abby's hands and face, she

saw a number — 177 — written in ink on the palm of Abby's left hand. "What is *that?*" the child's mother asked.

"That's how many days I stayed down in that bloody place," Abby said defiantly. (It had actually been 181 days, but Abby was, remarkably, only four days off in her calculations.)

"Where?" her mother asked. She was still confused by the sequence of events.

"At Don Hay's," explained Abby. "The guy who makes the campers. He knew the police were there tonight, and he ran upstairs once he thought they'd gone. Wendy screamed when I came out of the hole."

More tears streamed down Ruth's face.

At twenty minutes past midnight, Abby desperately wanted to go home but still had to be examined by the emergency room physician. As the doctor came into the room, Ruth reluctantly got up to wait outside while Constable Reed entered Treatment Room 2. Leaving the connecting door slightly ajar, the policeman had no difficulty hearing the doctor's initial diagnosis that severe inflammation would preclude a complete internal examination.

The policeman could also hear the remainder of the conversation, which he recorded in his notebook.

"Why was food cut off?" the doctor asked.

"He wouldn't come down," said Abby.

"When was the last time you saw him?"

"Today."

"Today?" the doctor repeated.

"Yes," replied Abby. "That's when the police found me."

"Have you had intercourse?" asked the doctor. "Do you know what intercourse is?"

"Yes," said Abby.

"Yes?"

"Yes. All the time."

"Did he put his penis anywhere else but your vagina?" asked the doctor.

"Yes," the girl replied. "My mouth."

"Did you bleed at all?"

Constable Reed craned his neck but was unable to hear Abby's response. The doctor made some general inquiries relating to previous illnesses before he continued to ask the girl about her six-month ordeal.

"Were you able to have a bath at all?" he asked.

"No," said Abby. "Just a face-cloth."

"Have you been out of that room at all? It's quite sore here. Have you been swollen up for a long time?"

"Yes."

"Has this just been sore today? You've quite obviously been swollen for some time. You say you had intercourse?"

"Yes."

"Tonight, around suppertime?"

"Yes."

"Did you just have intercourse or did he make you take it in your mouth?"

"Both."

"Did he use anything else besides his fingers or penis?"

Reed was unable to hear the girl's reply. At 1:45 a.m., Abby was transferred to another room, where the doctor continued his examination. "Spread your legs further," he requested.

"I've heard that so many times in the past six months," the girl sighed.

"Did he ever put anything in your back passage?" asked the doctor. "Just his finger, not his penis?"

Feeling the examination seemed to be taking forever, Abby brushed off the question. "Yes," she replied. "Just his finger."

Three hours after she had first entered the hospital, Abby heaved a huge sigh of relief upon being told that she could go home. Waiting in a hallway outside, Ruth and her sister felt pangs of sympathy as the child emerged in a wheelchair, a blanket draped partially over her head to keep her hidden from the prying eyes of curious onlookers. In that instant, Del realized just how fragile life was. Abby was incredibly strong and resilient, but it was obvious that she had been so close to death.

At 2:35 a.m. on September 7, Constable Reed escorted the family back to 1617 Barnet Highway. Kathy and Robyn were overjoyed by the safe return of their baby sister, but stood well back as their mother helped the filthy waif upstairs to the bathroom.

Constable Smith and Corporal Connell arrived back at the house, and waited in the living room as Ruth gently soaked her daughter in a hot bath. It was clear that the child was extremely malnourished, and Ruth gasped on seeing the full extent of her daughter's emaciated condition. Abby didn't even have the strength to bathe herself. *She's just like a skeleton*, Ruth thought.

Bathing her gently, Ruth paid careful attention to scrubbing the "177" from Abby's left hand. The marks blurred together and finally disappeared from sight, but both of them knew that that ink would be indelible on their minds.

After her bath, Abby put on a nightgown and crawled into her mother's bed. A lamp glowed dimly on the dresser as she attempted to swallow some soup that Del had made for her, but her stomach had shrunk so much that it hurt to eat, and she was unable to keep down more than a few spoonfuls.

Constable Smith and Corporal Connell relayed their concern to Ruth that it would probably be only a matter of time before a horde of newspapermen would be descending on the house seeking complete details of the story. The policemen indicated they would like to interview Abby right away, if possible, adding it might be prudent for all members of the family to stay elsewhere for the night.

"That's no problem," offered Del. "We've got a big house. Doug and I can drive everybody back to Surrey."

"Okay," said Connell, glancing over as Ruth nodded her head. "Let's see if Abby's ready to talk to us."

Ruth and her sister fetched Abby from the bedroom. The child was unable to walk without assistance, but both policemen sat forward on the edge of the sofa, amazed by her fortitude and maturity as she entered the living room.

With a brave smile, Abby gave them a look of gratitude as she sat down. She should have been more leery of Donald Hay, she began, because of an incident the day before he kidnapped her. On March 9, she explained, she had accepted a ride home from school with Hay and his stepson Brent. "I was wearing a navy blue dress," she recalled. "When he shifted the gears in his truck, he put his hand on my knee. It was such a fleeting thing that I didn't think much about it.

"He informed me he had driven Jackie, Wendy and my sisters to look for me. He thought it was a big joke. Here he was supposedly out looking for me — pulling the wool over everybody's eyes."

As Abby paused in her narrative, Smith took out his notebook. Despite the lateness of the hour, it was time to take down a complete statement. In his heavy Scottish accent, Connell conducted the interview as Smith recorded the child's statements for the first time in her own words. "Just start from the beginning," Connell said. "Can you tell us how he first kidnapped you?"

```
Statement of Abby Drover,
3:00 A.M. September 7, 1976:


"After Mom left, he [Donald Hay] phoned and said
he would give me a ride, so about 8:10 I went over.
He told me to cut through the yards. I was going
down the stairs when he came up and grabbed me. He
half picked me up and dragged me into the garage
and kind of pushed me in the hole, and made me go
down the ladder.
  "After he put me in the room, he came in. He
said, 'We're going to play house for a while.' He
took off all my clothes. He pushed my top up and
pulled my pants off. He then raped me. He couldn't
get in me so he handcuffed me and chained me to the
wall. After, he let me get dressed. He came back
and brought me my books.
```

"He came back every day after that. He used chains and metal handcuffs. He went away. I got out of the chains and shackles but the door was bolted. When he would come down, he would do the same thing.

"At first, he couldn't get in me, but after a while he did. Sometimes he would make me suck on him. After the first couple of times, he would keep the chains off. He was usually drunk when he would come down.

"He would talk to me about letting me out. Sometimes he threatened to kill me if I made any noise. He said he would strangle me. He was partially drunk, but he would attack me even if he was sober. Sometimes he would force his penis up my bum.

"He kept me in the room all the time. He used boards and chains to keep the room locked. He told me he was going to keep me for a ransom. He said he was going to make a camper, get the money and give it to Mrs. Hay.

"The first day, he said I was only going to stay for a day. He kept promising to let me go. I finally didn't believe him. This last night, he said he was going to let me go, but I didn't believe him.

"Before that, the last time he was down was a Saturday morning about two weeks ago. He came down about three o'clock a.m. and stayed to six o'clock a.m.

"I was lying down when he came in, but I was awake. He said if he ever came down and found me asleep he would use me, and I was never asleep when he came down.

"When he came in, I was wearing my clothes. He said, 'Take your clothes off.' He had been drinking, but not much. I took my clothes off except for my socks. He then raped me. He made me suck on him for a while and then he raped me. He entered into me. He climaxed in me then. He then got off me but wouldn't let me get dressed. He just sat there and drank and smoked, with his pants off. He would touch my breasts as he sat there.

"He would mainly talk about trying to get me out. The night before the police came, he came down about 6:15 and gave me two chocolate bars which is all I had had in six weeks. He had a drink and made me take my clothes off. He then shoved one of his fingers in me, then four fingers, then two.

"We were lying there when the police were upstairs. He had one hand on my neck, and one on my mouth. He threatened to kill me if I screamed. He then went out and I heard Mrs. Hay's voice so I climbed out. During the time he made threats to kill me all the time: if I did anything bad he would strangle me."

The interview — which left Smith and Connell shaking their heads in amazement — came to an end at 3:50 a.m. Abby Drover had just been to hell and back. Most adults would probably never have survived. She was indeed a very special child.

19 UNDER ARREST

SHORTLY BEFORE MIDNIGHT, while Abby was being taken to the hospital, Constable Paul Adams drove a handcuffed Donald Hay to the Port Moody Public Safety Building. Inexplicably — other than the fact that it was the night of a full moon — all of the adult cells were occupied. In the stark light of the police station, the officer and his prisoner were met by Constable Dunn, who escorted Hay to one of the juvenile cells before searching him.

Once in the cell, Hay bowed his head, staring at the floor in apparent dejection. "If I try to escape, will you guys blow me in the back of the head?" he offered. "That's what I deserve."

It was a tempting proposal, but the police officers remained outwardly calm as they completed their search. "We're not even wearing guns, Don," Adams replied.

Hay sounded desperate. "I can't take it anymore," he said. Ignoring the comment, Dunn and Adams closed the heavy steel door behind them, leaving the prisoner to reflect on his predicament.

At 12:01 a.m., Corporal Connell and Constable Smith entered the cell to escort the dishevelled prisoner to an interview room. Smith, a resolute calm masking his true emotions, opened the conversation. "It's our duty to inform you," he said, "that you are not obliged to say anything, but anything you do say may be given in evidence." Part-way into their interview, the police officers suddenly realized that their tape recorder wasn't switched on and had to start all over again.

Hay shifted uncomfortably in his chair. He acknowledged understanding the caution, but declined the opportunity to write down his own statement concerning the events of the past six months. The prisoner confirmed, however, that he would be willing to sign a statement upon perusal, if the officers would write it down for him based on his comments.

Holding his head in his hands, Hay began. "I had first started thinking about doing something like this because I wanted to save someone like Abby. I didn't really have her in mind at the time."

Connell looked at the prisoner with incredulity. *Saving* someone seemed a strange way of describing a six-month forcible confinement, but the police officer resisted the temptation to interject.

"I had built the room originally as an air raid shelter," Hay continued. "That morning when it all started, Abby had come over to get a ride to school. She came into the shop and was talking to me. It just so happened she came in at the wrong time and we got tangled up."

The man's euphemisms were causing Smith and Connell to raise their eyebrows. Noticing their skepticism, Hay seemed to backtrack a bit. "She didn't really go down there voluntarily," he acknowledged, "but she ended up in the room. I didn't mean to keep her down there that long, but I didn't know what to do about her when it had started.

"I thought about getting money for her through Cimbriani or whatever his name is. I told Abby she would get some of the money or she could write a story about it and sell it. I wanted to make her happy by keeping her from the world."

Hay seemed lucid and coherent, but was sprinkling his account with obvious deceptions. "I didn't hurt her or have any sex with her," he claimed. "We were on good terms from the start and had a good relationship together. I don't think it did her any good mind you, but I don't think it did her any harm.

"I used the handcuffs on her the first day but she got out of them. She is a clever girl. I never used any force on her after that. I would take her food and books at least twice a week at first. We would talk together sometimes for two or three hours. I started seeing her less when the room got messy. She wouldn't clean up, and the garbage spilled over. She would plug up the vent I had built, and the smell got terrible.

"I never got her new clothes because she never asked for any. The night the police came, I had planned to let her go, and had new clothes that I had taken from my younger daughter to give to her. The only new clothes she needed during that time was a bra because she had outgrown her own.

"During the summer, I could only see her about once every two weeks because the wife and kids were on holiday and were around all the time.

"The night I was going to let her go I hadn't seen her for about ten days. That night, I had planned on tying her up in the garage, leaving a note for my wife and driving away as far as I could get. I had $100 and a full tank of gas."

Connell and Smith had just about finished, but the corporal had a couple more questions before asking Hay to peruse and sign his statement.

"Did you make any sexual advances towards her?" the policeman asked.

"No," Hay claimed. "Just ask Abby."

Connell rephrased his question more explicitly. "Did you ever have sexual intercourse with her?" he repeated.

"No," said the prisoner. "She is all right. She is a healthy girl."

Hay perused his written version of the forty-five-minute interview and accepted Connell's pen. "I have read this statement and it is true and correct to the best of my knowledge and belief," he signed. Smith and Connell added their names as witnesses before escorting the prisoner back to his cell.

AT ALMOST EXACTLY the same moment, back at the garage on Gore Street, Constable Lylack sealed the cupboard doors, locked the workshop behind him and retained the key. Satisfied that the crime scene was properly secured, he walked over to the Hay residence where his colleague Constable James O'Connor was interviewing the suspect's wife.

Hilda Hay, he thought, looked absolutely devastated. "I have been living with Donald Alexander Hay since November 1,

1970," she told O'Connor. "We are not married and he is not the father of any of my children. We bought this house in April 1972 and we have lived here continuously since that time.

"His general behaviour during this time, except for his moods when drinking, was normal for him," she added. "In the time we were having sexual relations they were normal. Eventually, though, he became impotent on account of his heavy drinking and our sexual life for the next three years was nil."

Thinking the problem might have been caused by subconscious fear of fathering more children, Hay had undergone a vasectomy on April 13, 1974. "The doctor said he was chronically depressed but otherwise displayed no obviously abnormal tendencies," said Hilda.

After the operation, Hilda found that Hay still showed no interest in her, but did recall that her daughters had complained that their stepfather was making unwanted advances toward *them*. "They said that he sometimes pinched their backsides, or flicked their busts and said, 'Gee, you're getting chesty.'"

Hilda had dismissed the behaviour as playful teasing, but now realized she had been more than a little naïve. "The girls were a little leery of him," she conceded. "This was mainly due to his drinking and also to the fact that he had been charged with indecent assault when we lived on Davies Avenue, but he was not convicted of that offence."

"When did you last see Abby Drover before she went missing?" O'Connor asked.

"The night before," said Hilda. "She brought over her rock tumbler for Don to fix."

"Did Abby visit Don frequently?"

"About three times the week before she disappeared."

As O'Connor listened, the woman described how her common-law husband had ostensibly helped in the search for the missing child.

"I remember exactly the day Abby Drover disappeared," she recalled, shaking her head in continuing shock and disbelief.

"It was March 10, which was four days before my daughter Wendy's fifteenth birthday."

Hilda described how she had gotten a phone call from Robyn Drover asking if Brent had seen Abby. She told the police how they had gone to the Drover house that evening to offer their help, and how Don had taken her daughter and Abby's sisters to search local malls. She seemed sickened as she recalled how close she had been to the truth all along.

Hilda went on to report that, apart from going on benders, Donald had seemed quite normal, and never mentioned Abby unless someone else brought it up.

"Were you afraid of him?" O'Connor asked.

"No, except for the time he had the revolver."

"Did you contact Don's probation officer?"

O'Connor wondered how the suspect could have kept the missing girl for so long without arousing his family's suspicions.

"On the occasions when he was working in the shop," Hilda explained, "the doors were not locked and we had access at all times while he was home. I knew that there was a hole in the floor of the workshop as my son Brent had told me about it. I did not know how big the hole was, and I assumed that it was a place where he hid his booze. He always had jerrycans, paint and his chain-saw over it. I went to this area a couple of times to get paint and brushes and I did not notice anything unusual."

Hilda signed O'Connor's record of the conversation without hesitation. "I have requested that this statement be taken down for me as I feel unable to write it down myself," she acknowledged. "I have been advised that I can make any alterations to this statement that I wish. I have read this statement over and it is correct."

As O'Connor concluded his interview with Hilda, Constable Lylack decided it was as good a time as any to question the suspect's stepchildren to ascertain just how much *they* had known. All three of them seemed wide awake despite the lateness of the hour, but Lylack thought it wise to begin the first of his three interviews with twelve-year-old Brent, who might be getting tired.

"Did you know there was a room under the garage?" the policeman asked.

"No, he said he filled it in," the boy replied. "I think my sisters knew he didn't fill it in."

"Did you know where it was?"

"Yes," said Brent. "It was in the corner."

"Did you ever look for the hole?"

"I looked for it lots of times," the boy confirmed. "One day, when I was cleaning up the shop, I tried lifting up the floor in the cupboard, but all the stuff on top was too heavy."

AFTER TAKING DOWN the remainder of Brent's statement, Constable Lylack posed his next questions to Wendy Hay, who had been away visiting relatives for a week before returning home earlier that night to the shocking circumstances of her stepfather's arrest.

"Did you know there was a room under the garage?" O'Connor asked.

"Yes I did," Wendy admitted.

"Did you know how to get to this room?"

"Yes."

"Did you know what was kept in the room?"

"No."

"Did you know why he built the room?"

"He built it to make it easier to change the oil in the car."

"Did he tell you this?"

"Yes."

"Have you been in the workshop lately?"

"About a week and a half ago."

"Was Donald Hay there when you went in?"

"No."

"How did you get in?"

"I went through a hole just above the porch above the new addition."

"Did you hear or see anything different?"

"No."

NEXT, CONSTABLE LYLACK sat down to talk to Jackie Hay, a mature girl close to eighteen. Describing the underground cell, Jackie confirmed the others' versions of events.

"When the police left today, Mom found something spilled on the floor so she looked in the cupboard.... I heard Mom say, 'He's dead,' then I saw his head come up out of the hole. I ran to the front of the truck and the police came running down the driveway... Don climbed right up on the cupboard and the police got him down.

"Abby started to come out of the hole," the girl shivered. "At first I didn't know who it was, then I recognized her."

Still wondering how Hay's crime had gone unnoticed for six months, O'Connor continued.

"Have you been in the workshop lately?"

"I used to go in there and clean it up."

"Was he with you when you went in?"

"Sometimes, sometimes he wasn't. Sometimes he went to get supplies and he left the door unlocked and I was supposed to lock it when I was finished."

Having finished interviewing the suspect's eldest step-daughter, Lylack made a final check of the garage interior. Shocked but satisfied with the statements in his notebook, he ensured that the cupboard was still sealed and returned to the Port Moody police station.

STILL GUARDING HIS prisoner, Constable Dunn refused yet another request from Hay to put an end to his misery by allowing him to make a run for the back door and shooting him. Constable Reed had now returned to the police station to turn in Abby's clothing and to continue the evidence-gathering process by having the prisoner relinquish his clothes as well.

Aware that the clothes might yield crucial forensic evidence if Hay pleaded innocent, Reed again carefully placed each of the exhibits in separate plastic bags, and numbered them:

1 One pair, black socks
2 One pair, men's white undershorts
3 One pair, men's blue trousers
4 One blue shirt
5 One blue T-shirt

After six months of torturing a young child, it was not more than five minutes before Hay complained of his own privation. "When will I get my clothes back?" he whined. "I'm cold." Silently, Constable Dunn removed a blanket from an upper bunk and covered Hay with it to stifle his complaints. Finally, at 5:20 a.m., an adult cell became available, and Hay was moved from the juvenile facilities to the end of the cell block.

Saying nothing, the prisoner lay down on a lower bunk, closed his eyes and fell asleep.

20 CLOSE CALL

POLICE OFFICERS CAN be a dedicated lot, even if they don't always get the recognition and support they deserve. Ignoring physical and emotional exhaustion, all those involved with the case worked throughout the night and into the early morning hours, pressing ahead to document the evidence.

"We thought for sure one of you guys had been shot," the dispatcher was telling Adams. "When you called for the ambulance without any lights, you had us really worried."

The policeman nodded, giving the dispatcher a faint smile as he finished writing his report of the previous night's events. Adams and his colleagues wouldn't be returning to the garage until daylight.

Constable Dunn checked the prisoner throughout the night. At five, six and seven a.m., he was still sleeping.

At 7:30 a.m., intending to gather any remaining evidence, Constables Bill Reed and Paul Adams returned to the garage, in the company of Constable Lylack. Breaking the seal on the garage door, Lylack entered and found the cupboards above the dungeon still sealed as they had been the night before.

The two policemen who found Abby wondered what Hay had been reaching for atop the upper cabinets. As Lylack loaded his camera, Reed climbed a ladder beside the counter from which Hay had been dragged down the previous night.

"Careful, Bill," cautioned Adams, only half smiling. "You might get swept down some hidden chute into a pit full of alligators."

"Yeah," Reed replied. "After last night, who knows what to expect?"

On a top shelf above the counter, Reed found a box containing thirty .22-calibre long rifle bullets and a .22-calibre Cooey rifle. Descending the ladder, he held the weapon cautiously, noting that it was half-cocked and ready to fire.

Adams gazed at the weapon. The stock of the rifle had a

piece of masking tape bearing the letters E.T.H. and a white sticker with the number 168. As Reed pulled back the bolt, both policemen saw a live round in the breech and realized just how close they had been to imminent personal danger. On removing the weapon's magazine, Reed found a further eleven rounds.

"Phew!" said Adams, leaning back on his heels as Lylack photographed the weapon. If Adams had hesitated the previous night — instead of tackling the suspect without breaking his stride — the dispatcher's worst fears might very well have come true.

Lylack took several more pictures of the interior of the workshop before breaking the seal on the cupboard doors. None of the policemen was anxious to return below ground but it was a job that had to be done. At 7:50 a.m., Lylack finally undid the cabinets and descended the shaft to take more photographs.

Gagging as he gingerly sidestepped garbage strewn throughout the cell, he plodded through about two inches of water that covered the floor. The striped mattress on the bed was soaked and the walls seemed to close in on him as he went about his work. Unable to stand it any longer, the identification officer covered his mouth and nose and hurried back up the stepladder to escape the putrid surroundings.

Finding themselves unable to remain below for more than a few minutes at a time, each of the three policemen took turns descending into the pit to retrieve evidence. None of them could tolerate the oppressive environment for more than five minutes at a time, yet Abby had somehow survived there for six months.

"I don't see how she could have lasted much longer," Adams said. "If we hadn't found her, I think he would have killed her. After everything he did to her, he admitted to me that he was getting fed up with her crying all the time."

While speculating on whether Hay might have been planning to kill the girl on the night of her discovery, the officers were interrupted by police headquarters with a radio message. According to the dispatcher, reporters and photographers at that very moment were already on their way to the garage. The police chief had personally okayed media coverage and was instructing his officers to afford the press full cooperation.

Proud of his officers' work, McCabe had already notified the mayor, and was now instructing Adams and Reed to let the media know how they had found Abby the previous night. Not only that, the newspaper crews were to be allowed to go down into the cell to take photographs and see the shocking dungeon for themselves.

"This is a crime scene!" Adams protested. "We're still gathering evidence." Adams hadn't been a policeman very long but the chief's position struck him as being fraught with risks. Backed by his colleagues, Adams continued to protest that unrestricted media coverage might seriously jeopardize any future trial.

"The chief is giving you a direct order," Adams was told. "One of the reporters is a friend of his. Just tell them what happened."

It was futile to argue with an old-school cop who was a strict disciplinarian. Attempting to set aside their concerns as they awaited the media deluge, the officers in the garage continued methodically with their investigation.

Among other things, they retrieved a blue cup with latent fingerprints, which could later be examined to see if they matched those of Donald Hay. But as they continued with their work, the policemen were interrupted by a man with a notebook standing at the garage door. Accompanied by a photographer, it was Paul Musgrove from the *Sun*.

AT 8:35 A.M., Donald Hay was roused from his sleep and escorted back to the interview room. Sipping a cup of coffee, the prisoner peered through bloodshot eyes to find Constable Smith and Corporal Connell seated across from him once more. Having interviewed Abby Drover earlier that morning, the two policemen now suspected that Hay had not been forthright in his first account of the kidnapping.

Smith, attempting the faintest of smiles, again cautioned Hay that he was about to be asked some further questions for the court record. "Do you understand fully the initial statement taken from and signed by yourself?" the policeman asked.

"Yes," said Hay.

"Do you wish to add or take anything from that statement?"

"No."

Hay stroked the stubble on his chin. Perhaps he realized the police had now spoken to Abby herself and that it was time to come clean.

"Did you have any sexual relations with Abby?" Connell repeated.

"If Abby said so," Hay replied. "She wouldn't lie."

"Well, did you?" Connell asked, seeking a straight answer.

"Yes," Hay at last admitted. "I had sexual intercourse with her."

"More than once?" asked Connell.

"Yes," Hay agreed. "I hadn't had sex for months and months before that."

Now that Connell had been able to elicit the truth, Smith sought to defuse the tension by changing the subject. "Did you own a .22-calibre rifle?" he asked.

"No," said Hay. "I'm not allowed to have guns."

"Does any of your family own a .22-calibre rifle?" the policeman continued.

"No, not to my knowledge," said Hay.

In the face of Hay's duplicitous responses, Smith pressed ahead to corroborate the information he already had, but still found it difficult to pose his next questions in calm, matter-of-fact tones. Abby Drover was such a brave young girl, but how could she possibly overcome such long-term sexual and psychological abuse?

"Did you ever have anal intercourse with Abby?" the policeman asked.

"No," claimed Hay.

"Did you ever have oral sex with Abby?"

"What do you mean?" If Hay wanted to feign ignorance,

that was fine, but Smith wasn't about to let him off the hook. Patiently, the policeman rephrased his question. "Did you put your penis in her mouth?" he persisted.

"Not to my recollection."

"Did you ever fondle her breasts?"

"Yes."

The next questions were from Connell. "Do you remember ordering her to remove her clothes?"

"I must have," Hay conceded. "She wouldn't voluntarily do it."

"Did you ever remove her clothing?" asked the senior policeman.

"Probably," said Hay. "Christ, if I had intercourse with her, I must have."

Hay was getting uneasy but Smith turned up the heat. "Did you perform any other type of sexual act with Abby?"

"It was normal sexual relations as far as I know."

Smith framed his next question based on his knowledge of Hay's previous attempted rape conviction, and the fact that he'd been charged with assaulting a young girl in Coquitlam. "Have you ever been involved with young girls?" the policeman asked.

"Never since coming to B.C.," said Hay. "I had been charged in Manitoba for indecent assault and rape, but the rape was dismissed."

"Did Abby ever give any encouragement to you of any kind to make you believe that she would go along with sexual acts with you?"

"No, not really," Hay conceded. "She never gave me any encouragement."

"You seem to have trouble remembering things. Is there a reason for this?"

"When I get these blackouts, I don't remember or don't want to remember things I've done."

"What sort of things?" Smith pressed, barely managing to disguise his sarcasm.

"A variety of things," said Hay.

"How long have you been under treatment for blackouts?"

"I'm not," Hay admitted. "I stopped taking treatments. It's some time since I last saw the doctor."

"Do you have normal sexual relations with older women?" Smith asked.

"No."

"Do you have normal sexual relations with younger girls?"

"No, I'm impotent and have been for about three years."

The final questions came from Connell. "Did you ever threaten Abby, if she made a lot of noise or was bad?"

Hay shifted in his chair. "I told her a couple of times not to turn the radio up loud," he said, "but I don't think I threatened her."

"If you had other than normal sexual relations with Abby, would you remember it?"

"I would have to agree with Abby, if she said it."

"Did Abby at any time consent to you having sexual relations with her?"

"Not to my knowledge," the prisoner said.

Except for several attempts to minimize his sexual assaults and his denial of possessing a .22-calibre rifle, Hay's answers eventually amounted to a fairly frank confession. But would it hold up in court? Fervently, the policemen hoped they had done everything they could to ensure that Donald Alexander Hay would be convicted and put away for a long time.

21   FRONT PAGE NEWS

LIVING OUT OF TOWN, it usually took me about half an hour to get to work at Pacific Press. For the most part it was a pleasant country drive: vistas of dairy cattle grazing in verdant pastures, and seagulls never far in the distance circling over the Fraser River delta.

The morning of Tuesday, September 7 (the first day of school) dawned with clear skies and mild temperatures — predictable enough for late summer — but the news emanating from the car radio following the weather bulletin was another matter altogether.

Foregoing his normally dulcet tones, the newscaster excitedly related the first scant details of how a young Port Moody girl had been found alive after a six-month kidnapping.

As I approached the city, it was the first I had heard of it, but being a general news reporter, I knew there was a good possibility that I would be dispatched to cover the story as soon as I arrived for work.

And just as I expected, I was intercepted by a somewhat agitated Don MacLachlan the moment I walked into the cavernous, third floor newsroom. Ignoring the fact that I was ten minutes late, the city editor gruffly handed me a sheaf of notes on the *Province*'s distinctive green copy paper and pointed to the door. "You and Al Arnason are on your way to Port Moody," he said. "Have a nice trip."

Al was waiting for me as we teamed up in preparation for the assignment. Normally, only one reporter would cover a given story, but the circumstances surrounding the Abby Drover kidnapping were extraordinary. "I hate going out on a story completely cold," said Arnason, reviewing the notes. "I don't know anything about it."

"I couldn't agree more," I said, but both of us quickly perked up when we learned that the photographer who would accompany us knew virtually the whole story. Peter Hulbert was a talented cameraman trained on daily newspapers in England, where he had even photographed some of the same soccer matches that I had attended in my youth. Not only did Peter now live in Port Moody, but his wife sat on the municipal council there, and he had been intimately involved with the case from its outset.

"I took the pictures during the original search for Abby Drover six months ago," he explained. A pleasant, wiry man with glasses and a cleft chin, Hulbert had also helped the small Port Moody police department design the "missing" poster when Abby had first disappeared, and was more than slightly chagrined that the police chief hadn't reciprocated by tipping him off ahead of anyone else about the child's discovery.

Arnason and I followed Hulbert to the parking lot and climbed into his radio-equipped car. While reporters generally were sent on their assignments directly from the newsroom, photographers with their radios could be dispatched to news events quickly, and spent so much time on the road that most of them knew the city and environs like the backs of their hands.

Despite our being crammed into a compact car with not even enough time for a morning coffee, things would turn out to be much less stressful than we had thought. In his heavy British accent, Hulbert could give us most of the details on the way.

Hulbert got us to our assignment in what must have been record time. Under uncharacteristically clear skies at the head of Burrard Inlet, the industrial townsite of Port Moody had just come into view when the photographer turned sharply onto what otherwise would have been an easily missed hairpin bend to the right of Barnet Highway.

Sluggishly climbing to the top of the hill, our car arrived at 1601 Gore Street, where Constable Adams identified himself and advised us that Mrs. Drover was already in the process of giving some television interviews at her home, just four doors down the street. "I'll go talk to her," said Al, addressing

Hulbert and me. "You guys can stay here for a while and talk to the police."

"Thanks, Al," I said. "Leave the house of horrors just for me." We exchanged smiles, however, knowing he'd be back. Being an all-round reporter, Arnason would undoubtedly also want to see the dungeon for himself.

One thing that concerned both of us was the knowledge that our main competitor, Paul Musgrove, and his photographer had already visited the scene an hour or so earlier. That meant the afternoon *Sun* would be the first newspaper to hit the streets with the details of the case; the next edition of the *Province* could not be published until the following morning. It was all the luck of the draw: some stories broke on *Sun* time, some on *Province* time. Having time on our side, however, we hoped to come up with all the new angles, as well as the latest updates. It may have been impossible to be the first newspaper to carry the news, but at least we could attempt to provide the latest and most comprehensive coverage.

After Arnason left the garage, I met for the first time Constable Paul Adams, who was wearing a T-shirt and jeans rather than his standard police uniform. Aged thirty-two, Adams was exactly one year and one day older than I was. While my career had always been in the media — with whom the police coexisted in a strained, symbiotic sort of relationship — Adams seemed to have been born for a career in law enforcement; his stern, six-foot-four father was deputy warden at Oakalla Prison Farm, despite having lost a leg on account of a blood clot.

Adams pointed to the opening of the concealed underground chamber, showing me how he and Constable Reed had found Abby in the course of the previous evening's domestic complaint.

"I don't think we'll ever forget last night for the rest of our lives," Adams said. The policeman told me how he immediately recognized the girl having been the first officer to investigate her disappearance six months previously.

"Another thirty seconds and we'd have been away," added Reed. "The timing was perfect. If the cupboard had been locked up again, we might never have found her."

Each of the policemen had managed to slip home just long enough to change into work clothes for the dirty job of repeatedly going underground to retrieve various items of evidence. Later that day, they would be taking the battered mattress and most of the other exhibits to the Crime Detection Laboratory in Vancouver for forensic analysis.

It was now time for Hulbert and me to see what they were talking about. In turn, we each descended the shaft without much hesitation, but neither of us stayed below ground any longer than absolutely necessary. In a hybrid of abbreviated words and Pitman shorthand, I quickly scribbled down as many details as I could before dashing back for the surface.

It was indeed a subterranean chamber of horrors, which I attempted to describe in my first person newspaper account. We may not have been familiar with the ramifications of the story at first, but now it was all only too clear.

As expected, after interviewing Mrs. Drover, Al Arnason returned to the workshop to take a firsthand look for himself. "It gave me a sense of foreboding even to go down the ladder," he recalled later, describing the filthy dungeon. "Even though it was hot and clammy, my whole body felt cold as soon as I climbed down into the hole. It was certainly something I'll never forget."

Leaving the workshop, Arnason and I then spoke to Ken Woodward, the neighbour who had almost come to blows with Hay earlier that year in their dispute over the retaining wall between their properties.

Woodward, who had only just heard the news on the radio, felt like ripping down the national flag that Hay had so proudly been flying on a pole atop his camper business.

"I'm totally shocked," the neighbour seethed. "To think I could be so close to helping that little kid and not doing anything. We just moved in here and now my wife wants to move again," he groaned.

Twelve-year-old neighbour Mike Hoce also appeared and expressed disbelief. "We played all summer long with the boy who lived here and we never heard a thing."

IT WAS ALMOST NOON as Hulbert, Arnason and I left Gore Street to map out our afternoon strategy and compare notes over a quick lunch on St. John's Street in downtown Port Moody.

Between gulps of coffee, Al apprised us of his morning interview with Ruth Drover. The interview had been possible because Ruth had returned home to get a few things after dropping her older daughters off at school. Otherwise, said Ruth, we would have missed her because all members of the family, including Abby, were staying with relatives elsewhere.

Reiterating the details of that joyous moment when she learned Abby was alive, Ruth added, "We are trying to keep her out of the limelight, and I'm going to get her fattened up and mentally stable before we think about anything else."

According to the child's mother, Abby had been unable to sleep well since her rescue and had only managed an hour's nap since returning from the hospital. She had also been unable to take much food. "She said her stomach hurts when she eats," Ruth reported. "I guess her stomach has shrunk."

Mrs. Drover had also told Al how she had driven below the workshop every day for the past six months on her way to work. She had never entirely given up hope, she said, but lately she had come close. "When you don't hear anything for six months, I guess that's natural. I'm just so happy she's alive."

As he picked up the tab for lunch, Al told us Mrs. Drover had refused to speak about Donald Hay but had felt sorry for his family. "My own heart reached out for his wife and children," she had told him. "They had no idea. I just can't imagine what they must be feeling."

LEAVING THE RESTAURANT, we headed for the Port Moody police station. The officers in charge of the investigation, we'd been told, would be available for a brief interview. Certainly, we had no reason to complain about the help and cooperation we were receiving as we reached the old police building to talk with Constable Wayne Smith and Corporal Archie Connell.

With dark circles under their eyes, both officers admitted that the case had shocked them beyond belief. "It's been quite an emotional upheaval," said Smith, adding that the forty-three-year-old suspect would be appearing in court later that afternoon charged with kidnapping; holding a female person against her will with intent to have illicit sexual intercourse; and with rape and gross indecency.

"I would think the girl was mentally tormented in a quite extensive form," said Corporal Connell. "A perverted form of mental cruelty was exercised."

Because Port Moody had no provincial court facilities, Hay's first appearance would take place in the adjoining municipality of Coquitlam, so Peter Hulbert wasted no time finding a position where he could get a photograph of the suspect on his way to or from the court building.

Before the proceedings got under way, police searched everyone entering the courtroom, including startled lawyers arriving for other cases on the afternoon docket. The pale, unshaven suspect, wearing a short-sleeved shirt and brown slacks, stared straight ahead as three sheriffs escorted him to the prisoner's box to appear before Judge F.C. Giles.

The doors were guarded by a total of seven police officers as prosecutor Stewart Chambers rose to inform the judge of the serious nature of the charges. Chambers, a silver-haired man with a military bearing, would need a lot more time to prepare his case, but he also had to request an adjournment so that Hay could have time to find a lawyer.

Suddenly, Hay, who had been silent, spoke up. "I don't think I need counsel, Your Honour," he said. Judge Giles disagreed. "I think you do need counsel," he replied. Remanding the accused in custody, the judge proposed that legal aid officials should consult with him as soon as possible. The entire proceedings had lasted only three minutes, but Hulbert was able to snap a picture of Hay attempting to hide his face in his hands as he was driven away in the back of a police car.

It was time for Hulbert, Arnason and me to return to the office where, running on adrenaline, we put together a package for the next edition of the paper. In all, we came up with a total of two main articles, four sidebar stories and seven photographs. As daily newspapermen, we were used to meeting deadlines, but still felt more than satisfied with the results of an assignment that we had taken on completely cold.

22 STUNNED REACTIONS

DONALD HAY HAD been right. He did make the front pages after all. At the Port Moody police station, the switchboard lit up yet again, this time with calls from newspapers, magazines and television producers around the world, wanting to know if the details they had received over the wire services could possibly be true.

Some of them offered money for an exclusive interview with the family, but Ruth Drover was adamant that no such deals would be forthcoming. Her primary and overriding concern was for Abby's recovery — away from the disturbing glare of the media spotlight.

News that a family man had allegedly kidnapped and entombed his neighbour's daughter, while pretending to help find her for the past six months, was indeed of worldwide interest. Hay's former neighbour Leo Morin was stunned by the news — but nowhere were people as shocked yet enlightened as they were thirteen hundred miles away in Hay's former hometown of Brandon, Manitoba.

Despite the passage of time, Prairie farmers still remembered how Hay and his brother had assaulted a local teenage girl eighteen years before. One of them, a former employee of the *Brandon Sun*, had kept several old newspapers containing details of the case and showed them to a group of his friends in a local coffee shop.

"If ever there was a case of history repeating itself…." one of the farmers muttered as he and his colleagues thumbed through the newspaper articles.

Dated November 1958, the now-yellowing newspapers contained reports of a first-ever meeting in Paris between Canadian Prime Minister John Diefenbaker and French Premier Charles de Gaulle, but it was the account of the Hay court case that gripped the interest of the coffee shop quartet.

According to the newspaper, the trial had begun on November 4, 1958, when Hay, together with his twenty-year-old brother Malcolm, had pleaded not guilty to the rape of a fifteen-year-old Souris girl the previous March. "If ever there was trouble, you could always rest assured that Mac was in the middle of it," one of the farmers recalled.

The group fell silent, reminded as they re-read the old articles how another local youth by the name of Clyde Ernest Williamson had given evidence for the prosecution. Aged eighteen, Williamson testified that he and the Hay brothers had picked up three girls, including the complainant, while driving around Souris about 10:30 one night seven months before the court case. After returning to the Hay residence, the brothers had consumed several beers before taking two of the girls home shortly after midnight. The girls had had nothing to drink.

According to Williamson, the men had driven the victim to a dirt road four miles northwest of town, where Williamson had gotten out of the car because he had wanted no part of the assault. Hay and his brother, the young witness testified, had threatened the girl with physical harm if she didn't comply. Although the girl complained that she felt sick, the attack had continued for another hour.

The newspaper articles — noting that the victim was "pretty" and "attractive" — reported that Justice Paul Duval had excluded the public when the victim and her mother took the witness stand. The newspaper hadn't described the lurid details of their testimony but reported that both the victim and her mother broke down while describing the effects of the assault. One of the girl's friends, the report added, had also been reduced to tears when Donald Hay's Winnipeg lawyer had questioned her moral standards.

At the conclusion of the four-day trial, Harry Walsh, QC, the lawyer for Donald Hay, proposed that the brothers be set free because they had been attempting to get on with their lives, running a small restaurant in Saskatchewan.

Prosecutor F.O. Meighen, QC, resisted, however, maintaining that the brothers had set out from Souris with the common intention of holding a community rape. "These young men have got to be shown that they cannot gang up on a girl," he said.

After deliberating for five hours, members of the jury returned with a compromise, acquitting the brothers of rape, but finding both of them guilty of attempted rape and indecent assault. Saying that gang attacks on young women had to be "stamped out", the judge concluded that the brothers should be separated so that they would not be "a bad influence" on each other.

Both men received two years for the attempted rape, plus concurrent fifteen-month sentences for the indecent assault, but younger brother Malcolm had one day lopped off his sentence so that he could serve his time in the Brandon Jail. Just twenty-five, Donald Hay was sent to the federal penitentiary at Stony Mountain. According to the newspaper, the youthful prisoners showed no emotion when the verdict was announced.

"I don't know if I'd blame Mac," said the former newspaper employee. "Don was quite a bit older. Even when he was growing up, he invariably had a way of getting whatever he wanted. He was very manipulative."

Finishing his coffee, another of the farmers, who knew the Hay family, said the fact that Don's father George had worked for the Canadian Pacific Railway had sheltered the family from the worst of the economic depression, even though Don, born in 1933, was the third of four children. "His father had full-time work as a conductor on the Souris-Elm Creek-Glenboro subdivision," recalled the family acquaintance. "They were shipping lots of grain and coal in those days and anybody with a full-time job on the railroad was never short of money and respect.

"He can't say he didn't have a good childhood. I remember his mother Gladys regularly took Don to church with his sister and his brothers. He had all the athletic equipment he wanted, as much or more as any of us other kids. Even when he was little, if his parents said, 'You can't do that,' he would find a way around it. He used to climb out of the window at night after he was supposed to have gone to bed.

"You know, he was always very clever with his hands. He could do things that required a tremendous amount of thought and skill. I remember how he impressed his teachers and friends with one particular school project — that balsa wood model he whittled of a railroad trestle without any special tools other than a jackknife and some glue.

"He was an exceptionally good-looking young fellow and very smooth with it. He was outgoing and sociable, not at all the type to sit in the back row. He was an all-around, multi-talented person, active in every circle. He may even have had a job for a while as a dance instructor.

"He wasn't boisterous but he was very clever and had a lot of pizzazz about him. He could adapt to just about any environment. He was definitely of above-average intelligence."

The family acquaintance concluded how everyone felt Don was wasting his talents when he dropped out of school in Grade 8. "After that, there was always something about him that told you he could either rise to the top or end up at the bottom."

Nearby, at the Brandon police station, news reports of the case also shocked twenty-one-year-old Dwight Kirkup. Born in the same hospital on the same day as Donald Hay's daughter Vicki, the young man had recently been accepted to join the Royal Canadian Mounted Police. Now engaged to another woman, Kirkup still had fond memories of Vicki Hay, whom he had taken on one of his first-ever teenage dates to the Souris Choc Shop. "She was a very nice, decent young girl," he recalled "I don't think she ever knew her father. After her parents' divorce, she spent a lot of time with her grandmother."

But while his former Manitoba neighbours had long known of the suspect's knack for manipulation and deception, on the west coast, the discovery of Hay's dark secrets came as a total shock to just about everyone, including Port Moody Mayor Norm Patterson.

"I didn't think you'd ever find her," the mayor said when apprised of the details by Police Chief Len McCabe. Congratulating the chief on his department's good work, Patterson breathed a huge sigh of relief. He added he would seek council approval to give the city's $1,000 reward directly to the Drover family, plus any additional sum on which the council might agree. The family, he thought, might well be facing some unexpected costs. "Abby will probably need therapy and some private tuition," he suggested. "I doubt she'll be able to go back to school immediately."

In the meantime, while hundreds of newspaper subscribers also wanted to help after reading the September 8 issue of the *Province*, millionaire landlord Alexander Di Cimbriani said he would talk with the family before deciding what to do with the $7,500 reward he had offered.

Interest in the case remained at a fever pitch, and Hulbert, Arnason and I were assigned to visit Port Moody the next day to follow up on the latest developments. While Peter dashed off to photograph a large sign outside the Port Moody Inn — which praised God and the local police department — Al and I returned to the public safety building, where Constable Smith and Corporal Connell agreed to help us recreate the anatomy of the six-month search. According to Connell, Abby's discovery had been "a chance in a million".

Smith showed us the Oliver psychic's uncannily accurate drawings and added he had searched the area described by the psychic at the time but had not been able to find anything matching the drawings. In retrospect, the directions had been slightly incorrect in describing a nearby corner store — but incredibly the area Smith had searched had been just three blocks from where Abby was eventually found. "If there were any such thing as psychic phenomena, this comes about as close as you can get," the policeman admitted.

Now that Smith had sparked our curiosity, Arnason and I spent most of the day attempting to unearth as many other inside details of the case as we could.

Police chief Len McCabe said he had been amazed by the

girl's speedy recovery. "She's still very weak and taking it easy," he said, but only two days earlier the girl had been speaking in a whisper and had been unable to walk without assistance. Never during his thirty-year police career, the chief added, had he seen anyone "live through an experience like this little girl."

It was not surprising, he concluded, that people who had stood in the garage hadn't been able to hear anything. "One of our officers went down there, closed the opening behind him and shouted as loud as he could. It was so soundproof that our other members, standing upstairs, never heard a thing."

By the time Arnason and I departed for our homes, we agreed that neither of us had ever covered a more emotionally draining story in our lives.

23 GATHERING EVIDENCE

AT THE PORT MOODY police station, Constable Wayne Smith attempted to suppress a smile as he watched his colleagues arriving for work. Several of them he noticed were more than a little bleary-eyed following an impromptu celebration at the police station the night before. The festivities celebrating Abby's dramatic rescue had been sanctioned by the chief, but Smith and Connell had felt obligated to restrain themselves on account of the heavy caseload still ahead.

Now, discussing the case over morning coffee, the two policemen nodded in recognition as they compared the second statement they had obtained from Abby with the list of exhibits including those recovered from the underground cell.

"It's amazing how lucid she is after what she's been through," said Smith, thumbing through his files. "Just about everything she says corroborates her story."

"You're right," Connell concurred. "She's even described the needlepoint we got from Hay's bedroom."

Smith and Connell were encouraged that everything seemed to be falling into place. Not only had they recovered the note that Abby had hidden in her boot describing her kidnapper; colleagues in the identification section had also established that the whorls and ridges on the blue cup found in the underground cell were an undoubted match for the thumbprint of Donald Hay.

Such evidence seemed irrefutable, but both police officers still shared the nagging feeling that nothing these days could be taken for granted. Not only would the police officers have to organize their myriad pieces of information as effectively as possible in readiness for the anticipated trial, they also needed a complete background report on Donald Alexander Hay.

With its limited resources, Smith decided, the small Port Moody police department needed the help of the Royal Canadian Mounted Police, and Smith soon found himself grateful for their quick response to his requests for assistance. The Mounties, through credit card receipts and other records, even compiled a detailed calendar of Hay's activities for each of the thirty-six months preceding the abduction, causing Smith and Connell to note what appeared to be some especially significant entries. "Look at this," said Connell, pointing to a specific date. "It even shows us when Hay rented a cement mixer."

The significance of the information was not lost on Constable Smith either. As evidence, it may have been circumstantial but it more than likely pinpointed when Hay had first set about building his underground torture chamber.

In addition, with its national resources, it didn't take long for the RCMP to supply the two police officers with a detailed history of Hay's background and criminal activities over the past twenty-five years.

Solemnly, Smith and Connell raised their eyebrows as they read the detailed background report. According to the RCMP profile, Hay had joined the Department of National Defence in Souris when he was eighteen years old, but had quit the following year to work for Knowlton's Boot Shop at 819 Rosser Avenue in nearby Brandon.

Returning to Souris, he had become a volunteer fireman, which had led to a job as a fireman and wiper with the Canadian Pacific Railway. Occasionally laid off, he had worked as a painter and decorator with his older brother Bob. Other than one short stint on unemployment insurance, he'd always had work, even though he would eventually work at more than two dozen jobs throughout western Canada.

In 1952, when he was still only nineteen, Hay had begun dating and then married a Souris girl named Donna Baldwin, whose parents operated the town's Avalon Theatre. Although she was an only child, Donna had been described by her friends as a "super, very friendly" and family-oriented type of person.

With his young wife pregnant, Hay had taken extra employment as a lifeguard and as a ticket usher at the Avalon, where he had begun to flirt with other women. Soon after the birth of their daughter Vicki in August 1955, Donald and Donna Hay had divorced — a turning point that appeared to precipitate the first of several altercations with the law. Making an unsuccessful attempt to win back his wife at gunpoint, Hay had been sentenced to two years in prison — although everyone felt he got off lightly when the judge in Brandon, Manitoba suspended the sentence in lieu of a $200 bond.

Hay had continued to work for the railroad and married his second wife, Phyllis, from the neighbouring province of Saskatchewan. It had not been long, however, before Hay and his brother had gone to jail over the attempted rape in Brandon.

Freed from prison two years later, Hay operated the cafe at the Whitewood Service Station near Phyllis' home village of Kipling, Saskatchewan. In 1962, with newborn twins, the couple moved across the Qu'Appelle River valley to the larger community of Esterhazy, where Hay had found stable employment with the International Minerals and Chemical Corporation, mining and processing potash in the southeast part of the province.

Hay stayed with the company for five years, and had been in charge of five foremen and sixty-seven workers until June 1967, when he was sentenced to six months in jail for extortion in Yorkton, Saskatchewan. Although the District Court acceded to his request for a ban on publication, Hay had been rumoured to have assaulted a young woman — and lost his job at the potash mine as a result.

After completing his second term in prison, Hay drifted in pursuit of work to the Cominco smelter in Trail, British Columbia (coincidentally the same place where Ruth Drover's father had once worked), and to the docks of Vancouver where he had found brief employment as a longshoreman.

But none of these jobs had lasted either. With a résumé beginning to look like a telephone book, Hay moved back to Alberta as a travelling representative for the provincial telephone company. Shortly afterwards, his wife Phyllis divorced him and gained custody of their twin children after discovering that her husband had been using the company car for an affair with another woman in Minot, North Dakota.

Hay had apparently retained his interest in firearms and was charged yet again on April 22, 1968, with possession of an unregistered weapon. Although he won a stay of proceedings on that charge, he was fined $200 two weeks later and sentenced to one day in jail for possession of stolen property. Remaining in Alberta, he built metal granaries in the community of Milk River, then found employment with a masonry company in Lethbridge, where he met Hilda the following year.

"They've done a great job," said Smith, feeling somewhat enlightened after putting down the RCMP report. "I give them a lot of credit."

Smith and Connell agreed, however, that much remained to be done. Donning their jackets despite the late summer heat, they left the police station and began further inquiries by visiting two trailer supply businesses in nearby municipalities.

Unanimously, businessmen they interviewed told them that Hay had always seemed friendly and sober and paid his bills on time. One twenty-eight-year-old employee was able to describe the toilet found in Hay's underground cell as being a Tota Toilet distributed by Tedco Supplies Ltd. in Burnaby and by Sears department stores.

The policemen also visited medical clinics in an attempt to dig out information regarding Hay's previous treatments for alcoholism. Such information was confidential, but the policemen still learned that Hay had never complained of any blackouts or memory lapses during the course of his treatments. Neither, apparently, had he ever exhibited any indication of split personality or other mental disorders. Smith felt a tinge of satisfaction. Such evidence, if it were admissible, thought Smith, might make it difficult for Hay to avoid a prison sentence by claiming insanity and thereby serving his time in hospital.

For the remainder of the week, the police officers visited each of the establishments where Hay was believed to have stayed during the six months of Abby Drover's confinement. Photocopying room receipts, the officers spoke with various hotel desk clerks and recorded their statements. Near the Austin Hotel on south Granville Street, they couldn't help but notice the plethora of "adult" shops selling a variety of gadgets — including handcuffs.

Finally, Smith and Connell arranged long-awaited interviews with Robyn and Kathy Drover. Arriving at the police station, both girls shuddered as they recalled how Hay had supposedly helped them search for Abby the night she disappeared. Although Hay had subsequently begun locking his workshop, neither of the girls had ever thought of him as other than a friendly and sympathetic neighbour.

Smith and Connell were satisfied they'd now spoken with virtually all the potential witnesses, except the two people with whom Hay had had dealings just days before Abby was found.

The first was the "Scottish lady" Hay told them he'd contacted at the Coquitlam Crisis Centre the night before his arrest. Located by the police, an astounded Kathleen Selfridge reported she could still hear the sadness in Hay's voice on the night of his call. Having felt genuinely sorry for the man, she hoped she wouldn't have to testify. "If he had killed himself," she shuddered, "that girl might never have been found."

The next witness, Ernest Henry Buckle, described how he had gone to Donald Hay's garage to see about buying a camper just hours before the grim discovery. Buckle remembered the concrete floor of the workshop, having visited the premises with his wife and daughter to check on the progress of his camper. "It's hard to believe that we three were standing in there and didn't hear anything," he said. "It must have been pretty soundproof."

Back at the police station, Smith had to consider where Buckle and the others would fit into his list of potential witnesses. The evidence, he decided, should be presented chronologically so that a judge or jury could learn about the case from its outset.

Logically, he decided, the first witness should be Ruth Drover. Abby's mother would describe how she had reported her daughter missing six months previously, and testify as to her child's physical and mental state as the result of the abduction. Kathleen and Robyn Drover could then be called to testify how Donald Hay had ostensibly helped them in searching for their sister.

Working overtime, Smith considered that members of the Hay family were probably the next most important civilian witnesses. Hilda Hay and her children could describe how the accused had appeared to carry on business as normal throughout the six-month abduction.

Smith himself could take the witness stand to describe how Hay had denied all knowledge of Abby's disappearance; followed by Constables Paul Adams and Bill Reed describing how lucky they had been to find the kidnapped girl during their investigation of an apparently routine domestic disturbance.

There were several other potential witnesses of course, but Smith prayed it wouldn't be necessary for one of them in particular to have to go to court. After all she'd been through, Abby Drover he still hoped might be spared from having to appear on the witness stand — reliving all the horrors of her six-month confinement.

24 QUESTIONABLE THERAPY

WHILE ABBY DROVER continued to celebrate her freedom, hundreds of Port Moody schoolchildren gathered busily in their classrooms to make her get-well cards; everyone was wishing her a speedy recovery — or so it seemed. Following her ordeal, Abby had become remarkably adept in assessing people's motives, and had developed a healthy suspicion of strangers.

Abby frowned as she opened one letter from a man in his eighties who had written asking her to tell him all the intimate details of her confinement.

"I think this guy is some kind of sicko," she said dismissively, handing the letter to her mother.

Agreeing with her daughter's intuition, Ruth angrily absorbed the letter's contents but resisted the urge to tear it up. Instead, she forwarded it to the police, who in turn warned the man not to make any further contact with the family. It seemed incomprehensible that anyone might seek to exploit her daughter still further, but eventually Ruth felt reassured by the continuing widespread offers of support.

The latest interest in her daughter's well-being manifested itself when Ruth telephoned the family doctor to inform him that Abby still had serious abdominal pain. "She seems to be doing quite well psychologically," Ruth reported, "but I think she might have a kidney infection."

Responding with kindness as usual, Dr. Rubin was more than willing to make a housecall, but thought he might be able to offer a better suggestion. "I've just received a telephone call from a New Westminster pediatrician who wants to know how she's doing," Dr. Rubin said. "Apparently he's just moved here from Toronto and thinks he should see Abby personally."

According to Rubin's information, the pediatrician was a specialist in child sexual abuse and was probably just the expert needed to assist the young patient in her physical and mental recovery. "I'll give you his number," said Dr. Rubin. "I think it'd be a good idea if you arrange for her to see him. He wants to have her admitted to Royal Columbian Hospital."

After all that Abby had endured, her mother was unable to break the news immediately and allowed her to believe she was packing for a holiday with her father. Instead of travelling with her bags to the airport, however, Abby found her mother delivering her back to the hospital in New Westminster.

The pediatrician introduced himself to the family. He was a soft-spoken young man who assured Ruth that her daughter would be receiving the best treatment possible. Showing concern for her privacy, the doctor recommended that Abby be checked into hospital under an assumed name to avoid the prying news media, as well as the curiosity of other patients.

"We'll call you Ann Smith," said the doctor. "Ann is my daughter's name." He told the hospital staff to make out her hospital bracelet as "Patient X".

After her mother departed, the doctor instructed Abby to remove her clothes and lie on an examination table. Lying on her back, Abby complied but suddenly felt embarrassed. The doctor didn't touch her, but he seemed to be taking a long time and his expression made her feel uncomfortable. "It seemed weird," she recalled later. "There was something disconcerting about the way he looked me up and down."

Though Abby desperately wanted to be home with her family, the doctor seemed to be taking a special interest in her and brought her one of her favourite orange milkshakes from McDonald's. "After you get out of here," he told her, "maybe I can take you ice-skating with my daughter."

It was a bit odd that a doctor would suggest becoming her personal acquaintance, thought Abby, but she put the idea out of her mind as she underwent further tests and injections. Finally, after recommending that the patient should visit his office for some follow-up treatment, the doctor advised Abby that she could be discharged.

Still suffering from aches and pains after some time, Abby finally decided to visit the doctor in his office. When she arrived, the pediatrician asked Ruth to wait outside while he took Abby into the office.

After the doctor reiterated his offer to take Abby ice-skating, it suddenly seemed that he wanted her to come closer. Sitting on the couch in his office, he beckoned the girl to come over and sit on his knee. Abby felt nervous and eyed the door, her mind flooding with memories of how Donald Hay had touched her knee the night before he kidnapped her.

The doctor seemed perplexed. "How come you feel so uncomfortable around me?" he asked. "You can trust me. I want you to look at me."

Abby, however, had already experienced unwanted affections from a supposedly trustworthy man. The idea that a doctor whom she thought she could trust might be offering bodily contact filled her with revulsion and anger. Refusing to budge, she stared resolutely at the floor until the doctor relented, agreeing it might be better if she made an appointment for another day.

Escorting Abby from the waiting-room, Ruth could see that her daughter was upset. "I just had the creepiest feeling I was in the wrong place at the wrong time," said Abby.

Ruth could see that her daughter was shaking. "What on earth is wrong?" she asked, as they got into her car.

"Mom, I won't ever go there anymore!" Abby insisted. "He wanted me to sit on his knee." The doctor, she suggested, was even worse than Donald Hay because he was supposed to be someone she could trust.

"I'll let Dr. Rubin know about this," said Ruth, her voice rising.

"No, Mom," said Abby. "Nobody would believe me. After everything I went through, they'd say it was all my imagination. I would be accused of just being paranoid."

RETURNING TO HER FAMILY, Abby loved the sights, sounds and smells of the outdoors. Sleep remained difficult, but she rested by gazing at the stars in deep meditation. Although the girl continued to recover, Mayor Norm Patterson and members of the Port Moody Police Department were well aware that the young girl and her family still needed a considerable amount of help and support.

At some point, Patterson knew, the Drovers might be eligible for up to $15,000 from the provincial Criminal Injuries Compensation Fund, but meanwhile the mayor was able to persuade fellow councillors to release half of the city's reward moneys for any uninsured medical needs and a holiday. "Considering what the family has gone through," he said, "I must give my strong support."

Despite council's good intentions, however, Alexander Di Cimbriani heated up the debate by telling reporters he was "shocked" that Patterson and his colleagues hadn't given Abby the full $1,000 reward that the city had originally offered.

Still seething from the earlier name-calling, the Vancouver businessman was also angry that Port Moody council had never thanked him for his original reward offer of $7,500. "These politicians talk too much but they never dig into their pockets when something important like this comes up," Di Cimbriani blustered.

Even though the conditions of his $7,500 offer had not been met, he added, he would still give the Drovers a cheque for $1,000. "The people of Port Moody must be wondering why those politicians put up so little money while I, someone from Vancouver, am giving $1,000 with no questions asked."

Mayor Patterson was nonplussed by the diatribe, but deflected Di Cimbriani's bombast by informing the press he was meeting Ruth Drover to discuss further council assistance. The mayor also confirmed he had been appointed as one of three trustees overseeing a special fund for the Drover family. Public donations, he announced, could be delivered in the care of the *Enterprise* weekly newspaper, as well as at several banks in Port Moody and neighbouring municipalities.

BACK AT HOME after being in hospital, Abby not only suffered from insomnia but also found it difficult to walk on painfully swollen ankles. Taking extra-strength medication for arthritis, she amazed her mother and sisters by insisting she was ready to start attending her new school.

It would be therapeutic, all of them agreed, for Abby to resume her education. Despite having missed so many lessons, her teachers had given her a passing grade. That meant with the exception of gym classes, she could immediately start Grade 8 in junior secondary school.

Abby didn't know any of the students at her new school, but soon discovered that virtually all of them knew who she was. She also found that most of them were kind to her, but at least a couple of girls seemed jealous.

"Why should you should be getting any special treatment?" one of them taunted. "You're just trying to be some kind of queen!"

"No, I am *not*," Abby said defiantly. "I never wanted any special attention. I'd gladly change places with any of you. I just want my life back the way it was."

Soon, even her detractors respected her strength and independence, and Abby had a supportive group of new friends. Kids, she found, could be much more understanding than some of the adults who had tried to cheer her with incredibly inept comments. "I'm so happy you are back," she remembered one woman telling her. "You didn't miss anything. The weather was terrible."

Despite such insensitivity, Abby still managed to laugh. Even though she was only thirteen, she realized that her own attitude was probably going to be the main key to her recovery. She couldn't dwell constantly on her anger, she resolved, or else she would go crazy. "The kidnapping is something that happened," Abby told herself. "I have to deal with it as part of life. There's nothing I can do to change the fact that it happened."

Abby also found strong support and encouragement from the Port Moody police, who took her to western-style riding classes at nearby Ioco. Like most of the students, Abby loved riding and soon passed Levels 1 and 2 on a spirited mare named Wolf. She dreamed one day soon of getting a horse of her own.

For several weeks, different officers arrived at the Drover home each weekday morning to drive Abby to school. "We're here to make sure you get there safely," they told her. Swearing her in as a make-believe deputy with her own police hat and reserve badge, officers including Constable Paul Adams took the girl on patrol and showed her how radar was deployed to pull over speeding motorists. "Wow, that's bitchin'!" Abby said excitedly.

Constable Smith also spent time taking the girl for a walk around Rocky Point. As he directed her attention to the birds circling the inlet under unusually azure skies, Smith detected how very lucky Abby felt to be alive. Playfully, she plucked a buttercup and held it under the policeman's chin. "If it makes a reflection," she said, "that means you like butter."

The child's resilience filled the hardened policeman with tenderness and emotion. Superficially, she didn't seem much different from any other thirteen-year-old, yet she possessed an unmistakable aura of maturity and intensity. "It was almost as though there were two people there," Smith told colleagues on his return to the police station. "The child that she was before and the person she is now."

In his office, Constable Smith reached into his files to re-read an assessment that he and his colleagues had prepared in the event that such information might be needed for the benefit of the courts. It ended with a strong testimony to Abby's will:

There seems little doubt to the officers who investigated this incident that Hay's absence from the room for a six-week period was intended in the hope that the girl would have succumbed as a result of her treatment and neglect. It is in main part due to this individual girl's determination that she did not. This determination has also been a large factor in her recovery to date.

25 PLEA BARGAINNING

In Coquitlam, Crown Prosecutor Stewart Chambers met with Constable Smith to discuss preparations for the upcoming trial. Chambers, who was nearing retirement after a distinguished career in the courts, stubbed out the remains of yet another cigarette in the already full ashtray on his desk. The silver-haired lawyer was more than usually tense and anxious. Over the years, he had prosecuted all manner of villains, but he couldn't remember anything as inherently evil as the case that confronted him now.

It was amazing, he thought, that the girl had survived. As a former military man, Chambers recalled that prisoners of war had generally received better treatment. Nothing, he decided, could redress the crime. It was an abomination. He'd simply have to seek whatever justice he could.

The prosecutor opened what must have been his third cigarette package of the day. Once in court, he managed to run on adrenaline but in his office and elsewhere he was a hopelessly addicted chain-smoker. Reviewing the case with the police officer, the prosecutor was acutely aware of the responsibilities resting on his pinned-back shoulders.

Smith reached into his files and handed the prosecutor a list of police and civilian witnesses. "You can see what they'll be testifying," he said. "It seems like a pretty ironclad case."

Perusing the material, Chambers inhaled deeply and commended the policeman on his preparations. "You certainly caught this guy with his pants down," the prosecutor said without smiling. "There's no doubt about that, but I've still got lots of concerns."

Fourteen lawyers, the prosecutor told Smith, had been so disgusted by Hay's crime that they had refused to represent him, but Hay had managed to retain an attorney named Kenneth Baxter, a tenacious advocate who could be expected to mount a vigorous defence. "I expect they'll contend that Hay is unfit to stand trial," Chambers said. "They may propose

198 — John Griffiths

that he should be committed to a mental hospital rather than prison."

The prosecutor's fears also concerned Smith. "But it may not even get that far," the policeman suggested. "Everyone says he's waiting for the next possible chance to commit suicide."

Chambers nodded. He was apparently untroubled by thoughts of Hay's untimely demise but assumed the trial would eventually go ahead. Clearly, however, he remained determined that Abby should not have to testify, and he placed his hands together for a moment as he reflected on the possibilities. "We might be able to avoid that if Hay were to plead guilty," he said.

Smith's jaw dropped, revealing his concern. "You mean some kind of plea bargain?" he asked. "I'd be very much opposed to that."

Chambers sought to reassure him. "It might involve dropping one or two of the charges," he conceded, "but I still intend to argue that this man should spend the rest of his life in prison."

THE PROSECUTOR and the policeman were about to find out that Donald Hay might stop at nothing to manipulate the proceedings. When he next appeared before Provincial Court Judge Fred Giles on September 17, Hay again wore his short-sleeved shirt — this time in an apparent bid to gain sympathy by revealing bandages still held in place by adhesive tape around his right elbow.

So far, the accused had not entered a plea on the four charges against him, and defence lawyer Kenneth Baxter was indeed raising the possibility that his client might be mentally unfit to stand trial.

Baxter began by calling forensic psychiatrist Dr. Derek Eaves to testify that he had visited the accused in prison the previous day and had indeed concluded that Hay was suffering from a serious mental disorder.

The accused, Eaves told the crowded, hushed courtroom, had exhibited deep feelings of fear, depression and hopelessness and seemed resigned to the idea that his life was more or less over. "He said he had been feeling extremely tense, that he found it impossible to sleep and he found it difficult to concentrate on issues."

Cross-examined by Chambers, the doctor speculated that Hay was indeed waiting for the next opportunity to commit suicide, although he conceded that the prisoner was "fully oriented with his surroundings, and did not exhibit any signs of paranoia or schizophrenia."

Chambers had expected that the defence would play up Hay's suicidal tendencies, since the accused had already made an attempt to end his life in prison. A few weeks previously, while I was on vacation, my *Province* colleague Ed Simons had been assigned to pursue rumours that Donald Hay might seek to escape a prison term by pleading insanity. While following up on those rumours, the veteran reporter had discovered that the latest developments now cast doubt on whether the prisoner might ever make it to trial after all.

Simons reported that Hay — following his first appearances in court — had been taken to the Lower Mainland Regional Correctional Centre in Burnaby. More familiarly known as Oakalla Prison, the aging facility was scheduled for eventual demolition, but its stone walls still echoed with the misery of convicts who had lived and died there during the previous decades.

As an accused sex offender, Hay was not only considered to be at risk from other inmates but had also talked of committing suicide. Determined to prevent him from avoiding his day in court, prison officials placed him in a segregation unit where he was supposed to have been kept under observation every fifteen minutes.

Despite the precautions, however, Simons had discovered that other inmates had apparently managed to approach Hay and to slip him a razor blade.

"Either you do it," a burly prisoner had threatened him, "or we'll do it for you."

Taking the threat seriously, Hay had returned to his cell to roll up his bedding before placing it at the foot of the door.

Satisfied that the bedding would prevent his blood from trickling into the corridor outside, he had used the blade to slice through the flesh inside his right elbow.

Prison guards quickly discovered what had happened, and Hay, close to death, was rushed to Vancouver General Hospital. Stitching the deep gash in his right arm, doctors gave him a blood transfusion and saved him just in time. The wound was serious enough, they decided, that he should be hospitalized overnight while staff monitored his condition.

Prison director Henry Bjarnason told Simons that the prisoner had fully recovered and was now back in his cell. As before, he was not being kept in complete isolation but was being held in a section reserved for prisoners who feared violence from other inmates. "If he had been kept in isolation, we probably wouldn't have been able to save him," Bjarnason said.

After the incident, Simons had learned, prison guards had made a thorough search of the cell, but had been unable to find the instrument with which Hay had cut himself. "Whatever it was has probably been flushed down the toilet," Bjarnason had told the reporter. "It's finding a man guilty before he's been tried, but it's the law of the jungle that exists in here."

When Dr. Eaves left the witness stand, Chambers sought to undo the damage. Having predicted Hay's maneuvering, the prosecutor produced a letter that he had obtained two days earlier, offering a second opinion. Suggestions that Hay was suffering from a mental disorder, he maintained, were not borne out by the opinions of psychiatrist Dr. Gordon Stephenson.

The prosecutor obtained permission from the judge to read Stephenson's letter, which stated as follows:

I examined the above named man at your request on September 8 and again on September 15, 1976, at Lower Mainland Regional Correctional Centre, to determine his mental status.

Hay has several charges against him related to the confinement of a thirteen-year-old girl for several months. I identified myself, and he consented to be examined.

A summary of his personal history is to the effect that he is a carpenter by trade. He was first married in 1955 at age twenty-two and soon began to philander. The wife left, and he threatened her with a rifle to try to persuade her to return. He remarried about a year later, this marriage ending when the wife was unfaithful.

Hay has been involved in episodes with women all his adult life, several of these episodes resulting in criminal charges of a sexual nature. He has several times reestablished himself after a prison sentence only to waste his efforts by again becoming pathologically involved with a female.

For the past three years he has lived with his present common-law wife and her three children ages seventeen, fifteen, and thirteen years old. He has for many years been sexually inadequate being impotent a good deal of the time.

He has habitually abused alcohol, and has been subject to periods of depression, usually after some debacle related to his behaviour. He has made numerous serious suicidal attempts over the years.

At interview, he presented as a pale, middle-aged man with a tense, anxious expression and marked tremulousness. He was cooperative to examination. He was correctly oriented in all spheres, his memory was intact, and there was no confusion or clouding of consciousness.

He was appropriately dejected, but there was no evidence of severe depression, nor mood swings. Nor was there any evidence of disordered or dis-

```
torted thought processes such as to make him inca-
pable of appreciating the nature and quality of his
act, or of knowing an act to be wrong.
```
     Dr. Gordon H. Stephenson, M.D., F.R., C.P.

After a brief recess, the tall psychiatrist was called to present his evidence in person. While on the stand, he agreed with defence lawyer Kenneth Baxter that mental illness was "a lay term covering a whole host of things from temporary upset to severe psychosis."

Judge Giles was now faced with conflicting medical opinions. It *was* possible, he acknowledged, that Hay might be unfit to stand trial. Under the circumstances, the judge concluded, he had no alternative but to delay the proceedings yet again so that the accused could be remanded to Riverview Hospital for a full psychiatric assessment.

Outside the courtroom, Chambers lit another cigarette, refusing to comment as he was questioned by reporters. The latest psychiatric examination, he knew, would take thirty days — a tense time for the prosecutor, the police and members of the Drover family.

26 DISNEYLAND

WHILE THE MENTAL health of her kidnapper remained very much in question, Abby herself continued to impress members of her family and the Port Moody Police Department with her determination to recover.

After Abby's rescue, her estranged father had flown to Port Moody to attend celebrations of the birthday that Abby had missed while she was in Hay's dungeon. Sadly, Abby felt disconnected from the father she'd never known, but she put on the bravest face.

While in Vancouver, Cecil told *Sun* reporter Douglas Sagi: "Generally, she is in amazingly good spirits. She's even talking about going back to school but perhaps that won't be for some time. Right now, she's finding her way back to normal life, but slowly. She just wants to play in the sunshine, visit friends and let the ordeal she has endured fade from memory.

"It's a big adjustment," Abby's father admitted. "When she disappeared, it was winter and there wasn't a leaf on a tree. Six months went out of her life just like that. Now it's late summer and she's home again. She loves seeing the flowers in bloom and feeling the grass beneath her feet."

In the same September 10 newspaper article, the *Sun* also sought a prognosis on the child's recovery through an interview with local university psychologist Dr. Peter Suedfeld.

Emphasizing that he didn't know Abby personally and was speaking in general terms, Suedfeld speculated that the girl might have died had it not been for her strength and courage. "There are cases of psychogenic death," the psychologist said. "This means the death is psychologically caused, where people give up. They just turn their faces to the wall and die even though there is nothing physically wrong with them."

Suedfeld compared some aspects of Abby's ordeal to the case of newspaper heiress Patty Hearst who had recently been kidnapped and brainwashed by political extremists in the United States. "If you are in someone's power, it is better to be his friend than his enemy," the psychologist said.

According to Suedfeld, Abby seemed to have inadvertently stumbled upon some of the same survival techniques as prisoners of war by mentally detaching herself from her immediate surroundings. The child's religious faith, he added, was obviously a major factor in her recovery. "Some kids take very horrible things in their stride," he said. "They haven't the maturity to compare what has happened to them with what should have happened — with what things ought to be — so they more readily accept situations as they are."

Like everyone else, Mayor Patterson was amazed by Abby's efforts to put the dark days of the ordeal as far as possible behind her. "She was very weak two months ago but she has put on weight and is doing well at school," he told reporters. "She is in good spirits mentally and has a good attitude about the future."

Patterson announced that the local Lions Club had decided to join with radio station CKNW in financing a Drover family holiday to Disneyland. Expressing gratitude, Ruth Drover said she would take her children out of school to go on the trip in the latter part of December.

Meanwhile, neighbours, police officers and members of the public continued to contribute to the Drover family trust fund. In a letter typifying their sentiments, one woman wrote: "This is in memory of my granddaughter's sixteen-year-old girlfriend who was brutally murdered just over a year ago. God gave Abby the strength to survive those terrible days and I am sure will keep her from any further harm... ."

The Port Moody Parks and Recreation Department held a slide show to raise yet more funds, and Mayor Patterson valiantly tried to outshoot a neighbouring mayor with the longest kick at a benefit soccer match. Patterson's rival — a former professional football player with the Winnipeg Blue Bombers — was impossible to beat, but the event raised yet another $500 for the fund.

With donations approaching $10,000, Patterson and his fellow trustees were further encouraged when a Toronto entrepreneur named Tom Bennett telephoned asking permission to establish a similar fund on the opposite side of the country.

Bennett was a thirty-four-year-old entrepreneur who had connections through his business associates with various top ranking celebrities, including Frank Sinatra and his family. "I am amazed by this girl's stamina and her faith in God," Bennett told the mayor. "I know a lot of influential people and I think the fund is just gaining momentum."

Proving true to his word, the young businessman set about raising funds from the Ontario public, and even obtained a sizable donation from prison inmates in Brampton. Shortly afterwards, Bennett sent the mayor a bank draft for $10,000, matching and thereby doubling the amount already collected in Port Moody.

Speaking with reporters, Patterson said he and his fellow trustees would give some of the money to the Drovers as special needs arose, while the balance would be held in trust until Abby became an adult.

"MOM, THEY'RE HERE!"

The big day had finally arrived. Looking out of the window, Abby Drover was informing her mother and sisters that Mayor Norm Patterson and Police Chief Len McCabe had just pulled up at the house as promised to drive them to the airport for their pre-Christmas trip to Disneyland.

Even though reunited, the family had continued to experience psychological turmoil. They were thrilled, of course, to have her back, but Abby's sisters found themselves very much in the background with all the attention being devoted to their youngest sibling.

Unaccustomed to such celebrity, Ruth Drover also found herself overwhelmed by the sudden worldwide interest in her family. Frequently, Ruth was offered money if she and Abby would

206 — John Griffiths

give interviews to prominent international magazines but her answer was always the same. Determined to protect her daughter's privacy, she rejected them all.

Now, as the entourage arrived at Vancouver International Airport, Abby was excited. She had never been on a plane before. Noticing actor Leslie Nielsen waiting for a flight, she approached the Canadian celebrity and was thrilled to get his autograph.

Before the family headed for the departure lounge, the police chief had some more good news. Based on the psychiatric report from Riverview Hospital, he informed them, Judge Giles had indeed found that Donald Hay was fit to stand trial.

The mayor and police chief wished the family *bon voyage* and reminded Ruth that all of her expenses were paid. "Make sure you take a cab to your hotel when you get there," said McCabe.

In Los Angeles, Ruth was apprehensive when the cab fare came to $42. Her frugality told her it was just about a day's pay, even if she didn't have to pay the bill herself. After visiting some cousins in nearby Anaheim, however, she rented a car and took her daughters to various tourist attractions including Knotts Berry Farm and Seaworld in San Diego.

Finally Abby arrived at Disneyland. After receiving a wristwatch from Mickey Mouse, she hurried to ride twelve consecutive times on the new Matterhorn roller coaster. "Wow!" she told her sisters. "This is colossal."

There were more treats to come. The girl's Toronto benefactor, Tom Bennett, had not only visited the Drovers in Port Moody, but also had contacted acquaintances in California to advise Frank Sinatra Jr. of the family's itinerary. Apparently, the crooner's son had never forgotten the terror of his own kidnapping and had arranged to have Abby taken to Universal Studios in a chauffeur-driven limousine.

Coincidentally, a group of Port Moody schoolchildren was also visiting the studios at the very moment that the black limousine pulled up outside. The children craned their necks as they attempted to identify the arriving "celebrity" — and were amazed to see who stepped out of the vehicle.

"It's Abby Drover!" one of them said, and simultaneously all of the students burst into applause.

After the grand finale to their trip, Ruth and her daughters would still be home in time for Christmas. Abby knew it would be difficult but desperately hoped they might revert to being a normal family again. In the meantime, she had bought Mickey Mouse beer mugs for Mayor Patterson and Chief McCabe, who met them upon their return and drove them back to the less sunny climes of Port Moody.

Detouring via the police station, members of the family gazed with amazement at a giant plywood Christmas card erected for them by the Lions Club and signed by hundreds of well-wishers.

Finally they arrived back to the smell of home baking on Gore Street, where Grandma Adolphe had been looking after their house. They were also touched by the fact that Hilda Hay and her children had brought over and helped decorate a Christmas tree. Underneath it, brightly wrapped parcels were stacked several feet high and Abby gasped as she beheld more presents than she had ever seen in her life.

Ruth knew that Hay's wife was a "very honest person" who had been devastated by her husband's deceit. With Ruth's approval, Hilda returned on Christmas morning to watch Abby open a mountain of gifts, including numerous autographed record albums rounded up by Tom Bennett. Later, Hilda gave Ruth yet another present — a Pomeranian puppy named Nuffy that licked her face as she cradled it in her arms.

It was indeed, under the circumstances, a happy time. Each of the Drover girls received brand new ice-skates and Abby was able to laugh and joke with her cousins as the family sat down to Christmas dinner. They were sounds that filled her family with delight.

BEFORE THE NEW YEAR, however, family tensions once more resurfaced. Whether it was during a fit of anger or out of genuine concern for her sister, Robyn upset Abby by asking if Donald Hay might have made her pregnant. Abby's sister didn't know about Hay's vasectomy, but her family's disapproval of her lack of tact left her feeling unwanted and rejected.

Ruth tried to keep the bickering to a minimum, but the stress had already proved too much for one member of the household. Upset by the constant visits of police and newsmen, the bewildered university student who had recently rented the Drovers' basement suite had been unable to tolerate the disruptions any longer and moved out.

The family did its best to stay together through these trying times, but the alienation ran too deep and Robyn left the household to go live with her father. Ruth was devastated by the split — but other concerns soon surfaced, filling her with yet more apprehension. During the family's visit to California, she learned, there had been some disturbing new developments.

27 COVERT JUSTICE

THREE OF THE CHARGES against Donald Hay had been dropped.

The plea bargain that the police had so much dreaded was a *fait accompli*. Hay would no longer stand trial for rape, gross indecency or abducting a female with intent to have sexual intercourse. Instead, for his part of the bargain, he would simply plead guilty to kidnapping and to having sexual intercourse with a girl under fourteen.

Advised to stay out of the proceedings, Ruth felt very much neglected. She might have preferred the opportunity to address the court, but victim impact statements had not yet become a part of the justice system.

She could do little but watch as prosecutor Stewart Chambers explained the deal on television.

Abby, said the prosecutor, had met with court officials to discuss the trauma of having to testify. Having consistently opposed involving the family in the proceedings, Chambers was now quick to defend his decision.

"I have been seeking and will continue to seek a mandatory life sentence," he insisted. "The deal was made to keep the poor girl out of court."

For his part, defence counsel Kenneth Baxter concurred that the pleas were entered "as a result of reaching an agreement with the Crown."

The plea bargaining, however, prompted widespread public criticism, including an opinion piece entitled "Hush-Hush Justice" in the December 28 issue of the *Province*.

"Everyone will agree with the need to save young Abby Drover the suffering of recounting the story of her six-month confinement in a neighbour's underground room," the article stated. "But the plea bargain amounts to covert rather than open justice."

Condemning plea bargaining as an American practice, the article suggested that the judge could have cleared the courtroom while Abby testified, or alternatively have had her evidence taken at home.

The arguments, however, seemed almost academic in light of developments unknown to the newspaper at the time.

At Oakalla prison on Boxing Day, guards had once more found Hay semiconscious in his cell. Suspecting he had been saving sleeping pills for one massive overdose, they had rushed him to Vancouver General Hospital. In the emergency room, doctors pumped out the contents of his stomach, and the prisoner recovered.

JUST OVER TWO WEEKS later, the legal proceedings finally got under way. It was a cloudy day on January 13, 1977, when I went back to the court building in Coquitlam for the balance of the hearing.

I had already handed in my resignation at the *Province* and would be leaving early the following month. It was hard under the circumstances to be interested in day-to-day assignments, but the Abby Drover case was so dramatic that it continued to hold my attention right up until the end.

On the bench, a new judge had been appointed to preside over the case. The relatively young Judge Joel Groberman, generally considered one of the brightest legal minds in the province, would not be encumbered with responsibility for any of the court decisions to date.

Like everyone else, I was acutely aware of the tension that filled the courtroom. Uppermost in the minds of most spectators was what possible maneuvers the defence might have up its sleeve, but it was Stewart Chambers who rose to his feet to open the proceedings.

"*I am not asking you to consider retribution, because the law has no retribution appropriate to what has been done here.*" Ruddy-faced and indignant, the prosecutor argued that protection of the public, deterrence to the accused and deterrence to others demanded a life sentence.

Chambers was ready to begin tendering the evidence —

and began by handing a composed but obviously incredulous Judge Groberman sixteen photographs of the dungeon and its environs taken by Constable Lylack on the night Hay was arrested.

"I consider these necessary to deal with the situation in which the child in this case was confined," the prosecutor said. The first half-dozen photographs showed the judge the ingenious access to the underground chamber in Donald Hay's garage.

"Photograph Number Seven," the prosecutor continued, "is taken from inside the cell, showing the door leading to the shaft. That is a solid plank door, with planks approximately an inch and a half in thickness, and was lined on the inside with two inches of foam rubber. Above the cell is the concrete floor of the garage. The closing of the door made the cell for all practical purposes soundproof."

Methodically, Chambers produced another set of photographs depicting various chains affixed to the walls of the underground cell, before showing the judge a picture of how Abby had cut the lining of one of her boots to hide the letter describing the man who'd kidnapped her.

"In addition to that," the prosecutor said, "I wish to put in at this time two sets of handcuffs found in the cell, together with what appears to be a dog collar found in the cell and a pair of belts... ."

Judge Groberman was unable to resist shaking his head slightly as the prosecutor continued, recounting the details of Abby's abduction.

"On frequent occasions during those 181 days, this child was kept in a condition that I can only describe as chattel slavery. She had no access to any person other than the accused. He repeatedly came to that cell and had sexual intercourse with this child. On several occasions, he threatened that he would ultimately kill her."

Chambers went on to illustrate the extent to which Abby had been neglected while her kidnapper had carried on normal relations with his family.

212 — John Griffiths

"The accused — and the Crown says this was camouflage of the cruellest kind — took the older sisters of his victim out on search parties to look for her, knowing the whole time where she was, which would be not more than a hundred yards from her own home.

"Now, he continued to act as the friendly neighbour to the other children of his victim's family, and to other children in the neighbourhood throughout the time that this child was contained in the cell."

After describing Hay's long absences and abject neglect of Abby's nutrition, Chambers was ready to put his own perspective on the events he had eloquently described. "I referred Your Honour earlier to the expression — which I think is very appropriate to the condition in which that child was kept — as being one of chattel slavery. And I say that she was deprived of every conceivable human right.

"It occurred to me to look at the Canadian Bill of Rights, Section 1, where it states: *It is hereby recognized and declared that in Canada there have existed and shall continue to exist . . . the following human rights and fundamental freedoms: The right of the individual to life, liberty, security of the person and enjoyment of property, and the right not to be deprived thereof except by due process of the law. . . ."*

Chambers was presenting the case in ways that gibed with his own military experience, and his dramatic style seemed curiously effective as he continued. "All of those rights — except the right to life itself — the accused deprived this child of. And he very nearly deprived her of that."

The prosecutor went on to describe the frail condition in which Abby had been found as he outlined the circumstances of the rescue itself.

The judge appeared spellbound as the prosecutor continued with his story in increasingly dramatic fashion.

"She had heard the voices above when the door was opened. And she was in a state of complete hysteria, unable to say anything for some time except that she wanted her Mom.

"The accused at that point asked the police a strange request but one that is only consistent with his full knowledge of the extent of his guilt. He said, 'If I try to escape, will you guys blow me in the back of the head? That's what I deserve.'

"Again, at the police station, he made a request to the police in these terms, 'How much to let me get out the back door, then blow my head off?' I think it says a great deal for the discipline of our police forces and their regard for the rule of law that the very tempting request was not complied with."

Chambers then offered both Abby's and Hay's statements into the court record before continuing with his synopsis of the case.

"Earlier, Your Honour," he said, "I referred you to the note which was found in the girl's boot and which has been put in as an exhibit. The first portion of the note refers to this girl's very strong religious faith which may have had a good deal to do with her survival under these conditions.

"And then there follows a postscript: 'If you find me dead . . . my killer is Don Hay of 1601 Gore Street, Port Moody. He kidnapped me on the morning of March 10, 1976. I also died, if so, after my thirteenth birthday.'

"Her thirteenth birthday was May 3. It was September 6 that this child was finally rescued from this horrible situation."

There was a lengthy pause before Chambers continued. "Customarily," he said, "in considering sentence in major cases, precedents of previous decisions are cited. *I can find no precedent that fits this outrageous situation here.*"

The prosecutor did, however, point out that a Vancouver man had recently been given a life sentence for kidnapping a woman and chaining her to a tree — returning after three days to find that she had escaped.

"I find it difficult to draw a comparison between that situation, bad as it was, and this imprisonment and abuse that this man forced on this child for 181 days, and which, except for the discovery made on September 6, might have continued or ended even more tragically than it has.... .

"Your Honour has before you the pre-sentence report and the previous record of the accused. On November 7, 1953, in Brandon, Manitoba, he was convicted of attempted rape and indecent assault and given two years (but) that sentence did not deter him from the horrible acts committed in this case."

Even Hay's probation officer, said Chambers, found that he had a history of criminal and deviant behaviour dating back twenty years. The circumstances of his latest offences, the probation officer had added, were beyond most people's imagination. "He is described," said the probation officer's report, "as psychopathic and not future-oriented, and consequently not amenable to traditional therapy. It is, consequently, this officer's respectful suggestion that, in the matter of sentence, this is one of the few cases where the interests of both society in general and of the local community outweigh the interest of the accused."

Chambers threw down the probation officer's report. "I couldn't agree more," the prosecutor said emphatically. "I have looked carefully through the history of this confinement to see if there was any form of concern and kindness to this child. I can find none.

"It may well be that the accused may late in the day have extended some form of consideration to her in entering a guilty plea and saving her having to relive this whole matter through the courts, but it took him from the date of his arrest on September 6 until November 25 to make up his mind even to do that.

"The Crown's submission on this is that the maximum penalty provided for both of these two offences is designed for the protection of the public from men such as this accused.

"The Crown throughout this case has taken the position that the primary consideration here is to ensure that this man never gets the chance to get his hands on another girl child.

"And it is the Crown's submission that, within the powers given to the court, the only appropriate way to ensure that is to impose a term of life imprisonment with a recommendation against any parole."

Chambers, with a flourish, had finished his arguments, but Judge Groberman had one or two questions.

"There are a couple of things I want to know," said the judge, "if you have the information. First of all, do you have the dimensions of the room in which — "

"Yes, Your Honour," said the prosecutor. "The room is seven feet by eight feet, and its height from floor to ceiling is six feet seven inches. I had considered asking Your Honour to take a view of this, but I felt that the picture display of it would probably be adequate. I have no objection if you do take a view of the premises."

The judge sidestepped the idea. "I have one or two more questions," he continued. "With regard to ventilation for the room, I notice in one part of your submission you mentioned a vent. What was the ventilation?"

"If Your Honour would look at Photograph Number Eight," said Chambers, "you will see between that mirror and the door a dark circle up on the wall. That is the opening of a vent. It simply goes up into the furnace area of the garage above. It does not go into the outside air."

Groberman grimaced. "Is that the sole vent for the room?" he asked.

"Yes," said Chambers. "There was a fan installed in the room which was not functioning when the police arrived. It seems that it probably was functioning at the time this child was first imprisoned there."

"All right," the judge continued. "Now, with regard to the door, I think you mentioned in one other part of your submission that there was some locking facility on the outside of the door. Was that door the only access to the room?"

Chambers confirmed that it was. "This cell is completely underground," he said. "It can be entered only by descending that shaft."

"And what was the locking facility on the door?" asked the judge.

"I noticed that the child refers to him using boards and

chains," said Chambers. "There was a two by four in brackets used as a bolt on the outside of the door."

"One more question," said Groberman. "The health of the victim — both mentally and physically following this incident — do you have any information concerning that?"

"The immediate health of the victim was apparently surprisingly good as the doctors saw it," replied Chambers. "They anticipated a later relapse. The only occasion on which I saw this child would be before the guilty plea was entered. She was walking with a slight limp which apparently arose from something which happened down there. She had an internal infection of the urinary tract which has since cleared up. She was taken to hospital after her first release to have that done.

"As to her emotional future, all I can tell you, Your Honour, is that having spoken with her doctors, they are of the opinion, which I share, that the less notoriety and the less attention over this that is given to this girl the better her future will be — but they cannot guarantee that there will not be continuing emotional disturbances. She did return to school. I believe that she is still attending school."

"All right, thank you," said Groberman.

The judge had appeared shocked at times as he listened to all the lurid details of the case, although his general demeanour seemed one of dispassion. Could he now be swayed by submissions from the defence?

28 DEFENCE

KENNETH BAXTER, a portly, serious-looking defence attorney with greying hair, rose to his feet.

Waiving an option to wait until after the morning recess, Baxter immediately sought to dispel similarities with the case cited by Chambers involving the woman who had been kidnapped and tied to a tree.

"It so happens I was counsel for that defendant," Baxter hastened to point out. "The motive there was one of money.... There was no suggestion of mental disorder (or) sexual dysfunction."

It was clear as he addressed the judge that Baxter's defence of his client would be vigorous and thorough.

"I certainly do agree with my friend that the facts in the particular case before you are unique," he added. "I didn't even attempt to find another case with a similar fact pattern.

"The motivation here was not money. The actions of the accused — the actions that he took — are bizarre. The particular fact pattern is bizarre.

"In this particular case you are dealing with the actions of a man who is extremely sick. And that's what makes all of his actions bizarre."

Swivelling in his chair, Prosecutor Chambers appeared to wince at ongoing suggestions that Hay might be deserving of sympathy on account of mental illness, although he didn't yet rise to object as the defence lawyer continued.

"Your Honour asked my friend about the ventilation in the cell," said Baxter. "My instructions are that [during] the latter part of Abby Drover's confinement in this cell she took it upon herself to stuff up the ventilation pipe, as it were, so that it wouldn't work.

"Now, I don't know what the motivation was behind that, but I understand she was getting adequate air and that she chose to stuff it up herself, and that Donald Hay insisted on removing the stuffing within there. I don't think there is anything to indicate that there was insufficient air in regard to the efforts that Mr. Hay made."

Baxter went on to deliver a powerful opening statement, asserting that Hay's sexual dysfunction and alcoholism were the sole causes of his behaviour, and that both were treatable.

Stewart Chambers watched anxiously as Baxter called his first witness.

"At this time, with the court's leave," he said, "I'd ask to call Dr. Derek Eaves."

A hush fell over the courtroom, all eyes falling expectantly upon a sporty-looking man in a checked jacket, seated at the back of the chamber. Brushing a hand through his thick dark hair, Dr. Eaves wended his way to the witness stand, where the court clerk asked him to state his full name and occupation.

"My name is Derek Eaves," said the key witness for the defence. "Eaves is spelled E-A-V-E-S. I'm a psychiatrist."

On the bench, Judge Groberman turned deferentially to acknowledge the witness. "You may be seated if you would like, Doctor."

"Thank you," said the witness, settling in for what was expected to be a long period of testimony and cross examination.

Baxter began his examination in chief. "Dr. Eaves," he asked, "are you a member of the British Columbia College of Physicians and Surgeons?"

"Yes," replied the witness. "I am."

"How long have you so been?" Baxter continued.

"Three and a half years."

"Would you explain to the court what your background is in medicine — and your specialties?"

"Yes," the doctor replied readily. "I qualified in medicine, Your Honour, in 1966 from Liverpool. I have several English qualifications in psychiatry, including a diploma in psychological medicine from the University of Liverpool and also from the Royal College in London. I'm also a member of the Royal College of Psychiatrists. I hold the licentia to the Medical Council of Canada. And I am also a Fellow of the Royal College of Physicians in Ottawa in the specialty of psychiatry."

It was an impressive list of qualifications, but could the witness possibly demonstrate that Hay might yet be amenable to rehabilitation? Constable Smith and his colleagues shifted position in the spectators' gallery wondering what to expect.

"How long have you been practising in Canada?" Baxter continued.

"Over three and a half years," said the doctor.

"Now," Baxter continued, "have you had any experience in your practice with sexual dysfunction problems?"

"Yes, I have," said Dr. Eaves. "Even before I was a lecturer at the University of Liverpool for four years before I came to Canada, I did research in sexual deviation from 1969. And I have continued my interests in sexual deviants from that time."

"Can you describe what experience that you had at the B.C. Penitentiary and at the Matsqui Institution?"

The witness seemed somewhat unconvincing as he began his reply. "Well," he said, "I have visited B.C. Penitentiary during the time I was employed by the federal government when I first came to Canada.

"But I worked as a psychiatrist and later on as the acting clinical director of the Federal Psychiatric Centre in Matsqui. I was also and have been since 1973 clinical assistant professor at the University of British Columbia. And I also lecture at various places, including Simon Fraser."

Baxter sought to re-establish the doctor's qualifications. "How long were you actually at Matsqui as a director?"

"I was clinical director for a period of one year, on an acting basis."

Having set the stage, Baxter zeroed in on the crux of the matter. "Have you examined the defendant who is seated behind me, Donald Hay?"

"Yes, I have," said the doctor.

"Would you describe to the court the nature of the examinations that you had of him?"

"Yes," said the doctor. "I first met Mr. Hay in Oakalla before one of his court appearances. Subsequently, I've interviewed him at length on several occasions and had numerous short discussions with him, as well as longer discussions with him about his life history."

Baxter paused to make a note on the sheaf of papers in front of him. "Dr. Eaves," he continued, "are you familiar with the circumstances in this case, the facts that my learned friend informed the court of surrounding this case?"

"Yes," said the doctor. "I am. I have been present in the court and I have listened to the issue as described."

"Have you discussed with Donald Hay the facts surrounding this case?"

"Yes, I have, on several occasions."

"Now," asked Baxter, "have you formed an opinion as to what, if anything, caused Mr. Hay to act in the manner in which he did?"

In the courtroom, anticipation gripped the spectators as they wondered what possible explanations the witness might offer.

Eaves confirmed that he had formed some definite opinions on the matter. "I think that it would take me some time, Your Honour, to describe some of the facts which have led to certain opinions about... the crime which he is alleged to have had committed."

"Yes," said Baxter, bidding the witness to continue. "Would you explain that to us, doctor?"

Eaves looked at Judge Groberman on the bench. "Well, may I refer to my notes, Your Honour?"

"Yes," said the judge.

"Thank you," said the doctor, opening his notebook. "Mr. Hay is a person of Grade 8 education," the doctor began. "He's probably a person of average or probably considerably above-average intelligence.

"All his life he's been a very lonely, a very isolated person, a very withdrawn person socially. And I think one would use the label, the psychiatric label 'schizoid', to describe that personality.

"He has had a lifelong difficulty in his perceived acceptance by women. He's never accepted that anyone could love him, and he's often doubted whether he in fact could love people too.

"He's been chronically depressed. He's had feelings of social and sexual alienation, a feeling of personal hopelessness and a general feeling of hopelessness about the world...

"I think I have already mentioned that he had this — he had this difficulty in this area of being loved and this led — has led to him searching, if you like, for a loving relationship over a long period of time.

"I think when he was younger he tried to do it by acting in a somewhat sexually promiscuous way. He was married twice and I think his alcoholism and his promiscuity led to the demise of both marriages.

"For a long period of time, he's incubated a fantasy of a perfect life. We talked about this extensively — it consists of removing himself from the real world — and I think there is a lack of reality about his wishes.

"He talked about living a country, rural life in a cottage in the countryside by a lake. This was his kind of ideal. And I think he built a wish for himself that another person be involved in that ideal life with him.

"I think in his marriages, and more recently his common-law relationship, he was testing out some of those wishes and found them impracticable, in reality wanting.

"In particular, he idealized his relationship with his common-law wife's younger daughter. She, I think, is about fifteen or sixteen now and he expressed to me that he was in love with this girl.

"He thought for a long period of time how he could develop this loving relationship, and I think this included sexual love as well. He felt that if he could make his own daughter captive — if he could devise a scheme whereby he would do this — then he would do it, then he would capture her.

"And if he could put her in a place where she could be secure for a length of time, he could, I guess, involve himself in a way with her that could translate into reality his fantasy of what a perfect loving relationship could be. This, in fact, is what he intended to do.

"And this is what he told me: that he built the cell for her, that part of it was as a bomb shelter because he was afraid of a nuclear holocaust and, partly, it was in order to put his own daughter in there.

"In fact, for practical reasons, he felt that this wasn't appropriate to do because of the family complications it would cause. He told me that he had fleetingly thought about putting someone else in her place, but this would be as a substitute.

"He said he had never developed that idea for any length of time but had always dismissed it. And then on the day in question and somewhat impulsively, he put the girl in the case, in the cellar. He maintains this was impulsive.

"I think really one of his intents was to try to have a sexual relationship with the girl. And once he had done this, he found that he was committed to it and then couldn't get out of what he had done.

"In fact, he felt trapped as much as the girl felt trapped in that situation. I think, after she was placed there, his drinking escalated again. Drinking has been a lifelong problem for him. He could fairly be described as an alcoholic. And he has in fact been treated for alcoholism in the past.

"He's had no sexual relationships for a long time and had no sexual relationships with his common-law wife for several years. And the basis of this is probably his alcoholism, a complication of alcoholism and his impotence.

"He describes that he's been impotent. I think this impotence increased his feelings of inadequacy and decreased his feelings of self-esteem, that these have always in fact been low.

"He's made several suicidal gestures during his life, including several quite serious suicide attempts. He has in fact only been treated during one period of his life, from 1973 to 1974. I think when he was — when the girl in question was in captivity — he did make an attempt at suicide during one period and was treated medically in a local hospital."

As spectators whispered incredulity, Baxter returned to his earlier premise that Hay might yet respond to further medical treatment. "Now, you mentioned, doctor, his prior treatment," said Baxter. "What can you tell us that you know of that?"

"This was in 1973," said Dr. Eaves. "He was treated in Riverview Hospital for a short period of time as an in-patient for alcoholism and, as far as I know, he cooperated fully with the treatment regime there.

"He was then discharged, and he was followed up for a six-month period by Dr. Witt. She provided me with a copy of her notes and I have discussed his treatment with her.

"For the whole of that six months he was completely sober. She then saw him at more distant periods, and in fact he remained sober as far as I know for a period of sixteen months altogether. It's documented in the medical notes that he remained completely sober for at least a year. And this was confirmed by his wife."

The doctor appeared uncomfortable, despite his role on the accused's behalf.

"How," asked Baxter, "would you evaluate the treatment or the success of the treatment that he took during this course of time?"

"Well," said the doctor, "it clearly shows when he's under medical and psychiatric guidance that he can respond, given certain circumstances, to medical treatment."

"Now, you have outlined, Doctor, some of the problems that led up to the action. You have explained what led up to the action on the part of Mr. Hay.... In your opinion is there anything that can be done to cure Mr. Hay of the causes of his action?"

It seemed impossible that the doctor might be able to offer any hopeful prognosis, but his testimony indicated otherwise. "Yes," he continued. "I think Mr. Hay clearly has considerable psychiatric problems. I have already stated that he is an alcoholic and that he had a — has a schizoid personality — and he also has substantial sexual problems as well. And I think — sorry, can I — can you just remind me of the question again?"

"Yes," said Baxter, patiently. "I'm asking your opinion as to whether or not Mr. Hay's problems are treatable."

"Yes," Eaves confirmed. "I think all these aspects of him are in fact potentially treatable."

"Now," said Baxter, showing satisfaction, "can you tell us, where could such treatment be found within the existing penal institution that you are aware of?"

Eaves paused for a moment. His voice was becoming hoarse. He sipped from a glass of water before continuing. "The only place of treatment that I think is at all appropriate for him is maximum security at Penitentiary Hospital at Matsqui. I think this is the only place that would provide those kind of facilities. And there are in fact treatment programs which I in fact developed there for treating such people as Mr. Hay."

"People with similar sexual and alcoholic problems?"

"Yes."

"Now, could you describe some of these programs to the court that would be available to Mr. Hay if he was placed at Matsqui?"

"Well, the Regional Psychiatric Centre was only opened in 1972, I think. So, the programs themselves have only been running for five years. There are in fact two programs in the Regional Psychiatric Centre which cater to sexual offenders and dangerous sexual offenders. And most of the people have spent up to three or perhaps even more years in a treatment situation there. This includes group therapy — very, very intense group therapy — up to twenty hours per week for several years. So, this is a very, very intense treatment program."

"Doctor, do these programs include Mr. Hay's particular sexual problems?"

"Well, I think every person's unique, and I think every treatment program has to be devised for an individual. But I think in general terms they would include people such as Mr. Hay."

"Now, can you tell us what treatments for problems that Mr. Hay has exist at the B.C. Penitentiary?"

"None at all."

"Have you any opinion as to the effect on Mr. Hay's actions of a great punishment such as death or life imprisonment? Any great punishment for the acts he was contemplating, would that have any effect on his actions, the actions that he did take?"

"As a deterrent, you mean?"

"Yes."

"No, I don't think anything would deter a person from committing acts which he committed once he was embarked upon them."

"Why do you say that? Can you explain why that is?"

"I think because to some extent... his mental processes were quite irrational and they were devoid of a reality basis, and it precluded him from thinking logically as to what might be the consequences of his actions... . I mean that in the general sense and not in the psychiatric sense. I think he's aware of the consequences of his actions in the very narrow, medical, legal sense of the word, but I mean in the widest sense."

"You're saying he didn't care what happened to him?"

"Yes. And I think that was indicated to some extent by his withdrawn fantasy which precluded him from appreciating his situation properly. I don't think there is any way that deterrence would affect that kind of behaviour."

"Have you any opinion as to the effectiveness of any deterrent on persons with problems similar to Mr. Hay's?"

"I think deterrence has an effect on people of normal psychological functioning. I don't think it has any effect on people such as Mr. Hay or people similar to him."

"Have you any opinion as to the likelihood of Mr. Hay's

successful treatment of the problems which you have described if he was sent to Matsqui?"

"A rough indication of time?"

"Yes."

"I'm not sure that I can answer specifically about him. I can only say that his problems are quite tremendous. I think they would require a very long period of treatment and a very, very gradual rehabilitation process. I think the actual medical treatment or psychiatric treatment itself might take several years, perhaps three or four years and then followed by a very, very gradual rehabilitation program."

"Can you tell us what the likelihood of a cure for his problems would be if he does not get this psychiatric help available at Matsqui?"

"If he gets no treatment at all?"

"If he does not go to Matsqui?"

"There is no — no chance at all for him."

Baxter let the doctor's answer hang in the air for a moment before he proceeded.

"Have you formed any opinion as to what would happen to him if he were to be placed, let's say, in the B. C. Penitentiary?"

"I think if he didn't go to the regular psychiatric centre for treatment, he wouldn't live very long."

"Why do you say that, because of actions of other persons in the prison or because of his response to himself?"

"I think both. I think when the times I've seen him, he's had a great suicidal preoccupation. I think he's tried to commit suicide twice while he's been held in custody. One of the attempts I know about was a very serious one and required hospital treatment and he only just survived from it. I think that there is a very real risk if he was not given any hope, that is if he was given a life sentence that he might well kill himself. I think too he might well attract retribution from other inmates who would find his actions somewhat repugnant."

"What is the usual course of actions of persons who have gone through the program that you have described? Do you know where they go after they have taken the treatment?"

"Yes, I do.... Some dangerous sexual offenders have been treated to the point that there is good reason to believe that they will respond quite well.... I can confirm that several of them in fact are going out on passes and are undergoing a very gradual rehabilitation program. And none of them to my mind has relapsed so far."

"Now, would the length of Mr. Hay's sentence influence the effectiveness of the treatment?"

"The length of the sentence?"

"Yes."

"I have already said that if he was given a life sentence, that would remove any hope that he had. He's not forward-looking — I would agree with that part of the pre-sentence report — and I think that would remove any potential that he had for forward-thinking and would in fact be very deleterious to his mental functioning."

"The pre-sentence report has described Mr. Hay as being psychopathic. Do you have any opinion on that?"

"Yes, there is no evidence that he suffers from psychopathic traits. I have already described him as schizoid which I think is a more adequate term. In fact, as far as I'm aware, none of the previous psychiatric assessments have ever described him as psychopathic. They have referred to his chronic depression, his hopelessness, his alcoholism — but never to any psychopathic traits.

"I think to some extent the fact that he responded immediately during that period, 1973 to 1974, would remove that label because the diagnosis of psychopathy means a person who won't respond to any conventional therapies. He very clearly did respond to treatment at that time, even though it was short-lived and he relapsed after his medical supervision was removed."

The doctor had finished giving his evidence, and it was time for Stewart Chambers to call those opinions into question on cross-examination.

"I think, Your Honour, that I might be some time," Chambers said. "Perhaps we should take the break before I commence."

"All right," said Judge Groberman. "We will take the afternoon recess now. And we'll commence with the cross-examination when we return, Doctor."

29 CROSS-EXAMINATION

STEWART CHAMBERS began his cross-examination mildly enough by getting Dr. Eaves to agree that a person sent to a regular penitentiary might still eventually be transferred to a prison offering treatment programs. "It's done regularly, isn't it?" the prosecutor asked.

"Yes," the doctor agreed.

"Now," Chambers asked, "you have spent some time examining the accused in the case?"

"Yes."

"Have you ever examined the victim?"

Defence lawyer Baxter rushed to his feet: "Objection, Your Honour! Surely that's not relevant to the evidence that this doctor has been giving."

"Yes," Judge Groberman concurred. "What's the relevancy of that, Mr. Chambers? And if he had, what are you driving at?"

Chambers began his reply. "Well," he said, "Your Honour asked me some questions earlier as to the present condition of this child. And this man, having specialist qualifications — if he had any knowledge of that — I would like to bring it out. If he has not. . ."

The judge interrupted. "Why don't we take this one step at a time. Why don't we perhaps, if you don't mind, cross-examine on the purpose for which the doctor is here? And if the doctor *has* examined the girl, then he could perhaps be recalled again on that point. I would be interested in that myself, quite frankly, because that would assist me. But I don't think we should go at it necessarily now."

"Well," said Chambers, seeking to resolve the dispute, "if the answer is that he has no knowledge, that would be the end of it."

Groberman finally concurred. "Let's have the answer anyway, Doctor," the judge said.

"The answer, Your Honour, is that I haven't examined the victim."

"All right," said Groberman. "So much for that."

Chambers had made his point with a flourish, but resisted any gloating as he continued with his questions.

"Looking at your evidence here, or my notes of it," he asked the doctor, "I gather it is your opinion that the accused in this case is a person of better than average intelligence?"

"Yes, that is so."

"And you are not suggesting that he is in any way unfit to stand trial at this point?"

"No."

Chambers got the witness to agree that two other doctors had also found that Donald Hay exhibited no symptoms of mental incompetence.

"Have you seen the report of Dr. Joseph filed in this case from the Forensic Psychiatric Service?"

"I think I have, yes."

"This followed the thirty-day assessment at Riverview Clinic?"

"Yes."

"And this report, I take it that you agree with the reference that he does not suffer from any psychotic mental disorder?"

"Yes, I agree with that."

"Now, going back to my notes of your evidence, if I understand you correctly, the accused regards himself as a lonely failure, is that right?"

"They are your words. I don't think I used those words."

"Well, he has a low opinion of himself as a man, does he not?"

"That is correct."

"He has found — one of his complaints — is that he is not accepted by women, is that right?"

"That's the feeling that he's not accepted by women."

"That is a feeling that you find he has?"

"Indeed so."

"Yes. And that he has a fantasy of a perfect life?"

"He has incubated that fantasy for a long period."

"What in your opinion would eradicate that fantasy?"

"I think I have expressed in general terms a prolonged course of psychotherapy. I think it will be difficult to discuss that in great detail. I think it would require a very prolonged form of therapy. I think during the time that he was abstinent from alcohol, his sense of self-esteem in fact improved. I think it's a great shame that that treatment wasn't continued."

"During those periods that he has not been under treatment he has again returned to the excessive use of alcohol, has he not?"

"That is correct."

The prosecutor appeared to be struggling not to sound sarcastic as he continued. "Is it not so that he simply responds when someone else is dominating him and not when he is left on his own?"

"I don't think Dr. Witt dominated him," replied the witness. "I think she supervised his treatment program, and he cooperated with that treatment program fully. And I think if he were to be treated, that he would require that prolonged treatment and, if necessary, supervision for an extremely protracted period of time."

"If I understood you correctly, he desired to make his common-law wife's daughter captive, is that right?"

"Yes, he expressed that thought to me."

"And that the child who ultimately became his victim was a substitute for that other child?"

"Yes."

Again, the prosecutor was barely able to conceal his sarcasm as he phrased his next question. "Can you see any limitations to the number of substitutes that might appeal to him?"

"I think if he weren't treated, there would be a likelihood that he might relapse to that pattern of activity. I think in particular — if his sexual problems weren't dealt with — that that sense of inadequacy might propel him into similar kinds of situations. There is no doubt of that."

"To what extent do you have confidence that the treatment you advocate would eradicate the danger of this man treating another child in the same way?"

Dr. Eaves attempted an answer. "I have treated many sexual offenders, and I think I have successfully treated many sexual offenders to the point that, for example, people with pedophile tendencies have lost those tendencies and lost any fantasy that was associated with them. And people who were attracted, for example, to adolescent girls have been able to refocus on grown women and reformed adult and mature relationships with them."

"I take it that you are not in a position to guarantee that any treatment will necessarily eradicate this danger?"

"I think there is no guarantee in any individual case that you can eradicate that danger."

"Would you recommend castration as treatment here?"

If Hay was alarmed by this unexpected question, he didn't show it, but his lawyer jumped quickly to his feet. "Your Honour," Baxter protested, "I wonder if that question is relevant inasmuch as I don't believe it's possible even if it was going to assist? Unless my friend knows of a way of having that brought about."

"Yes," the judge concurred. "Perhaps you could establish the groundwork for that question, Mr. Chambers."

"Well," said the prosecutor, "is it fair to say doctor that basically this man has an abnormal sexual problem?"

"Yes," said the witness.

"And if he were rendered permanently impotent, what effect would that have on his problem?"

"Castration would not make him permanently impotent."

"It would not. I see."

Hay seemed impassive but twisted slightly in his seat as Eaves modified his answer. "It might," he added. "But there would be no guarantee."

"There would be no guarantee. All right. The thing that has struck me, doctor, in looking at this evidence is that it appears to me that the accused is unable to appreciate or care about the feelings of other persons with whom he comes into contact. Have you any comment?"

Eaves paused for a moment before giving a reply. "I think at times he's shown an extreme lack of concern for other people. I think at other times he's shown a great deal of remorse and guilt about his actions. And I think it was this guilt and remorse that motivated some of his suicide attempts."

"Well," said Chambers, "it would certainly be an awareness of guilt in his requests to the police to shoot him at the time he was captured, would it not?"

"I think that would be indicated."

Chambers asked the doctor about Hay's suicide attempts since his arrest. "On one of those occasions, is it not correct that he slashed himself on the inside of his elbow?"

"Yes, he did," said the doctor. "He made a deep laceration there and he severed his brachial artery. He almost bled to death and he had, I think, a transfusion of many pints of blood and plasma in order for him to recover."

Chambers, however, seemed skeptical — as though wondering whether the incident had in reality been a ploy for sympathy. "It seems to be common practice for the people who want to commit suicide to slash their wrists," he suggested. "Can you give me any explanation as to why this man would choose the elbow joint?"

"The artery is bigger there and you are more likely to bleed faster if you sever your artery at that point than if you cut your wrist. It's difficult to get at the arteries in your wrist anyway."

"An attempt to sever the major artery of the throat is usually a very painful process, is it not?"

"It is. And it usually doesn't work because the person puts their head back. As they put their head back it retracts their vessels so people attempting to slash their throat usually only cause superficial damage."

Chambers then asked the witness about reports that Hay had made another suicide attempt in prison around Christmas time. "I have read an article he had been taken to hospital and pumped out about that time. Was that one of the attempts you are referring to?"

"That's the only (other) attempt that I'm aware of, yes," confirmed the doctor.

"And actually there was no toxic substance found in him at that time, was there?"

"I don't know of the details of that particular episode. I did say that I was only acquainted with the first one personally."

Chambers seemed satisfied that he had made his point.

"Now, I understand, doctor — and correct me if I'm wrong — that you're of the opinion that punishment would not deter this man from future acts of this sort we are talking about here?"

"I think in general terms I would accept that view, yes."

"Can you enlarge on that?"

Judge Groberman concurred. "Yes, would you please, doctor?"

Eaves continued. "Because I think that punishment which is a huge threat has little effect on modifying people's behaviour. If punishment is given at the time that people perform miscreant actions, then I think punishment is likely to prevent people continuing that kind of behaviour.

"I'm using punishment in the technical sense at this point. And I think that, for example, one might invoke a therapeutic model which led him to understanding the consequences of his behaviour, and I think in that sense I believe that punishment would deter, but not punishment in the global sense of something held over his head, such as a life sentence. These things I don't think have any real meaning. Most people can't perceive what the meaning of that is."

Chambers could barely conceal yet another hint of contempt as he sought clarification. "Are you suggesting that a lesser term of imprisonment would deter him?"

"I'm saying that if he were not given a life sentence but were given a finite sentence, it might offer some motivation to be involved in the therapeutic process, and therefore, that that would offer him as an individual some hope for the future."

"Now, are you saying that with specific reference to this accused, or is that a generalization of anyone?"

"I would say that generally speaking, applied to anyone, but it specifically applies to him because he's had — and still has as far as I know — a total preoccupation with suicide. And I think he needs to be offered some motivation in order to be involved in a therapeutic process."

"Is this a fair way to put that, doctor: if you remove all hope of release, he has no incentive to take treatment. If you give him some hope of release by taking treatment, he does have an incentive to take treatment?"

"I think that would be true in general, yes. I have already said that this man has a great sense of personal hopelessness."

On that note, Chambers apparently felt he had done enough. "I have no further questions," said the prosecutor. Hay had listened impassively throughout. On the bench, Judge Groberman directed his attention to the accused man's lawyer. "Re-examination?" he inquired.

"I have no re-examination, Your Honour," said Baxter.

"I have a question or two myself," said Groberman, turning to address the doctor. "At the present stage of his mental health," the judge asked, "is he (Hay) dangerous to the public right now?"

Eaves phrased his reply carefully. "I haven't examined Mr. Hay for some time, Your Honour. I'd think he's more likely at the moment to be a danger to himself than a danger to others, but I couldn't reply that there was a danger to others."

"Well," Judge Groberman continued politely, "considering what he stands charged with and what he has done, if he did not receive treatment, would you say that he would perhaps go out and do the same thing again?"

Eaves seemed persuaded to agree. "I think there would be an increased likelihood that he would do, yes. Not perhaps in the immediate future, but certainly in the more distant future."

"You mean," said Groberman, "sort of whenever certain

236 — John Griffiths

things reach a type of atmosphere? Something is liable to trigger this again? When certain things, say, are right or wrong? Depending on his environment at the time, and how he feels and how he's compelled at the time?"

"I think that's right, depending on the external circumstances of his life. For example, if he weren't treated for his sexual dysfunction, that would propel him into that kind of situation. It might propel him into the use of alcohol again, and that might diminish his inhibitions."

"Of course," the judge continued, "as has been pointed out, there was a successful treatment given to him for alcohol, but then he fell back?"

"That is so," said Eaves. "...The treatment at that time concentrated on his alcoholism. I don't think there was a full appreciation of the severity of all his problems at that time. And I think there is a fuller appreciation at this point."

Patient and thorough, Judge Groberman seemed eager to clarify the medical evidence before him. "You say that he has a schizoid personality now?" he asked.

"Yes."

"If he were a member of society now, that would not be sufficient to have him confined to a mental institution, would it?"

"No, it would not. Schizoid personalities are predisposed, I suppose, to developing schizophrenic illnesses, but there is no evidence that he has ever gone beyond that stage."

"Now, looking at the situation as it now stands — with his being in what you have described as a depressive state — would that not make him less inclined to accept therapy?"

"I have discussed therapy with Mr. Hay. He has expressed some interest to be involved in treatment at the Regional Psychiatric Centre."

"You say he's expressed an interest?"

"Yes, I think he sees this as the only chance that he has to lead anything like a meaningful life in even the distant future."

"There are two things, then. One is to get him to cooperate

because doctors can do him no good unless he wants help, isn't that correct?"

"I think that's true."

"There is that problem to overcome?"

"Yes. I have seen nothing about Mr. Hay to suggest that he wouldn't cooperate with any therapy."

"Except that he's made two suicide attempts. You say that…"

"I think this is because he's preoccupied with the current hopelessness of the situation."

"Well, let's put it this way: how long has he, to your opinion, suffered from this schizoid personality?"

"It's been more or less lifelong I think."

The judge then asked whether antisocial behaviour resulting from such a personality could be expected to change in a man who was now forty-three years old, and who had relapsed despite treatment in the past. "What is the prognosis?" he asked. "Having pleaded guilty to an horrendous crime, wouldn't you tend to think that his chances of recovery, even if he were to cooperate, are really quite slim?"

The witness seemed to agree. "I don't think one could be overly optimistic about his chances," said Eaves.

"Well, call it the way you see it, doctor. Give me your prognosis."

"I would say there was a fifty-fifty chance… after a course of treatment… that he wouldn't get into further trouble again of this nature."

"It would have to accomplish a tremendous amount of psychotherapy, wouldn't it?"

"Oh, I think so, yes."

"It would have to involve an entire personality change — that is, a personality different than what this man has demonstrated his entire life?"

"Yes. I think I have seen this occur."

"With men his age?"

"Yes, with men his age. Many of the dangerous sexual offenders who are confined, I think, have made substantial changes in their social skills. Many of these people have consistently avoided medical treatment, and I think that can substantially shift them around. I think it's very difficult to put figures on it."

"No, I can appreciate that. But I'm just asking you to make your best calculated professional guess. Will he accept treatment — and if he will — then you think there is a fifty-fifty chance that his antisocial behaviour will be cured but it will take a long time?"

"Yes, I think that's a fair assessment of it."

"I want your assessment. If you disagree with me — "

"No, I agree with that. I think that's essentially what I have said."

Judge Groberman turned to the lawyers. "Anything arising out of my questions?"

"Nothing," said Baxter. "Thank you."

"No, Your Honour," said Chambers.

After being on the witness stand for several hours, the doctor was now excused. He had been afforded every opportunity to speak in Hay's defence but it was impossible to gauge whether Judge Groberman had been swayed by his testimony. It had been a long day but the judge still had to hear final arguments from both the prosecution and the defence.

30 SUMMING UP

DONALD HAY showed no sign of emotion as he sat in the prisoner's box listening to the arguments swirling around him. After hearing the extent of his crimes, some of those in the audience were muttering that they would have liked to have leapt at his throat — but the proceedings continued without incident.

As usual, Kenneth Baxter was well-prepared, quiet yet forceful, as he presented each of his concluding arguments. Immediately he sought to dispel suggestions that Hay might have left his victim to perish if he had killed himself.

"Your Honour," he began, "I have no basic quarrel with the facts as set out by my learned friend... with one exception. My friend indicated that the defendant, on the day that he was captured, told his wife that he was going out to the garage to commit suicide. My instructions are that that is not correct. He didn't tell anybody... that he intended to commit suicide at that time.

"I suspect that his wife became suspicious when he disappeared in a bad mood and in a state of alcoholic fog — that she suspected that he might be up to that.

"During the times that Abby was in the cell, the defendant made two suicide attempts..... At one point he went away and left her for some days while he was in the hospital.

"After some period of time that he had Abby in the cell, his sexual fantasy was not working the way he had planned it. He didn't overcome his impotency. The fantasy world that he had created in his mind before this offence took place just did not develop.

"So, he was left in a dilemma in his own mind as to what to do. He thought he couldn't let her go. He didn't think he could convince her that she could tell her mother that she had been off to Calgary for two months.

"That obviously wasn't going to work. He was unwilling,

incapable and undesirous of doing the obvious thing that many other persons might have done which would be to kill her at that point. He wasn't going to do that.

"Instead, what he did was he wrote a note. He left it in his workshop, and the note was addressed to whoever came in to see it that Abby was being hidden in the place in which the pictures describe.

"He left this note. He went into his home. He took an overdose of drugs believing that his wife would be at work for several hours and the children away, confident that he would indeed die, that the note would be found and that she would be released.

"It was ironic that the medication that he consumed in large quantities was medication that had been prescribed by Dr. Witt that he had left over from his treatment program. I don't know what that medication was. But what happened was, his wife came home unexpectedly, apparently, found him there in this state, presumably called an ambulance. At any rate, he was taken to the Royal Columbian Hospital. And I understand he was there about ten days recovering. His suicide attempt at that time was close, I understand, to being successful.

"There is a particular irony in that act…. No one found the note that he left in his garage during the ten days that he was away. Whether or not anybody had gone in there… and hadn't seen it, I can't inform the court as to that.

"So, he recovers. Approximately two months later he's still facing the same dilemma, what to do, so he decides to do this again — only this time he makes the note more obvious. It's put in an extremely obvious place inside the door of his workshop.

"He goes downtown. He's got $100 and he goes to an area of Vancouver — I believe it was on Granville Street — and attempts to purchase drugs.

"Now, Donald Hay was not a drug user. He wasn't a heroin addict. As I understand it, he never had any particular drug problem. So, he didn't know very much about drugs, but he found somebody that was willing to sell him drugs.

"He inquired as to how many pills he'd have to take to get high and how many were safe to take.... He paid $100 for quantities of pills. He was told that... if he took ten percent of the lot that he would get extremely high. Any more than that, it was going to be dangerous.

"Donald Hay goes to the Blackstone Hotel, rents a room, gets a bottle, takes the pills. A day and a half later he wakes up with a great thumping headache. That's all.

"So, he goes back. He's still got the same problem. My instructions are that on the day that he was captured ... that he had indeed planned to let Abby go, that he went down to her.

"He was waiting for his family to go out — which he believed they were going to do.... He was going to get clothing from his daughter, tie her (Abby) up inside the garage, but in a position where she could eventually secure her release by making a noise or whatever.

"In the meantime, he'd allow himself a little headstart. In one of the statements, he indicated that he told the authorities that he planned to drive as far as he could go for $100. My instructions are that his actual plan was again to attempt an immediate suicide.... When he was caught, he did again ask the police to do away with him.

"So, this young girl, Abby, was taken down into this terrible place because of a fantasy on his part and a sexual dysfunction. The fantasy disappeared for him. There was no fantasy about it for her, certainly. It disappeared for him, and he was left in a dilemma....

"I think it's important that his solution to that dilemma was in fact not an attempt to do away with her, but an attempt to do away with himself and thereby save her."

Several spectators in the courtroom exchanged looks of cynicism, but the lawyer continued to portray his client as a suicidal man deserving of some sympathy.

"Now, Dr. Eaves has given his expert opinion dealing with all of these matters.... It's my submission that at least part of the motivation behind these (attempted) suicides was a self-loathing for the deeds and the offence that he had committed against Abby.

"Certainly it wasn't a matter of him being insane. It was a matter of him having this terrible impulse to do this terrible thing for which there was a loathing.

"He's not a psychopath. He's not a person who said, 'I did it, and I don't give a damn.' This man will be amenable to treatment and has in the past.

"I think it's important he had ample opportunity, 181 days, to kill Abby, but chose instead, and attempted on three occasions, to kill himself and inform others as to where Abby was."

Baxter went on to remind the court that Hay had confessed and pled guilty to the crime. Having done his best to put forward as many mitigating circumstances as possible on behalf of his client, the defence attorney now sought to minimize the damage that Hay had done to his victim; and not a murmur could be heard from the spectators as he discussed the question that remained on everyone's mind.

"I have never met Abby Drover," said Baxter. "I do understand from the little information I have that her recovery back into a normal life of a girl her age has been quite remarkable, very fortunately so. She must be a lady of tremendous strength and courage. But from what I understand she's not left with any particular problem that she can't overcome and hasn't mastered."

Several spectators in the public gallery shook their heads in disbelief, but sat quietly as Hay's lawyer began to address the key issue. "In regard to the principles of sentencing," Baxter said, "the court, of course, must take into consideration all factors touching the case and impose a sentence tailored to the particular circumstances before it.

"I agree with my friend firstly that this is a serious case. And I certainly agree that the two most important factors in sentencing in serious cases are the factors of deterrence and the protection of the public." But although developments such as the breathalyzer might deter drinking drivers, said Baxter, deterrence would not be a factor against crimes such as that committed by his client.

"It doesn't work, and it wouldn't have worked to deter Donald Hay from committing the offences that he committed. He committed these offences because he had a fantasy. He had a sexual dysfunction coupled with an alcohol problem that resulted in his actions.

"We have had the expert evidence of Dr. Eaves that no deterrent would have had any effect on whether he committed the actions he did or not. His motivations were removed from his rational being when he committed the initial act.

"So, a severe sentence in this case is not going to deter him from doing it again… and it is my submission it would not deter anyone of a like mind — if there is anybody out there with a like mind to do what Donald Hay has done — a like mind being a person with a sexual disorder that results in a fantasy that is devoid of rationale.

"You cannot deter that kind of a person. You might deter a shoplifter. You might deter anybody doing an act because of a profit motive, but in cases of this nature, it's not a rational process: 'I do this and I receive that.' They are driven. He was driven. And anybody with a like mind would be driven as well. So deterrence is just not a factor, in my submission, that is appropriate in this kind of a case, because it simply won't work.

"Protection for the public: I agree with my friend that that is perhaps the most important consideration in serious cases, and in this one too. My friend asks for a life sentence. It is my submission that a life sentence is not the best protection for the public against further possible actions from Donald Hay. And I say this because Donald Hay will eventually be released no matter what sentence this court imposes.

"The question, then, in my submission, is what sentence is likely to result in him — when he leaves — being safe for the public or what sentence increases the possibility or the probability of the public being safe?

244 — John Griffiths

"Fortunately, we have expert evidence from Dr. Eaves as to what steps can be taken. There are programs to cure Donald Hay. Those have been outlined generally by Dr. Eaves.

"Dr. Eaves gives evidence that if he doesn't receive the kind of treatment that is available, there will be no cure for Donald Hay.... . He could quite possibly be a worse menace to the public when he's released — and he will be eventually."

Finally, Baxter was ready to play his hand. "I suggest to this court that a sentence in the neighbourhood of eight years is appropriate in this case as it would allow for Donald Hay's successful treatment and also allow the authorities ample scope to evaluate his treatment before his release."

Prison officials, said the lawyer, were prepared to speed up their normal two-week evaluation processes. "They might be able to get it down to one day in order that Donald Hay commence immediate treatment for his problems. Thank you, Your Honour. That's my submission."

As HE STOOD to refute the defence's arguments, Stewart Chambers reflected the skepticism of those in the gallery — who continued shaking their heads and whispering among themselves.

"Now, I don't know what makes my friend so sure that everybody that goes to prison is going to get out no matter what sentence the court imposes," said the prosecutor. "I would think that in this case the chances of parole would be extremely slim."

Chambers referred to Dr. Eaves' testimony about Hay's chances for rehabilitation. "I think, Your Honour, that the public is entitled to better odds than that — that we cannot take a fifty-fifty chance that this offence may be repeated....

"I am interested in this expression of the accused being filled with self-loathing. It calls to mind the expression of Winston Churchill about Clement Attlee being a modest man with a great deal to be modest about. I would think that this man has a great deal to loathe himself about.

"My friend has added one point which I find even more horrible than before. He says the accused made two suicide attempts while the child was confined in that cellar. He left a note somewhere in the upper part of that garage so somebody could find her if he happened to die.

"He was hospitalized, according to my friend, for some ten days when that attempt failed. He must have known that that child had not been found or there would have been police down there standing guard over him. He continued during that period to leave that child there, where she could well have died, had his suicide attempt been successful. And it appears that he then went back and continued to use that child sexually.

"I don't think there is a concern for the survival of the child. I think there was a concern of her *still being available* to him when he found that he was going to get back out of hospital."

On that note, Chambers concluded what seemed to be a very brief submission.

"I want some time to consider this," said the judge, as he adjourned the proceedings. "We'll make it February 3 at 1:30 p.m. for sentence. Thank you."

31   SENTENCE

IT WOULD BE over two weeks before Donald Hay would reappear in court to learn his fate, but the Drover family was hardly aware of what was going on. Having been advised not to attend the proceedings, Ruth Drover focussed a day at a time on the slow and painful attempts to assist in her youngest daughter's recovery.

Again, they stayed away from the proceedings on February 3, 1977, when Donald Hay was brought back before Judge Groberman as scheduled. Outside the stark concrete court building, the chill in the mid-winter air reached deep into the bones of Constable Wayne Smith and Corporal Archie Connell as they arrived to learn of the kidnapper's fate.

Several uniformed police officers were also present to assist sheriffs, who thoroughly searched all members of the public entering the courtroom amid tight security.

For me, after ten years, it was my last week as a reporter at the *Province*, yet like everyone else in the courtroom, I was acutely aware of the tension.

In the prisoner's box, Hay sat ashen faced as Judge Groberman entered and took his place on the bench.

Dispassionately, Groberman began with a review of the proceedings. "On November 25, 1976," he began, "the accused elected to be tried by this court and pleaded guilty to one count of kidnapping and one count of having sexual intercourse with a female person, not his wife, under the age of fourteen years...."

As Groberman went on to recap the details of the crime, it seemed he was imbued with the same outrage as that felt by the spectators; but his calm recital of the child's ordeal kept everyone guessing. The judge's reiteration of the crimes committed against Abby Drover seemed to take an unbearably long time as everyone waited to hear what Donald Hay's fate would be.

"It is difficult to appreciate the suffering experienced by

the child at the hands of the accused. A lesser person may not have survived.

"She was physically and mentally punished for 181 straight days and in constant fear of death. The suffering of her family must have been immense."

Groberman paused for a moment to keep his composure as he read out the note that Abby had concealed in her boot while contemplating her own death.

Putting the note aside, he maintained his calm, professional demeanour as he went on to interpret the psychiatric evidence. He agreed with Baxter that the prosecution's assertion that Hay was a psychopath had been shaky; the author of that statement had never been identified or called as a witness. But Groberman, after all, had not been moved by the testimony of Dr. Eaves — psychiatric expert for the defence.

"The doctor believes the accused could respond to treatment which is available at the Regional Psychiatric Centre and be cured, but such would involve extended treatment for several years — perhaps six, seven to ten years.

"In other words, the length of the treatment required is not known. If there is no treatment, then there is no hope for recovery, according to Dr. Eaves.

"The doctor said that the accused responded to treatment before. It is to be noted that after sixteen sober months the accused fell back to alcoholism, so the treatment worked on a temporary basis. The doctor's prognosis for recovery is a fifty-fifty chance with no guarantees.

"Before plea, the accused was examined with regard to his fitness to stand trial. Two psychiatric reports were filed and both reports concluded that the accused is not incapable of appreciating the nature and quality of his acts or knowing that an act is wrong."

The judge referred to Dr. G.H. Stephenson's assessment that Hay had a severe personality disorder characterized by obsessive sexual preoccupation. At last, it seemed, Groberman was ready to speak his mind on the evidence before him.

"I cannot help but feel that the prognosis of Dr. Eaves is overly optimistic," said the judge. "The accused is forty-three. He has suffered from a schizoid personality all his life. He is an alcoholic, a sexual deviate and a chronic depressive, to mention only a few of his serious emotional symptoms... .

"There is no doubt in my mind that the accused in his present condition represents a real danger to the public. He is a very sick man with tremendous emotional problems and requires many years of psychiatric treatment that may or may not be successful.

"I am skeptical. I cannot accept that there is a fifty-fifty chance for a complete recovery of the accused.... I must conclude that his chances for a complete recovery are slim.

"The defence says that the accused tried suicide twice while the victim was being held prisoner. He left a note in his workshop that no one found. The workshop is cluttered, to say the least, and unless someone was looking for something, it is not surprising that the note was not found, if indeed there was a note.

"The defence submitted that on the day of his capture he intended to let [Abby] go and again attempt suicide. I do not believe that he was going to let her go."

Among the police contingent in the courtroom, there was palpable relief as the judge continued.

"Defence counsel submits that the accused has shown remorse and has admitted his guilt. This will be considered. He also points out that he did not kill his victim. Why should he? That's not what she was there for.

"Guidelines for sentencing have been set down in many cases by the British Columbia Court of Appeal. I must consider firstly the safety and protection of the public; secondly, the deterrent effect of sentence; thirdly, punishment of the offender; and fourthly, reformation and rehabilitation of the offender.

"It is obvious that the paramount consideration in this case is the protection of the public. I am dealing with a crime of exceptional gravity committed by an emotionally disturbed, forty-three-year-old man who at present represents a serious danger to the public, who requires years of psychiatric treatment with only some possibility for recovery and who has a criminal record of some significance.

"The six convictions span twenty-three years with one offence of attempted rape for which the accused was sentenced to two years' imprisonment."

Groberman cited other cases he had reviewed in pondering an appropriate sentence, one of them involving the "vicious rape" of a fourteen-year-old by a twenty-six-year-old man with no previous record. A doctor in that case also had testified that the rapist might respond to psychotherapy — but the man had still received a life sentence.

"I have considered the possibility of the rehabilitation of the accused and the possible effects that a life sentence may have upon him, but it is my opinion that the public should receive all the protection possible under the law."

"Having taken all the principles of sentencing into account," said the judge, "I conclude that the protection of the public far outweighs any other consideration and that it is appropriate in this case to impose a maximum sentence. Stand up, please, Mr. Hay."

Appearing resigned to his fate, Hay braced himself against the prisoner's dock. Still expressionless, he rose slowly to his feet to hear Groberman's judgment.

"On count one, the kidnapping charge, I sentence you to imprisonment for life with a recommendation that you be transferred to the appropriate facility for psychiatric treatment which, I believe, is the Regional Psychiatric Centre at Matsqui.

"On count three, which was the sexual intercourse with a female under fourteen years old charge, I sentence you to imprisonment for a term of eight years concurrent. That concludes the sentence of this Court."

With great relief for Constable Smith and Corporal Connell, it was finally over. As they prepared to leave, however, Stewart Chambers rose once more to make a concluding remark.

"If our Honour would allow me one minute before leaving this distressing case, I think that we must take note that my friend (Kenneth Baxter) has under very difficult circumstances taken on a case which many lawyers might not, and has followed the highest traditions of the defence bar, and I can see nothing that he could have done more for this man than he has done."

"Yes," said Groberman. "I entirely agree, Mr. Chambers. Will the clerk please adjourn court."

As soon as the despondent Donald Hay was led from the courtroom, reporters gathered in the hallway outside to get his lawyer's opinion. Surrounded by newsmen, Baxter said he considered the outcome "unsatisfactory", even though he believed his client would still be eligible for parole within ten years. Tenacious as ever, Baxter added he would be contacting his client with a view to appealing the life sentence.

"We're not exactly having a party here," he said.

32 AFTERMATH

WITHIN DAYS OF Hay's conviction, I quit journalism and had no further involvement in the story until two decades later, when I learned how the intervening years had continued to take their toll on both the kidnapper and his victims.

Indeed, it turned out there had been more than one victim.

For the Drover family, the initial relief that Hay was to spend the rest of his life in prison was tempered by press confirmation through the National Parole Board that the kidnapper technically would be eligible for release after only seven years.

Adding to the family's concern was the fact that Hay's lawyer, true to his word, was indeed seeking to have the sentence overturned by the British Columbia Court of Appeal.

According to Kenneth Baxter, the trial judge had erred in concluding that a life sentence was the best way of ensuring public safety, when the psychiatric evidence had shown that the culprit could in fact be rehabilitated. Documents filed with the Court of Appeal also contended that Groberman had no basis for having concluded that the victim might never recover fully from her ordeal.

The family would have to wait another three months to learn if the appeal would be successful. In the meantime, Abby resolved to enjoy her freedom even though she was in fact receiving no professional therapy.

"I still managed to laugh," she told me later. "That was probably the key if I was going to recover. I didn't carry all the anger around with me or else I would have gone crazy. I tried to deal with it as part of life. It happened. There was nothing I could do to change the fact that it happened, but in some ways I'm still in my prison, I'm still serving a life sentence."

For weeks, Abby had to avoid many foods and follow a diet rich in calcium and iron. She found it difficult to sleep on her right side, sore from six months of lying on a damp mattress.

It was quite likely, she learned, that the damage would be permanent and that she might eventually need hip replacement surgery.

Proving her loyalty, Abby remained close friends with each of the Hay children, whose stepfather's appeal finally made it to court.

Just before the children recessed for their summer holidays, the British Columbia Court of Appeal handed down a decision completely dismissing all of Hay's machinations. "He should never be released from prison," said an outraged Chief Justice J.L. Farris. "I am *not* concerned about this man at all. I'm concerned about this girl and the protection of the public."

Farris paid short shrift to the notion that Hay might be amenable to treatment, dismissing any suggestions that the accused should be shown some kind of sympathy.

"I cannot imagine a more horrible crime, and it was not an isolated case. I do not care what a psychiatrist says now all this time later. This man has engaged in deviant practices for twenty years."

Finally, sighed Abby's mother, the courts had put an end to the legal mumbo-jumbo. But she had reached another important decision as well. The house on Gore Street, as far as she was concerned, would be forever haunted. The memories were too unbearable. As soon as school was out, she resolved, the property would go up for sale and the family would move to Kelowna — a sunny lakeside resort some 250 miles east of Vancouver in the Okanagan Valley.

It would be a fresh start. Encouraged by her real estate agent, Ruth had passed a four-month correspondence course and was set to embark on a new career in real estate. In Kelowna, Ruth met with the principal of Abby's new high school and urged him to protect the child's anonymity so that her daughter might resume as normal a life as possible. Once she started school, they agreed, she would be known as Becky.

While her mother was out showing houses, Abby pitched in with the housework. Outside, she tended the yard and relished having her own vegetable garden. The relationship between mother and daughter, however, often flared into disagreements as the maturing teenager experimented with ever increasing amounts of makeup and with what Ruth perceived to be unduly immodest fashions.

Ruth and her daughter had never really been able to speak to each other about the horrors that Abby had suffered. Arguments typical of mother-daughter relationships were much more exaggerated and frequent than might otherwise have been the case.

ABBY WOULD NEVER have admitted it at the time but a frightening encounter with a stranger perhaps indicated that her mother's concerns were not without justification.

It began late one night when Abby stormed away from a date in Kelowna after getting into a row with her boyfriend. Pacing the sidewalk with tears in her eyes, the girl was walking home alone when a young man in a blue pickup truck pulled up alongside offering her a ride. Soon after accepting, she became concerned as the driver headed farther and farther out of town.

"Where are we going?" asked Abby. "We should have turned the other way at the last traffic lights."

Ignoring her question, the driver pulled off the road into a darkened area. "We can do it right here," he growled.

Backing away in the front seat of the truck, Abby took off one of her spiked heel shoes and held it menacingly between them. She had already been a victim and had no intention of being so again.

"That won't do you any good," the driver leered, removing his greasy baseball cap. "We're gonna have sex."

"Come any closer and I'll beat you about the face and head with this!" warned Abby, eyes aflame with anger.

"You can't fight me," said the man, but Abby heard a waver in his voice as he hesitated.

"I'll die trying," she said.

Something about her tone caused the driver to back away. He restarted his truck and dropped her off in an isolated area.

Stumbling back into town, Abby reported the incident to the local police and was not surprised to learn that the driver fit the description of a man suspected of having raped several local girls over the past few months.

She later learned there had been no similar complaints after hers, and hoped the fact that she had stood her ground might have made a difference. If *all* women could be so assertive, she thought, perhaps there might be fewer victims.

THE REAL ESTATE market eventually soured and, with little money coming in, Ruth found herself forced to take employment as a home care worker back on the coast. Abby announced she would stay in Kelowna to share an apartment with her oldest sister.

"If you want to come home, you know where to find me," said Ruth.

Abby, however, managed to make ends meet by working part time in a pizza parlour after school. Local boys often asked the pretty young waitress for a date, but Abby inevitably found herself uninterested in young men her own age. Although she realized this obviously stemmed from her own loss of innocence, she couldn't help the fact that she found them too immature for her.

Soon she found herself attracted to a local scuba-diving instructor almost twenty years her senior. Moving in with him, Abby told her sister that he treated her well, but soon realized she was not yet ready to settle down. Instead, she would accept her mother's standing invitation to move back to the coast and finish Grade 12.

Shortly afterwards, while Ruth was at work, Abby answered a telephone call from a man with a vaguely familiar voice. "Is Ruth there?" he asked.

"Who's calling?" asked the girl.

"This must be Abby," said the man. "It's Cecil, your father."

Taken by surprise, Abby felt her father had shown too little interest in her since her rescue, and gave a typically quick-tempered response. "I don't have a father," she retorted.

Cecil, who was visiting from Calgary, did his best to ignore the rebuff. He called on Ruth and his daughter that evening with heaping cartons of food from a local Chinese restaurant.

It was the first time that Abby could ever recall having sat down to dinner with both of her parents.

Cecil was making an effort but, sadly, Abby still felt no closer than before. Not only that, other developments were also about to cause seemingly irreconcilable differences with her mother.

MEANWHILE, INCARCERATED with other sex offenders, Donald Hay had begun serving his life sentence at the Matsqui Regional Psychiatric Centre, which afforded him not only protection from the general prison population but also access to programs ostensibly offering treatment.

Ever since his arrest, Hay had found himself ostracized and alone, reluctantly accepting the fact that Hilda and her children would have nothing to do with him.

"I didn't have visits, phone calls, letters or anything," he later recalled. "I thought that was okay because this is my life now and I didn't need any outside contacts. After what I'd done, I didn't think anybody would want to see me."

Hay at first expressed shock over the "heinous" sex crimes of some of his fellow inmates. "It boggles my mind — some guys, their fantasies and what they've done," he told outsiders. "I don't fit in this category." It wasn't until he dried out from alcoholism, he added, that he finally admitted he did belong in the program after all.

In jail, Hay bemoaned that he had never felt loved as a child, but then claimed that he had no recollections of growing up until he was ten, eleven or twelve, and only little bits and pieces at that. "Nothing pertinent, nothing special — other than my dog or first bike — and a lot of it I remember from pictures I saw, and albums, and I said, 'Well, this is me, what am I doing and who am I with?' Like a picture with my Grade 2 schoolteacher…"

Had something awful happened in those first ten years that he had repressed?

"No," Hay insisted. "There was no physical abuse, no sexual abuse. I didn't run away when I was twelve and I wasn't beaten."

He complained, however, that he felt he had been raised without any expressions of love. "Unless you're shown love, you can't learn how to love," he postulated. "I compared my home to a boarding house. Like there was no interaction between mother, father, children.

"I found out recently that I was probably an illegitimate son. My father probably wasn't my father. I can understand that — and maybe that's why we were always so distant from each other — and I can live with that. It's not a problem any more."

No, he insisted, his problems stemmed not from childhood but from his heavy use of alcohol, which he attributed to the peculiarities of his employment in railroading, mining and construction.

"It's through the alcohol, my lifestyle as a loner. I never felt I really fit in on my jobs. Like railroading — there you had two choices when you got to the end of the line, either gambling or drinking. I'm a lousy gambler so I drank."

This caused him to have a "low self-image" and to begin lying about his past, such as not telling his second wife about his first wife. "I lived my whole life as a lie. I didn't know how to tell the truth."

Shortly before the kidnapping, he said, his doctor told him he was developing cirrhosis of the liver and had only six months to live, which caused him to fantasize about escaping to a cabin by a lake. "In my drunken stupor, I just couldn't face life. I'd go to this cabin all alone and eventually a young girl was with me."

It wasn't until he came out of his alcoholic fog, he claimed, that he realized the psychological damage he had caused to his victim. Hay continued to insist, however, that he had built the cell under his garage as a bomb shelter and not as a dungeon.

"It was something I always had in my mind," he said. "Back

in the 1940s and 1950s, they were talking about atomic bombs and everyone should have a bomb shelter… even during Vietnam and those years when they were talking about bomb shelters and invasions and all the rest of it… . I never told my family or anybody. I felt a little stupid, self-conscious — about, you know, people don't build them anymore — but I figured, 'Well, I'm building my shop… . I've got the material.' "

At first, he said, the dugout had been intended as a pit for working under his truck, but the cavity had filled with water because his property was on the side of a mountain. "So then this bomb shelter comes to mind and I said, 'Oh well, why not? You've always wanted one and you've got the summer to do it' — so I did it. It was stupid, and nobody believes me to this day.

"The chains on the wall were there to roll up blankets or sheets instead of a shelf, which you'd bang your head on. If they weren't in use, well you could just hang them up."

No one asked Hay the next logical question — whether the handcuffs were towel holders — and he sidestepped his earlier admissions that he had originally planned the "bomb shelter" as a prison for his own stepdaughter.

The prison psychiatrist also noticed that Hay minimized his previous record of sexual assault. Questioned about his 1958 attempted rape conviction in Manitoba, Hay vociferously argued that he had only been guilty of what he preferred to term as an attempted seduction.

"There were three of us," he said. "My brother was going into the army… this other young fellow (Scott Williamson) was going into the navy… my brother was going to Germany so we were going to have a going away party and they wanted to pick up these three girls."

After taking two of the girls home, he said, the rest of them drank more beer "and one thing led to another." The girl's parents, he said, were angry because she was two hours late, and she and her family accused him of attacking her.

"Williamson was with the girl originally. He had a fight with her and got in the front seat, so my young brother got back there. He got up in the front seat, then I got back there and he (Williamson) said it was our doing. Well, I guess it was in a sense because we got back there — so they found us guilty anyway."

Hay said his brother was just one of the many people who had cut him off since the Abby Drover kidnapping. "He's got about as much use for me now as I expected."

Despite being cut off from friends and family, however, Hay told prison officials that being sent to jail had saved his life. "It was a godsend. I would have been dead within a year. In fact I'm surprised that I haven't had any problems with my body because of what I did when I was drinking."

Hay now wanted to live after all, and to make the most of his treatment. "I'll jump through the hoops and do whatever people feel is necessary," he said. His life sentence, he believed, had only been imposed as a precaution — and he might be ready for release in seven years if he could prove that his treatment was working.

"The treatment works whether you have one fantasy or twenty fantasies," he said later. "I used to spend many, many sleepless nights. The only way you can eliminate them is not to allow them to come in. You have to fight them. When you lay down at night, naturally the first thing that wants to come in is your fantasy. That's when you have to try to think of something else — or get to sleep or get up. I'd get up and have coffee and have a cigarette Lots of nights, I never got any sleep but eventually it's gone, and you can't allow it to ever come back."

Believing now that he might have some kind of future, Hay was encouraged when he finally received a visit from one of his old neighbours on Gore Street, Leo Morin.

Both Morin and his wife Lois felt many of their former neighbour's problems resulted from alcohol. If Donald responded to treatment, and eventually got out of prison and stayed sober, they might be able to offer him a job and a place to stay.

33 NEW BEGINNINGS

THE WORLD OUTSIDE the prison walls turned out to be not quite as safe a place for several of the people involved in the kidnapping story.

In Port Moody, the stress of police work led to a marriage breakup for Constable Wayne Smith, who was also devastated by the suicide of one of his own three children. He eventually remarried and consoled himself with "the reality that life has to go on".

Investigating another disturbance, his former colleague Paul Adams (who had transferred to the Vancouver police) was shot at through a rooming-house door. Although he was struck in the face by splinters of wood, he somehow managed to avoid the bullet itself.

Norm Patterson, who had quit politics, also had a brush with death, only narrowly escaping a hotel fire that claimed eighty-five lives while he was attending a 1980 convention at the MGM Grand casino in Las Vegas.

Meanwhile, that same day, I walked away from a near-fatal car crash with merely a broken hand, unaware until years later that Ruth Drover had also only just recovered from serious injuries in yet another vehicle collision.

Ruth, in fact, had survived so much devastation that perhaps she should have been better prepared for the revelations with which her youngest daughter confronted her now, in June 1981. She was, however, an old-fashioned mother, not easily diverted from her strict Christian background.

The truth surfaced one evening while Ruth prepared dinner. As she glanced out the kitchen window, she noticed that eighteen-year-old Abby had suddenly stopped mowing the lawn and appeared to be doubled over in pain.

Ruth slammed down her cooking utensils and rushed outside. "What's the matter?" she said, filled with panic as she approached her daughter.

Abby, clutching her midriff, struggled to reply. She had been playing basketball at school, she told her mother. One of the boys had thrown the ball, hitting her in the stomach.

"I guess it's time I told you the truth," she added, the colour draining from her face. "I'm pregnant."

"What!" Ruth shrieked. "What on earth is going on? I didn't bring you up for this. Who's the father?"

Abby admitted that it had been the scuba-diving teacher. She insisted she would keep the baby, whether or not she got support from the father.

At that moment, Ruth Drover's expression might have been enough to strike fear into the heart of just about anyone — with the possible exception of her own youngest daughter. With her pregnancy in its third month, Abby was steadfastly opposed to an abortion and Ruth's own convictions prevented her from making strong arguments to the contrary.

Nonetheless, for Ruth, single parenthood was an embarrassment that would bring shame upon the family. "If you don't leave town," she said, "I am leaving the country."

Dinner, under the circumstances, was off. Amid much yelling, Abby hurled the fewest of necessities into an overnight bag and walked almost two miles to the home of a girlfriend in Maple Ridge.

Borrowing $27.50 from her friend's parents, Abby boarded a bus to Kelowna where once again she could move back in with her oldest sister. After a few weeks, however, she wanted to be even more independent, and slept one night on a park bench. "I was still angry at my Mom and wouldn't speak to her," Abby told me later.

Finally, she moved in with "very understanding" foster parents named Ron and Pauline Irvine, who had cared for dozens of other unwed mothers and even gave her a key to their house. They, too, however, were about to move back to the coast and they offered Abby the chance to return with them.

The Irvines convinced the teenager to reconcile with her

mother, and a proud and forgiving Ruth was present at Maple Ridge Hospital on November 30, 1981, for the birth of her first grandchild. "The day my son was born," Abby said later, "was the happiest day of my life."

Always concerned for the welfare of others, Abby was distraught not long afterwards as her foster mother Pauline Irvine lay dying of cancer. "I took turns at her bedside and was with her when she died," Abby sobbed. "Her husband couldn't bear to be there. They were the kindest, most wonderful people in the world."

Abby was still on good terms with her former boyfriend and was able to obtain financial support for their newborn son. It was not enough, however, for them to live on, and Abby took a job as a cocktail waitress at a local cabaret, where she met a recently divorced glazier named Gerry.

Gerry had invested some money in the nightclub where she worked and sat there most nights quietly gazing into the mirror behind the bar. Late at night, he seemed to have time on his hands as he became accustomed to being single again after five years of marriage.

With four children of his own, Gerry had financial obligations, and Abby found him a "really poor tipper". There was something about him, however, that she did like. Thirteen years older than Abby, he had an easy, friendly air and was not at all pushy.

Nonetheless, at first Abby gave him the wrong telephone number and it wasn't until eight months later that she agreed to go out with him on their first date. Gerry, she noticed, immediately made her feel at ease as they sat enjoying a Japanese dinner. "You're the first man I've met who I feel I can really trust," she told him as she got into his car afterwards.

With trepidation, Abby finally informed Gerry about her terrible childhood ordeal. She could tell that he had already sensed something about her past life, but she felt comfortable with the fact that he had never pressed her for details. Suddenly, he understood her a lot better. She was relieved that nothing changed and Gerry continued to lend her a sympathetic ear.

Soon he began visiting Abby at the townhouse where she was living with her young son in Port Coquitlam. Gerry had known little about the kidnapping, but realized now as he listened to Abby's story that his own brother George had been one of the volunteers who had combed Port Moody looking for her. His brother had been only thirty-eight but had since died of cancer.

"It's amazing how you've still got a sense of humour," Gerry told Abby. Eventually, he thought, now that he was divorced, he would ask her to marry him. He regarded her as probably the most assertive, straightforward but caring woman he'd ever met. Abby, for her part, felt safe in the arms of this man — able to dissociate herself from past nightmares while sharing intimacy and trust.

ABBY DROVER MIGHT not have felt quite so safe, however, if she had known that at the time, just eight years after receiving his life sentence, the man convicted of kidnapping her was frequently being allowed out of jail on unescorted passes.

After completing his psychiatric treatment in 1984, Hay had been transferred to a minimum security prison farm outside the federal penitentiary at Prince Albert, Saskatchewan, where he was befriended by several respected members of the Mennonite community.

Every other Saturday morning for the past six months, he had been boarding the bus at the prison gates and spending weekends at the homes of some of his newly acquired friends, as far as ninety miles away in Saskatoon.

Churchgoers Albert and Hilda Kornelson and their friend Leola Epp had met Hay through the prison visitor program and felt that he was making genuine efforts to turn his life around.

"I'm so disgusted with my life, my first forty-three years," Don Hay told them. "If God can use me for the rest of my life, I give it to Him."

"We consider you one of the family," his new friends replied, impressed that Hay had painstakingly sewn them a 250,000-stitch needlepoint of *The Last Supper*. The Kornelsons proudly hung the picture on the wall of their Saskatoon home, where grand-children leapt into the arms of their newfound "Uncle Don".

"Scripturally, if we say an eye for an eye and a tooth for a tooth, he's certainly given a whole lot of teeth," said church member Leola Epp. "He started to tell me about what he had done, and he didn't even minimize what he did. I came to believe him. I believed that he wanted to change. I believe he's strong enough to change if he wants to — and he definitely wants to. Maybe he can never make amends for it. He knows he can't, but serving more time doesn't change that."

Despite his apparent progress, however, Hay was suddenly returned to maximum security and told that the National Parole Board was denying him further passes because it felt his offence outweighed his institutional progress.

Hay appealed the decision, arguing that he was being un-fairly treated because of unexplained policy changes aimed at prisoners convicted of sex offences. "If I was a paranoid type of person I would almost feel there was somebody out there with a lot of power who said this guy will never get out," he complained.

Federal Court Judge F.C. Muldoon upheld his appeal saying the decision had been arbitrary and unfair because Hay had done nothing to deserve it. "It does seem that Hay has been caught in the crossfire of competing exertions of authority by the parole board and the correctional service."

According to the judge, the fifty-two-year-old Hay was a model prisoner who was making "solid progress" as a member of Al-coholics Anonymous, and he appeared ready for temporary leaves in Saskatoon, where a family was ready to care for him.

Putting Hay back in maximum security, said the judge, offended fairness and violated Charter of Rights and Freedoms guarantees against arbitrary imprisonment, unjust treatment and cruel and unusual punishment.

Muldoon ordered Hay returned to the farm prison at once and urged the parole board to reconsider his request for temporary releases. Rehabilitation, said the judge, remained an important tenet of penal law and prison authorities had no right to move sex offenders around "like cordwood".

In Port Moody, former prosecutor Stewart Chambers read of the decision in the July 19, 1985 edition of the *Vancouver Sun*. Now retired, Chambers shook his head in disbelief. He had poured his heart and soul into obtaining the life sentence. Although he was disturbed by what he regarded as overly lenient attitudes on the part of the judiciary, he was unable to take any action. His health was failing and he was rapidly losing weight from his already gaunt body. Within a year, the former prosecutor would slip away from smoking-related illness.

LIVING ON LIMITED income, Abby had to spend most of the money that had been in her trust fund to cover day-to-day expenses. She remained grateful for the public generosity, but it had been short-lived — and ten years after the kidnapping it seemed she had long since been forgotten.

Abby had previously discounted the idea of selling her story, but friends continued to suggest that her tale of survival might serve as an inspiration to other victims. Finally, through a mutual acquaintance, she agreed to sit down with CBC television reporter Wayne Williams to discuss telling her story in a book.

Williams, a big shambling man who was the network's legislative reporter in Victoria, dug up numerous files and transcripts about the case, and wrote to prison authorities in June 1988 to inquire whether Donald Hay had been released or was still serving his sentence.

Assuming such information probably would be unavailable, Abby was surprised when prison officials promptly responded, informing her that Hay was still serving his sentence in Saskatchewan.

Hay had been granted some escorted passes, said the reply, but these had been revoked, and despite more than ten years in prison he had been denied day parole as recently as the previous fall.

The letter explained that members of the public attending parole board hearings were usually present to speak on behalf of the offender. "Thus it would not be appropriate for you to attend Hay's next parole hearing," Abby was told. "Besides, we would suggest that it would be most difficult for you to sit in the same room with this man and discuss the offence."

But the letter provided relevant addresses and telephone numbers, and concluded that Abby could express her views to the National Parole Board. "The policy of the board clearly emphasizes the need for victim participation."

Subsequently, Wayne Williams advised Abby that he was unable to take sufficient time from work to complete the book project, but he was willing to continue indefinitely as a go-between in assisting her with further National Parole Board correspondence.

Having gone this far, Abby decided to write yet another letter in 1989 when Hay once more became eligible for release, and again she received a prompt reply.

"The concerns you expressed in your letter of August 15, 1989, were taken into consideration by the Board reviewing Mr. Hay's case," said a letter by return post. "The Board's decisions of August 16, 1989, were unescorted temporary absence denied and full parole denied.

"Unless the Board is able to assess that Hay no longer presents a risk to society if granted some form of conditional release, he could well serve life imprisonment."

Even if he was eventually released, said the letter, the board would advise her of his destination and impose a special condition requiring him not to have any contact with her.

It was somewhat comforting, but Abby still felt more than a twinge of concern. She was haunted by memories of what her captor had told her back in 1976: Hay had warned her that if she ever caused him to go to prison he would one day get out and spend the rest of his life hunting her down.

34 SECRETS FINALLY SHARED

ON NEW YEAR'S EVE, 1992, Abby and Gerry got married. Although the temperature outside dipped to thirty degrees below zero, Abby was filled with warmth as her eleven-year-old son gave her away at a moving ceremony attended by three dozen of their friends and relatives.

Awaiting them at the reception was a very special centre-piece. The wedding cake, which evoked many happy memories, had been made lovingly by her mother.

"If she'd asked anybody else," smiled Ruth, "there would have been one very ticked-off mother of the bride!"

With her husband back at work after their honeymoon, Abby spent many happy hours in her craft room turning out a plethora of candles, beadwork and dolls.

At night, she gazed meditatively at the stars, and when spring arrived she delighted in the outdoors as she prepared to plant her vegetable garden.

Abby Drover felt happy most of the time, but never a complete day went by when she was not haunted to some degree or another by the darkest, most terrible memories of her past.

She was also extremely protective of her son and panicked even more than most mothers when a young girl was sexually assaulted and murdered in the neighbourhood.

Abby had never intended to tell her son about what had happened to her as a child, but after the murder, the boy objected so much to being grounded that she finally had to tell him. "You never let me do anything!" he complained. "It's not fair. You treat me like a baby."

Exasperated that her son thought he was invincible, just like any other kid, Abby rummaged through hidden newspaper accounts of her own kidnapping until she found what she was looking for.

"You've always wondered why I'm so concerned about your safety," she said as she followed her son into his room and showed him the now-yellowing headline story from the September 8, 1976, edition of *The Province*.

"This is about you?" her son asked, tears of concern welling in his eyes.

Abby nodded and hugged the boy as she fought to hold back her own tears. "I've got to tell you, when I was your age, one of our neighbours kidnapped me," she said. "This explains how I survived. Maybe it'll help you understand how upset I would be if anything ever happened to you."

EVERYTHING, THOUGHT ABBY, seemed to have its own strange and inexorable way of coming full circle. She had never forgotten the doctor who had sought her out for treatment and was not surprised now as she read about his latest woes in successive 1994 editions of the *Vancouver Sun*.

According to the newspaper, the pediatrician had been suspended for six months for hugging and kissing one of his female patients, although a special prosecutor had found insufficient evidence that he had also molested twenty-two children. The parents of one five-year-old girl, however, were still suing him, claiming that the doctor had persuaded their daughter to sit on his knee, touching her "in the area of her breasts, vagina and buttocks" and causing psychological damage by leading her to believe that she was unloved.

Abby felt vindicated as she read the articles but her sense of satisfaction turned to dismay as she read that the doctor had since satisfied the College of Physicians and Surgeons of his psychiatric fitness to resume his practice.

"He's even worse than Donald Hay!" she told Gerry, perturbed as she put down the newspaper. "This man was supposed to be in a position of trust."

IN SASKATCHEWAN, meanwhile, Hay had once again been enjoying several passes following the federal court decision. For quite some time, he had been able to go shopping and to get out of the prison farm to play golf and attend hockey games.

In 1994, however, he was sent back to the penitentiary yet again and denied further passes after being found guilty of mishandling prison canteen funds. The parole board believed Hay's sex drive had diminished with age, but expressed concern that pedophilia remained a possibility, since Hay couldn't achieve sexual satisfaction unless his partner was a young female.

"There is an emotional coldness when Hay claims that maltreatment of the victim was not as severe as documented," the board found.

It also expressed concern that Hay might re-offend if he began drinking again; that he dwelled on his own pain; and that he felt he was as much a victim as Abby. It concluded that Hay "remains quite antisocial, allegedly continues to be somewhat unscrupulous in his business affairs and that his credibility is very much a concern."

Hay's hopes were dashed further still when his case management worker Dennis Nowoselsky, who had "sweated blood" to get him released, was suddenly taken off the file.

Since then, Hay complained, he'd had four case management workers in the last four years. "It's not fair to me and it's not fair to them because they don't get the chance to read tons of paperwork to get to know a case."

35 "THEY'VE GOT THEIR POUND OF FLESH"

WHILE I VAGUELY recalled having read about Donald Hay in prison, I still had no idea what had become of Abby Drover; and it was not until twenty years later that we spoke together for the first time, in a telephone conversation arranged by her mother.

I tried to be as gentle as possible but she still sobbed as we discussed the miracle of her rescue. It was one of the most dramatic interviews I could ever recall.

"Are you all right?" I asked. "Would you prefer to postpone this until another time?"

"It's okay," she replied bravely. "I've made it this far so I guess I can carry on."

Abby agreed it was logical for me to tell her story, as one of the few reporters who had seen the exact location of her confinement. She explained how she had always kept the articles I had written and had finally shown them to her son.

She wasn't sure if a book about the case would help her personally, but hoped that it might be an inspiration to others. I was not surprised that the brave little girl I had written about had grown into a stoic young woman.

Eventually she would be comforted to know that public concern for her had not waned during the intervening twenty years.

Within a few weeks of our telephone conversation, I met Abby in person, and was impressed by her courage as we sat down for the first of several interviews.

Since first speaking with her on the phone, I had discovered that only recently Donald Hay had been entered in the new police computer system known as ViCLAS. There, he was labelled a "bondage practitioner". Abby was relieved to know that her abductor had not been forgotten by the authorities.

Despite the passage of twenty years, specific details of Donald Hay's crimes were now available to police departments throughout North America. At the time of the kidnapping, rapists and murderers could often escape attention by moving across the continent, but all that changed when the notorious Ted Bundy committed his string of murders in the burgeoning age of the computer.

Almost overnight, law enforcement agencies had come to realize that the modus operandi of rapists such as Bundy might just as easily be recognized through data in the northwestern United States, where he began his murder spree, as in Florida, where he ended it before going to the electric chair.

Thus was born the computer-matching system known as ViCAP (the Violent Criminal Apprehension Program), which was soon followed by its Canadian counterpart, ViCLAS (the Violent Crime Linkage Analysis System).

Even though he was back under the police microscope, however, Hay had a parole hearing scheduled for November 1997, and he wanted to show Abby that he was a changed man. Prior to his hearing, Abby learned, Hay and his friends would be willing to do a series of interviews with CBC reporter Wayne Williams to demonstrate the fact that he was finally deserving of his freedom.

Williams travelled to Saskatchewan to interview him, but first met outside the prison with several of his friends, including Dennis Nowoselsky, the former case management worker who was now a Prince Albert council member and who strongly supported Donald Hay's bid for parole. "He was at my daughter's christening," said Nowoselsky. "They all call him Uncle Don. He's a caring, sensitive, responsible individual. At some point, when a man or woman makes an effort to change and displays it, when does the punishment end and the healing and return to the community begin?

"I see a man that has shown significant change, a man that's deserving of freedom to go on with his life. I guess the ultimate evil·here is the man can die inside. He's done his whole life."

Williams also interviewed Hay's former neighbours Leo and Lois Morin, who had since moved to Saskatoon and who remained equally supportive of their friend's bid for freedom. "Okay, it happened," said Morin, gesturing with a cigarette at his kitchen table. "Yes, it still bothers Abby — there's no way that anybody should have to grow up with that, but you can't change it. It's done. Is it going to make her life any better by him staying there?

"He's got people here that want him, that love him, that will back him. We've proved that we'll back him."

Finally, Williams sat down with Hay in the prison visiting area and told him about the loyal comments of his friends.

"It just boggles my mind — their support and the stick-to-it-iveness," Hay said.

Despite having the grey pallor of a prison inmate, Hay appeared to Williams to be in good physical shape. He had a neatly clipped white mustache and beard. His hair was thinner than before, there were liver spots on his hands and forehead and he now wore glasses — but the absence of alcohol had indeed left him looking healthier than the gaunt, haggard man of twenty years before.

Hay said it was easy for people to be cynical about his conversion to Christianity but *he* knew how he felt when he walked into church. "It's like a big family. I wish I could say what's in my heart, once you get to feel that, how you could never hurt another human being again. I know I'd never re-offend."

Hay said he used to talk to offenders, church groups and children — mostly about alcohol and the importance of family, which he claimed was something he had never had.

"The family is a big part of your life," he postulated. "The church is a big part of life. For people that know me, the shock waves are over as far as my crime is concerned and they get onto the bigger picture of who I am today."

Treatment, he said, had taught him the only way to keep his friends was to be open and honest with them so there would be "no surprises down the road." His friends, he added, knew everything about him.

"My crimes have been against people I know — against family, friends or neighbours, or whatever. It's never strangers, so therefore if anybody has anything to fear from me it's them. It's all my friends and their families and that — and they know that."

His friends were very special to him now, he said, even though he reiterated that he had grown up without love himself. "I'm still pretty immature in that area," he said, "because other than through my friends — I'm receiving this type of love — I'm beyond the point of having a wife and a family and all that. Like I'm now at the point where I'd be happy to enjoy my grandchildren a little bit."

It didn't bother him, he said, that he couldn't be alone with children if he were paroled, but he thought it was sad that such restrictions would prevent him from living with his friends because they all had children or grandchildren.

Hay said he wanted freedom more for the sake of his friends than for himself — to save them from driving ninety miles and giving up family time to see him. Being almost sixty-five, all he wanted to do was retire to his hobbies. He had enjoyed needlepoint for twenty years, and he freely admitted that he had tried to get Abby involved in it, too.

Williams asked Hay if he remembered telling Abby he had taken her into the cell to play house.

"Probably, yeah. That was more or less my intention, yeah. I didn't feel like I was in control. I felt like I was — the best way to explain it is I was at the controls of a big machine. My body was a machine and I controlled it up the stairs and I controlled it into the shop, but I didn't feel like it — it was a weird sensation."

"How did you keep a straight face when the police and Ruth were around?" asked Williams.

"I couldn't have done it sober," Hay shrugged. "Well, it wouldn't have happened if I was sober…. As far as alcohol, a lot of people take a thermos of coffee in the car, I used to take a thermos of vodka.

"The plan was ... er ... like, I thought they'd all think she ran away, and then I'd get an apartment somewhere and she'd be... er... my friend until I died. Like I didn't realize the uproar."

"You really thought, though, at the time that a forty-three-year-old man and a twelve-year-old girl were going to be able to move out and move on?" asked the reporter.

"That should tell you a lot about my mental state at that time," said Hay, shaking his head. "There was no way I could let her go and carry on with my life and ... er ... that was when I think I got suicidal and I did attempt suicide twice while she was down there."

Before attempting suicide, Hay reiterated, he had left a note in his garage disclosing Abby's whereabouts, although it was never found. At the time, he recalled, he was desperate to bring the situation to an end. Questioned by Williams, he admitted he had indeed thought of killing Abby but he couldn't bring himself — or even imagine how — to do it. "I got myself into something I didn't know how to get myself out of."

He reiterated that he had never physically struck his victim and thought he was on good terms with her. "I remember the first day talking to Abby down there. We laughed about her being out of the cuffs," he remarked, apparently oblivious to the absurdity of his attempt to mitigate his actions.

Hay continued to minimize his actions. "She had lots of food," he insisted. "A lot of it rotted and wasted. She had no appetite, I guess.... I worried about the workshop catching fire, about noises during the night, about her getting sick down there."

Hay recalled that he had felt great relief when he was finally arrested. "A load came off my shoulders like you wouldn't believe," he claimed. "Once I sobered up and realized just what I had done — like how horrific it had to be for her — I didn't want to live. I didn't think I should live. I didn't think I was fit to live."

He now felt differently, however, and believed the people "in control" also felt he was a reasonable risk. He said he had worked to prove that he could be an asset to society — not a drain or a victimizer. Hay indicated he was a well-behaved and frugal prisoner.

"I don't waste food. I don't waste clothing," he offered. "They've got their pound of flesh out of me. They've given me the opportunity to turn my life around.

"My case management has been trying to get me back to the farm for two or three years. I miss my visits and passes at the farm. It's frustrating at times when things don't happen as fast as you expect them to. They never do in this system.

"If they turn me down again, they turn me down. It's God's will. What makes it easy to do the time, I know it's not my time, its God's time, he's given me this time."

Hay agreed that Abby had had her hopes for freedom dashed again and again, but that he had also. "I've had my hopes dashed for the past fourteen years," he said. "I have to hope some day sanity will prevail."

Hay specifically denied suggestions by the reporter that Abby had not been his only victim. "Yeah, she was," he insisted. Speaking in soft, matter-of-fact tones, Hay startled the CBC reporter by suggesting that he might be able to ease Abby's suffering if only he could meet with her face to face.

Referring to a pilot project in which a Mennonite minister had comforted rape victims by arranging such meetings, Hay complained prison authorities had wrongly inferred that he was stalking Abby simply because he had discussed the idea with the prison chaplain.

Hay couldn't understand reports that Abby was still afraid of him. "I've never felt any animosity towards Abby," he said. "Never. She was a victim. Whatever happened to me, none of it was her fault." He seemed not to realize that Abby's fear of him could scarcely be wiped out now by his supposed acceptance of the blame.

The parole board should explain to her, he said, that he would never go back to British Columbia. "Like, even if I get parole, I'll be serving time for the rest of my life. I still have to report to the police, I still have to take the programs deemed necessary, I have to get approval to buy a car or get married ... but at least I'd be on the street where I'd be an asset to society. In here I can give nothing."

In the absence of meeting with Abby, the best he could do was give her his apology. "I'm just so very, very sorry it had to happen," he said. "Like, words — there aren't words — I don't know words strong enough to express how bad I feel about what I did to her.

"Abby was a good kid. She never gave me a minute's trouble down there, like, even after the fact. She was just a beautiful child and I don't know why it happened. I'm really, really sorry it happened. She was in the wrong place at the wrong time."

36 TELL, TELL, TELL

WATCHING THE INTERVIEW at her home outside Vancouver, a slim middle-aged mother named Faith Gilpin was outraged as she listened to Hay's televised insistence that Abby Drover had been his only victim.

The former Coquitlam resident was only too painfully aware that Hay was not telling the truth, for it was her own young daughter, also named Faith, that Hay had molested twenty-five years earlier — with devastatingly tragic consequences.

Four years before kidnapping Abby, Hay had been charged on May 15, 1972, after luring Faith and another ten-year-old girl named Brenda into his vehicle on their way home from school. According to a doctor, his tampering with the girls had given both of them internal infections.

"He threatened to harm them if they testified against him," Faith's mother recalled. "When it went to court, he acted as his own lawyer and got the judge to agree that the families should be excluded from the courtroom so as not to influence the proceedings.

"When he asked each of the girls questions, they cried. They didn't answer, they just cried. Hay walked out and he laughed. We couldn't believe it. We promised her he would be locked up. The police promised her, and we failed her."

Afterwards, her once happy, smiling little girl, affectionately known as Chickie, became anorexic and withdrawn. Throughout her teenage years, she required constant therapy but she never recovered. Fourteen years after the assault, Faith had returned home to take all of her prescribed medications in one massive overdose.

Faith's mother had tried to find forgiveness but still blamed Hay for her daughter's suicide. "He took my daughter's life," she maintained. "I'm convinced of that."

After coming forward to tell her story, she heard for the first time from Ruth Drover. "I had no idea what you'd been through," said Abby's mother, as both women commiserated through their tears, agreeing to stay in touch.

"It's haunted me for twenty-one years," replied Faith. "It's crucial that Abby stays strong and well so that he can't destroy her like he did my daughter."

Shortly afterwards, Faith's mother also heard from Brenda, the other little girl whom Hay had terrified and assaulted. "It needn't happen if parents, schools and television commercials encourage children to speak up," the two women concurred. "His gig is up the minute someone else knows. If someone is threatening you, tell, tell, tell."

Broadcast over three days in mid-November, Hay's televised parole bid touched off a storm of viewer protest, with callers jamming the switchboard of the CBC affiliate in Vancouver to demand that Hay not be released.

Some of the callers were in tears as they responded to the story, while virtually all of them seemed to think that Hay was still devious and unrepentant. "He's telling the psychoanalysts only what they want to hear," said one.

Several callers remembered growing up in Port Moody and always being frightened after the kidnapping to play outside. Many of them were now afraid to let their own children out of their sight. "Mr. Hay taught us what fear was," said one.

Some callers were leery that Hay continued to blame alcohol and "everything except himself" while others said he should never be released because he had crossed the line. "Once a pedophile, always a pedophile," summed up one viewer.

"If he is let out, what are you going to do?" asked another. "Check every week that he doesn't have a little girl in his cellar that he's abusing on a daily basis?"

Finally one viewer was outraged by Hay's suggestion that he should meet with Abby Drover face to face. "What a self-serving scum," said the caller. "His desecration of her child-hood is beyond all human comprehension... ."

Having seen her abductor twenty years later on television,

Abby Drover no longer felt afraid of him, but she was unmoved by Hay's apology. "All I heard was him making excuses," she said. "I want to be his last victim."

This time, Abby learned, her appeal to the National Parole Board was being supported by additional letters of opposition from Faith's mother, as well as Ruth Drover and the City of Port Moody.

Faced with increasing protest, Hay was reported to be afraid to leave his cell, and withdrew his parole application the day before the hearing. "Uncle Don's" public relations gamble appeared to have failed — but the Drovers still had to live with the fact that Hay remained eligible for parole and could reapply at any time.

ABBY WAS RELIEVED for the time being but there was still one more disclosure that opened up painful memories for her, and it was like salt being poured into an open wound.

After Hay had been sentenced in 1977, everyone had been led to believe that his "bomb shelter" had been filled in, but the present owner of the house had found that it still existed. The few cubic yards of sand that had been poured into the pit had settled over the years, revealing the old bedframe and the wall anchors, evoking their chilling reminders of the chains.

Distressed by his mother's tears, Abby's son joined her in writing to Port Moody council; and city officials — who also assumed the job had been done properly years ago — arranged to have the bunker sealed within seventy-two hours.

The following Monday morning, Ruth Drover heard the hum of machinery and cement mixers as once more she drove back up the hill to Donald Hay's old house at the top of Gore Street.

It was painful for her to stand above the "chamber of horrors" where Abby had been entombed, but Ruth felt she needed to be there. This time, for the sake of her daughter, she wanted to ensure that the terrible blight would be removed once and for all.

With her case back in the headlines, Abby and members of her family accepted an invitation to tell their story on U.S. network television. Returning to Los Angeles more than twenty years after the kidnapping, Abby bravely answered questions by syndicated talk show host Leeza Gibbons, who praised the young woman for her courage.

After getting back home, Abby learned that three other women had come forward, as a result of the publicity, to allege that Donald Hay had sexually assaulted them also back in the 1970s. The Port Moody police, she discovered, had dispatched two officers to arrest Hay in his prison cell and had escorted him back to their jurisdiction to face the new charges, effectively quashing his latest bid for parole.

In November 1998, Hay appeared, stiff and minus the beard he'd sported in his televised prison interviews, at a preliminary hearing in Coquitlam and was committed for trial on the new allegations. The new charges are scheduled to be heard in the Supreme Court in Vancouver, beginning in November 1999.